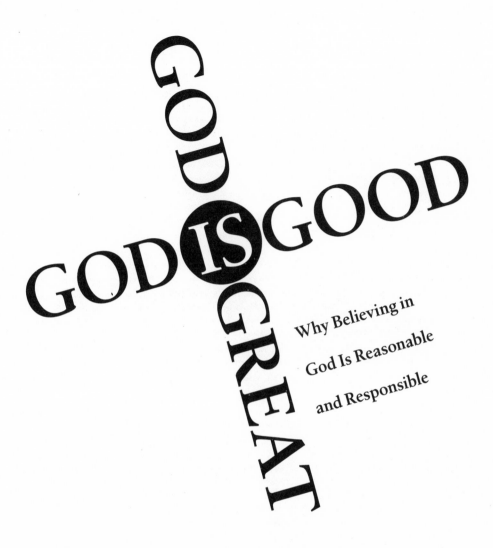

GOD IS GREAT
GOD IS GOOD

Why Believing in
God Is Reasonable
and Responsible

EDITED BY
William Lane Craig & Chad Meister

IVP Books
An imprint of InterVarsity Press
Downers Grove, Illinois

InterVarsity Press, USA
P.O. Box 1400, Downers Grove, IL 60515-1426
World Wide Web: www.ivpress.com
E-mail: email@ivpress.com

Inter-Varsity Press, England
Norton Street, Nottingham NG7 3HR
Website: www.ivpbooks.com
Email: ivp@ivpbooks.com

InterVarsity Press®, USA, is the book-publishing division of InterVarsity Christian Fellowship/USA® <www.intervarsity.org> and a member movement of the International Fellowship of Evangelical Students.

Inter-Varsity Press, England, is closely linked with the Universities and Colleges Christian Fellowship, a student movement connecting Christian Unions in universities and colleges throughout Great Britain, and a member movement of the International Fellowship of Evangelical Students. Website: www.uccf.org.uk.

All Scripture quotations, unless otherwise indicated, are taken from the Holy Bible, New International Version®. NIV®. Copyright © 1973, 1978, 1984 by International Bible Society. Used by permission of Zondervan Publishing House. Distributed in the U.K. by permission of Hodder and Stoughton Ltd. All rights reserved. "NIV" is a registered trademark of International Bible Society. UK trademark number 1448790.

Permission was granted by the Editor of Philolophia Christi *to reprint the interview between Gary Habermas and Antony Flew from the Winter 2004 issue. More about this interview can be found at <www.epsociety.org>.*

Permission was granted by Alvin Plantinga to reprint the essay "The Dawkins Confusion," originally published in Books and Culture, *March/April 2007.*

Design: Cindy Kiple

ISBN 978-0-8308-3726-7
UK ISBN 978-1-84474-417-6

Printed in the United States of America ∞

Library of Congress Cataloging-in-Publication Data

God is great, God is good: why belief in God is reasonable & responsible
  / edited by William Lane Craig and Chad Meister.
    p. cm.
  Includes bibliographical references and index.
  ISBN 978-0-8308-3726-7 (pbk.: alk. paper)
  1. Dawkins, Richard, 1941- God delusion. 2. Hitchens, Christopher. God is not great. 3. Harris, Sam, 1967- End of faith. 4. Apologetics. 5. Christianity and atheism. I. Craig, William Lane. II. Meister, Chad V., 1965-
  BL2775.3.D393G64 2009
  239'.7—dc22

                    2009026580

British Library Cataloguing in Publication Data
A catalogue rocord for this book is available from the British Library.

P	19	18	17	16	15	14	13	12	11	10	9	8	7	6	5	4	3
Y	24	23	22	21	20	19	18	17	16	15	14	13	12	11			

Contents

PART FOUR: WHY IT MATTERS

Introduction

In recent years theism—the view that God exists—has been on the rise and atheism on the decline worldwide.[1] Perhaps as a result, a movement dubbed the "New Atheism" has emerged, propagated by a flurry of provocative atheist publications. *WIRED* magazine (the publication which coined the name) noted the group's simple message: "No heaven. No hell. Just science."

> The New Atheists will not let us off the hook simply because we are not doctrinaire believers. They condemn not just belief in God but respect for belief in God. Religion is not only wrong; it's evil.[2]

Indeed, the New Atheists do not merely attempt to convince people to quit believing in God; they endeavor to make respect for belief in God socially unacceptable.[3]

Lest you think this movement is ineffective or not getting a wide hearing, consider this: through their writings, the New Atheists have created a flourishing worldwide, antireligious, atheistic movement. Their books have been national and international bestsellers for sev-

---

[1]See, for example, the United Press International article by Uwe Siemon-Netto titled "God Not So Dead: Atheism in Decline Worldwide," *World Tribune,* March 3, 2005, at <www.worldtribune.com/worldtribune/05/breaking2453432.91875.html>. See also the admission that "worldwide atheism overall may be in decline" in Phil Zuckerman, "Atheism: Contemporary Numbers and Patterns," in *The Cambridge Companion to Atheism*, ed. Michael Martin (Cambridge: Cambridge University Press, 2007), p. 59.

[2]Gary Wolf, "The Church of the Non-Believers," *WIRED,* November 2006 at <www.wired.com/wired/archive/14.11/atheism_pr.html>.

[3]Aptly put by Albert Mohler in his article "The New Atheism," homepage (November 21, 2006) <www.albertmohler.com/commentary_read.php?cdate=2006-11-21>.

eral years and include such stirring titles as *The God Delusion* by Richard Dawkins, *Letter to a Christian Nation* by Sam Harris, *Breaking the Spell: Religion as a Natural Phenomenon* by Daniel Dennett and *God Is Not Great: How Religion Poisons Everything* by Christopher Hitchens. The list goes on.

A central theme of these books is that belief in God (and religious belief in general) is not only false but dangerous—dangerous both to individuals and societies—and should therefore be rejected, criticized and denounced whenever and wherever possible. The New Atheists are not inconspicuous about their agenda. Richard Dawkins boldly proclaims: "I am attacking God, all gods, anything and everything supernatural, wherever and whenever they have been or will be invented."[4] Sam Harris opines, "It is time that we admitted that faith is nothing more than the license religious people give one another to keep believing when reasons fail."[5] He says elsewhere that "at some point, there's going to be enough pressure that it is just going to be too embarrassing to believe in God."[6] Michael Onfray, a French atheist with over thirty books to his credit (the latest of which, *Atheist Manifesto*, is a bestseller in France, Italy, and Spain), argues that atheism is facing a "final battle" against "theological hocus-pocus" and thus must organize and rally its troops. "We can no longer tolerate neutrality and benevolence. . . . The turbulent times we live in suggest that change is at hand and the time has come for a new order."[7] Christopher Hitchens ends his not-so-subtly titled book *God Is Not Great* with these words: "It has become necessary to know the enemy, and to prepare to fight it." The enemy, of course, is

---

[4]Richard Dawkins, *The God Delusion* (New York: Houghton Mifflin, 2006), p. 36.

[5]Sam Harris, *Letter to a Christian Nation* (New York: Knopf, 2006), p. 67. He adds, "I would be the first to admit that the prospects for eradicating religion in our time do not seem good. Still, the same could have been said about efforts to abolish slavery at the end of the eighteenth century. Anyone who spoke with confidence about eradicating slavery in the United States in the year 1775 surely appeared to be wasting his time, and wasting it dangerously. The analogy is not perfect, but it is suggestive. If we ever do transcend our religious bewilderment, we will look back upon this period in human history with horror and amazement. How could it have been possible for people to believe such things in the twenty-first century? How could it be that they allowed their societies to become so dangerously fragmented by empty notions about God and Paradise? The truth is, some of your [that is, Christians'] most cherished beliefs are as embarrassing as those that sent the last slave ship sailing to America as late as 1859 (the same year that Darwin published *The Origin of Species*)."

[6]Wolf, "Church of the Non-Believers."

[7]As quoted by Andrew Higgins, "The New Crusaders," *Wall Street Journal*, April 12, 2007, p. A1.

religion—all religion. As one author recently describes the situation, atheism has become militant.[8]

While the New Atheists attack religion in general, Christianity is typically singled out as their primary target. Dawkins candidly expresses in *The God Delusion* that he has "Christianity mostly in mind,"[9] Sam Harris titles his book *Letter to a Christian Nation*, and Daniel Dennett claims that religion generally but *Christianity* in particular is addicted to blind faith.[10] Given these relentless attacks on God, religion and Christian faith, we think the time is ripe for a comprehensive response by a number of top-notch scholars from across the disciplines.

PURPOSE OF THIS BOOK

Our primary objective in compiling this book is to answer challenges advanced by the New Atheists and others raising objections to belief in God and the Christian faith. Despite our overall impression of the New Atheists' writings as fresh packaging for "tired, weak, and recycled arguments" (to borrow a phrase from Alister and Joanna Collicutt McGrath's assessment of Dawkins's *The God Delusion*),[11] they are making much more headway with their message than many religious believers are willing to admit. Their rhetoric is powerful and often persuasive enough to convince people to think that (1) in order to believe in God and Christ, a person must be either uneducated or intellectually dishonest, and (2) religion is actually dangerous—a harm to humanity. In the past few years we have been in dialogue with a number of folks—students, churchgoers and others—who have been either convinced by the New Atheists' writings and lost their faith or persuaded in some way that Christian faith is unreasonable. This is unfortunate, especially since the material swaying them, while often witty and engaging, is generally poorly argued and lacking in substance.

We have sought out leading thinkers representing a wide range of expertise—from cosmology, astrophysics and biology to New Testa-

---

[8]Dinesh D'Souza, debate with Christopher Hitchens, accessed April 28, 2009, at <http://216.75.61.152/xstream/neproductions/tkc/debate.wmv>.
[9]Dawkins, *God Delusion*, p. 37.
[10]See Daniel C. Dennett, *Breaking the Spell: Religion as a Natural Phenomenon* (New York: Viking Press, 2006), pp. 200-248, esp. pp. 230-31.
[11]Alister McGrath and Joanna Collicutt McGrath, *The Dawkins Delusion* (Downers Grove, Ill.: InterVarsity Press, 2007), p. 12.

ment studies, theology and philosophy—to join us in responding to these arguments and claims. Throughout these pages we tackle some of the most vexing and perplexing challenges currently facing believers in God, some of which are formidable but none of which is insurmountable. We also go on the offensive and present some of the significant challenges confronting atheists.

The book is divided into four parts.

Part one tackles *God's existence.* Contrary to New Atheist allegations, there are a number of robust arguments and evidences for God which many philosophers and scientists find convincing, and some of them are explored in this section.

Part two focuses on challenges to *God's creative design* in the world, both at the cosmological and biological levels. Is naturalistic Darwinian evolution reasonable to affirm given the most recent scientific findings? Does cosmic evolution count against the belief that God is the grand designer of our world? These and other important questions are taken up here.

Part three addresses questions of *God's goodness,* a major bone of contention of the New Atheists. For example, how could a perfectly good God coexist with evil or hell? And what about the Old Testament laws that seem so revolting, if not malevolent? Does it make sense to believe in a good and wise God who ordained such things? These and other topics are tackled in these chapters.

Part four shifts from theistic issues generally to *Christianity specifically.* It hones in on issues related to divine revelation and Jesus' life, death and resurrection. It also addresses the question of why all this is relevant. Why does it really matter what we believe about these things?

Our aim with this project is to provide a well-argued resource—one that is irenic in spirit and not a vitriolic attack on any persons or groups. We wish to offer positive engagement in the ongoing dialogue between those who believe in God and Christ and those who do not. As you read through the following pages we challenge you to carefully weigh the arguments and evidences on both sides of these issues and, as Augustine exhorted, follow the truth wherever it leads.

Part 1

GOD IS

1

Richard Dawkins on Arguments for God

WILLIAM LANE CRAIG

I was fascinated to read the reactions in the blogosphere to my *Christianity Today* cover story on the revival of arguments for the existence of God among philosophers today.[1] Along with expressions of appreciation, there were comments like these:

- "Dawkins's *The God Delusion* soundly deals with [these] arguments. Did you even do any research?"

- "Have you even read Dawkin's [*sic*] book? He answers every one of those arguments quite well."

- "I was dismayed that someone as well known as Dr. Craig has used these arguments to defend the existence of God. As someone mentioned before, has he even read Dawkins's book?"[2]

It's not surprising that nonbelievers should turn to Richard Dawkins for refutations of arguments for God's existence, since none of the other New Atheists has much to say on the subject. Still, what's remarkable about these comments is the *confidence* placed in Dawkins's supposed refutation. Are they right? Has Dawkins dealt the death blow to the arguments I discussed?

Well, let's look at those arguments and see what Dawkins has to say

---

[1]William Lane Craig, "God Is Not Dead Yet" *Christianity Today,* July 2008, pp. 22-27.
[2]These were among the scores of comments posted to the article <www.christianitytoday.com/ct/2008/july/13.22.html>.

about each one.[3] But before we look at specific arguments, we need to be clear what makes for a good argument.

By an argument I mean a series of statements (called premises) leading to a conclusion. To be a good argument, an argument must meet three conditions: (1) it obeys the rules of logic; (2) its premises are true; (3) its premises are more plausible than their opposites. So defined, are there good arguments for God's existence?

THE COSMOLOGICAL ARGUMENT

The first argument I discussed in my article in *Christianity Today* was a form of the cosmological argument known as the argument from contingency. Dawkins doesn't even mention this form of the argument—a remarkable oversight, since it's the most famous version of the argument. So obviously he hasn't refuted it.

But Dawkins does discuss a different form of the cosmological argument, which may be formulated as follows:

(1) Everything that begins to exist has a cause.

(2) The universe began to exist.

(3) Therefore, the universe has a cause.

Once we reach the conclusion that the universe has a cause, we can analyze what properties such a cause must have.

Premise (1) seems obviously true—at the least, more so than its negation. First and foremost, it's rooted in the necessary truth that something cannot come into being from nothing. To suggest that things could just pop into being uncaused out of nothing is to quit doing serious philosophy and to resort to magic. Second, if things really could come into being uncaused out of nothing, then it becomes inexplicable why just anything and everything does not come into existence uncaused from nothing. Finally, premise (1) is constantly confirmed in our experience. We thus have the strongest of motivations to accept it.

Premise (2) can be supported by both philosophical argument and

---

[3]Since my space is limited, I can consider only the objections that Dawkins himself raises. You can probably think of other objections that he doesn't raise. Good for you—that shows you're thinking for yourself! If you're interested in exploring these arguments further, then I'd invite you to take a look at my book *Reasonable Faith,* 3rd ed. (Wheaton, Ill.: Crossway, 2008). If you're ready to go even deeper, look at some of the books listed in the bibliography at the end of this chapter.

scientific evidence. The philosophical arguments aim to show that there cannot have been an infinite regress of past events—in other words, that the series of past events must have had a beginning. The philosophical arguments against an infinite regress of events are fascinating and mind-expanding,[4] but fortunately we needn't consider them here, since Dawkins doesn't object to any of the premises of these arguments.

The scientific evidence for the beginning of the universe is based on the expansion of the universe. According to the big bang model of the origin of the universe, physical space and time themselves, along with all the matter and energy in the universe, came into being at a point in the past about 13.7 billion years ago (see figure 1.1).

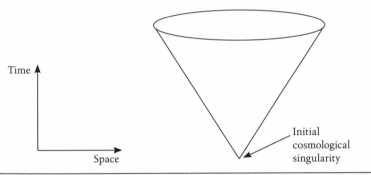

Figure 1.1. Geometrical representation of standard model space-time. Space and time begin at the initial cosmological singularity, before which literally nothing exists.

What makes the big bang so startling is that it represents the origin of the universe from literally nothing. As the physicist P. C. W. Davies explains,

> The coming into being of the universe, as discussed in modern science . . . is not just a matter of imposing some sort of organization . . . upon a previous incoherent state, but literally the coming-into-being of all physical things from nothing.[5]

---

[4]For discussion of such arguments see my *Reasonable Faith*, pp. 116-24.
[5]Interview of Paul Davies by Philip Adams, "The Big Questions: In the Beginning," ABC Science Online, January 17, 2002 <www.abc.net.au/science/bigquestions/s460625.htm>.

Of course, alternative theories have been crafted over the years to try to avoid this absolute beginning, but none of these theories has commended itself to the scientific community as more plausible than the big bang theory. In fact, in 2003 Arvind Borde, Alan Guth and Alexander Vilenkin were able to prove that *any* universe which is, on average, in a state of cosmic expansion cannot be eternal in the past but must have an absolute beginning. Vilenkin pulls no punches:

> It is said that an argument is what convinces reasonable men and a proof is what it takes to convince even an unreasonable man. With the proof now in place, cosmologists can no longer hide behind the possibility of a past-eternal universe. There is no escape, they have to face the problem of a cosmic beginning.[6]

It follows from the two premises that the universe has a cause.

What properties must such a cause of the universe possess? By the very nature of the case, the cause of space and time must transcend space and time and therefore exist timelessly and nonspatially (at least without the universe). This transcendent cause must therefore be changeless and immaterial, since anything that is timeless must also be unchanging, and anything that is changeless must be nonphysical and immaterial (since material things are constantly changing at the molecular and atomic levels). Such an entity must be beginningless and uncaused, at least in the sense of lacking any prior causal conditions, since there cannot be an infinite regress of causes. Ockham's razor—the principle which states that we should not multiply causes beyond necessity—will shave away any other causes, since only one cause is required to explain the effect. This entity must be unimaginably powerful, if not omnipotent, since it created the universe without any material cause.

Finally, and most remarkably, such a transcendent first cause is plausibly personal. Two reasons can be given for this conclusion. First, the personhood of the first cause of the universe is implied by its timelessness and immateriality. The only entities which can possess such properties are either minds or abstract objects, like numbers. But abstract objects don't stand in causal relations. The number 7, for example, can't cause anything. Therefore, the transcendent cause of the ori-

---

[6]Alex Vilenkin, *Many Worlds in One: The Search for Other Universes* (New York: Hill and Wang, 2006), p. 176.

gin of the universe must be an unembodied mind.

Second, this same conclusion is implied by the origin of an effect with a beginning from a beginningless cause. We've concluded that the beginning of the universe was the effect of a first cause. By the nature of the case, that cause cannot have either a beginning of its existence or any prior cause. It just exists changelessly without beginning, and a finite time ago it brought the universe into existence. Now this is exceedingly odd. The cause is in some sense eternal and yet the effect which it produced is not eternal but began to exist a finite time ago. How can this be? If the necessary and sufficient conditions for the effect are eternal, then why isn't the effect also eternal? How can the cause exist without the effect?

There seems to be only one way out of this dilemma, and that is to say that the cause of the universe's beginning is a personal agent who freely chooses to create a universe in time. Philosophers call this type of causation "agent causation," and because the agent is free, he can initiate new effects by freely bringing about conditions which were not previously present. Thus, a finite time ago a Creator endowed with free will could have freely brought the world into being at that moment. In this way, the Creator could exist changelessly and eternally but freely create the world in time. By exercising his causal power, he brings it about that a world with a beginning comes to exist.[7] So the cause is eternal, but the effect is not. In this way, then, it is possible for the temporal universe to have come to exist from an eternal cause: through the free will of a personal Creator.

We may therefore conclude that a personal Creator of the universe exists, who is uncaused, beginningless, changeless, immaterial, timeless, spaceless and unimaginably powerful.

Dawkins does, as I said, address this version of the cosmological argument. Remarkably, however, he doesn't dispute either premise! Instead, he questions the *theological significance* of the argument's conclusion:

> Even if we allow the dubious luxury of arbitrarily conjuring up a terminator to an infinite regress and giving it a name, there is absolutely no reason to endow that terminator with any of the properties normally ascribed to God: omnipotence, omniscience, goodness, creativity of design, to say nothing of such human attributes as listening to prayers, forgiving sins and reading innermost thoughts.[8]

---

[7]Such an exercise of causal power plausibly brings God into time at the very moment of creation.
[8]Richard Dawkins, *The God Delusion* (New York: Houghton Mifflin, 2006), p. 77.

Apart from the opening slur, this is an amazingly concessionary statement. Dawkins doesn't dispute that the argument proves the existence of an uncaused, beginningless, changeless, immaterial, timeless, spaceless and unimaginably powerful personal Creator of the universe. He merely complains that this cause hasn't been shown to be omnipotent, omniscient, good, creative of design, listening to prayers, forgiving sins and reading innermost thoughts. So what? The argument doesn't aspire to prove such things. It would be a bizarre form of atheism—indeed, one not worth the name—which admitted that there exists an uncaused, beginningless, changeless, immaterial, timeless, spaceless and unimaginably powerful personal Creator of the universe who *may*, for all we know, also possess the further properties listed by Dawkins!

We needn't call the personal Creator of the universe "God" if Dawkins finds this unhelpful or misleading; the point remains that a being such as described above must exist.

THE MORAL ARGUMENT

Here's a simple moral argument for God's existence:

(1) If God does not exist, objective moral values and duties do not exist.

(2) Objective moral values and duties do exist.

(3) Therefore, God exists.

What makes this little argument so powerful is not only that it is logically ironclad but also that people generally believe both premises. In fact, Dawkins himself seems to be committed to both premises.

With respect to premise (1) Dawkins informs us, "There is at bottom no design, no purpose, no evil, no good, nothing but pointless indifference. . . . We are machines for propagating DNA. . . . It is every living object's sole reason for being."[9] But although he *says* that there is no evil, no good, nothing but pointless indifference, the fact is that Dawkins is a

---

[9]Cited in Lewis Wolpert, *Six Impossible Things Before Breakfast* (New York: W. W. Norton, 2008), p. 215. Unfortunately, Wolpert's reference is mistaken. The quotation seems to be a pastiche from Richard Dawkins, *River Out of Eden: A Darwinian View of Life* (New York: Basic Books, 1996), p. 133, and Richard Dawkins, "The Ultraviolet Garden," Lecture 4 of 7, Royal Institution Christmas Lectures (1992), <http://physicshead.blogspot.com/2007/01/richard-dawkins-lecture-4-ultraviolet.html>. Thanks to my assistant Joe Gorra for tracking down this reference. See also chap. 7 n. 25 of this volume.

stubborn moralist. He declares himself "mortified" that Enron executive Jeff Skilling regards Dawkins's *The Selfish Gene* as his favorite book because of its perceived Social Darwinism.[10] He calls compassion and generosity "noble emotions."[11] He denounces the doctrine of original sin as "morally obnoxious."[12] He vigorously condemns such actions as the harassment and abuse of homosexuals, the religious indoctrination of children, the Incan practice of human sacrifice, and people's prizing cultural diversity over the interests of Amish children. He even goes so far as to offer his own amended Ten Commandments for guiding moral behavior, all the while marvelously oblivious to the contradiction with his ethical subjectivism.[13]

In his survey of arguments for God's existence, Dawkins touches on a sort of moral argument which he calls "the argument from degree,"[14] but it bears little resemblance to the argument presented above. We're arguing not from degrees of goodness to a greatest good but from the objective reality of moral values and duties to their foundation in reality. It's hard to believe that all of Dawkins's heated moral denunciations and affirmations are really intended to be no more than his subjective opinion, as if to whisper an aside, "Of course, I don't think that child abuse and homophobia and religious intolerance are really wrong! Do whatever you want—there's no moral difference!" But the affirmation of objective values and duties is incompatible with his atheism, for under naturalism we are just animals, relatively advanced primates, and animals are not moral agents. Affirming both of the premises of the moral argument, Dawkins is thus, on pain of irrationality, committed to the argument's conclusion, namely, that God exists.[15]

THE TELEOLOGICAL ARGUMENT

Dawkins is 0 for 2 so far on the arguments for God's existence. Surely he'll not strike out on the teleological argument, or the argument for design. Sorry to disappoint, but Dawkins's response to the most discussed form of the argument for design today—namely, the argument

---

[10]Dawkins, *God Delusion*, p. 215.
[11]Ibid., p. 221.
[12]Ibid., p. 251.
[13]Ibid., pp. 23, 264, 313-17, 326, 328, 330.
[14]Ibid., pp. 78-79.
[15]For more on the moral argment see chap. 7 of this volume.

from the fine-tuning of the universe for intelligent life—turns out to be very weak. Although advocates of the so-called Intelligent Design movement have continued the tradition of focusing on examples of design in biological systems, the cutting edge of the contemporary discussion concerns the remarkable fine-tuning of the cosmos for life. Dawkins responds to this form of the argument in chapter four of *The God Delusion* under the heading "The Anthropic Principle: Cosmological Version."

Here's a simple formulation of a teleological argument based on fine-tuning:

(1) The fine-tuning of the universe is due to either physical necessity, chance or design.

(2) It is not due to physical necessity or chance.

(3) Therefore, it is due to design.

With respect to premise (1), it's important to understand what is meant by "fine-tuning." This expression does *not* mean "designed" (otherwise the argument would be obviously circular). Rather, during the last forty years or so, scientists have discovered that the existence of intelligent life depends on a complex and delicate balance of initial conditions given in the big bang itself. This is known as the fine-tuning of the universe.

This fine-tuning is of two sorts. First, when the laws of nature are expressed as mathematical equations, you find appearing in them certain constants, such as the constant representing the force of gravity. These constants are *not* determined by the laws of nature. The laws of nature are consistent with a wide range of values for these constants. For example, Newton's law of gravity states $F = Gm_1m_2/d^2$, where F is the force of gravity between two masses, m_1 and m_2, separated by a distance d, and G is the gravitational constant. This equation for calculating F would hold even if G had a different value than it does. The world would look very different if G had a different value—if it were much stronger everything would collapse, and if it were much weaker everything would drift apart—but the law for how you calculate F would still be the same in such worlds. The value of G is independent of the law itself.

Second, in addition to these constants there are certain arbitrary quantities which are just put in as initial conditions on which the laws of nature operate—for example, the amount of entropy or the balance between matter and antimatter in the universe. These constants and quantities fall into an incomprehensibly narrow range of life-permitting values. Were these constants or quantities to be altered by less than a hair's breadth, the life-permitting balance would be destroyed and no living organisms of any kind could exist. Dawkins himself, citing the work of the Astronomer Royal Sir Martin Rees, acknowledges that the universe does exhibit this remarkable fine-tuning.

So how do you explain this fine-tuning of the universe? Premise (1) of our argument simply lists the alternatives: physical necessity, chance or design. The question is which of these alternatives is the most plausible?

Premise (2) addresses that question. The first alternative for explaining the fine-tuning of the universe, physical necessity, is extraordinarily implausible because, as we've seen, the constants and quantities are *independent* of the laws of nature. So, for example, the most promising candidate for a "theory of everything" to date, super-string theory or M-Theory, allows a "cosmic landscape" of around 10^{500} different possible universes governed by the present laws of nature. Dawkins notes that Sir Martin Rees rejects this first alternative, and Dawkins adds, "I think I agree."[16]

So what about the second alternative, that the fine-tuning of the universe is due to chance? The problem with this alternative is that the odds against the universe's being life-permitting are so incomprehensibly great that they cannot be reasonably faced. In order to rescue the alternative of chance, its proponents have therefore been forced to adopt the hypothesis that there exists an infinite number of randomly ordered universes composing a sort of world ensemble or multiverse, of which our universe is but a part. Somewhere in this infinite world ensemble, finely tuned universes will appear by chance alone, and we happen to be one such world. This is the explanation that Dawkins finds most plausible.[17]

Dawkins is acutely sensitive to the charge that postulating a world ensemble of randomly ordered universes seems to be an unparsimonious extravagance. But he retorts, "The multiverse may seem extravagant in sheer *number* of universes. But if each one of those universes is simple in its fundamental laws, we are still not postulating anything highly improbable."[18]

---

[16]Dawkins, *God Delusion*, p. 144.
[17]Ibid., p. 145.
[18]Ibid., p. 147.

This response is just confused. First, each universe in the ensemble is *not* simple; it is characterized by a multiplicity of constants and quantities. If each universe were simple, then why did Dawkins feel the need to resort to the hypothesis of a world ensemble in the first place?

Second, Dawkins assumes that the simplicity of the whole is a function of the simplicity of the parts. This is an obvious mistake. A complex mosaic is made up of a great number of individually simple parts. In the same way, an ensemble of simple universes will still be complex if those universes are randomly ordered in the values of their fundamental constants and quantities, rather than all sharing the same values.

Third, Ockham's razor tells us not to multiply entities beyond necessity, so that the number of universes being postulated simply to explain fine-tuning is at face value extravagant. Appealing to a world ensemble is like using a sledge hammer to crack a peanut.

Fourth, Dawkins tries to minimize the extravagance of the postulate of a world ensemble by claiming that despite its extravagant number of entities, nevertheless such a postulate is not highly improbable. It's not clear why this is relevant or what this even means. The objection under consideration is not that the postulate of a world ensemble is improbable but that it is extravagant and unparsimonious. To say that the postulate isn't also highly improbable is to fail to address the objection. Indeed, it's hard to know what probability Dawkins is talking about here. He seems to mean the intrinsic probability of the postulate of a world ensemble, considered apart from the evidence of fine-tuning. But how is such a probability to be determined? By simplicity? But then Dawkins hasn't shown the world-ensemble hypothesis to be simple.

What Dawkins needs to say, it seems to me, is that the postulate of an ensemble of universes may still be simple *if* there is a simple mechanism which, through a repetitive process, generates the many worlds. In that way the huge number of entities postulated is not a deficit of the theory; the entities all issue from a very simple fundamental mechanism. So what mechanisms does Dawkins suggest for generating such an infinite, randomly ordered world ensemble?

First, he suggests an oscillating model of the universe, according to which the universe has gone through an infinite series of expansions and contractions. Dawkins is apparently unaware of the many difficulties of oscillatory models of the universe, which have made contemporary cosmologists skeptical of them. In the 1960s and 1970s some theorists proposed oscillating models of the universe in an attempt to avert the initial singularity predicted by the standard model. The prospects of such models were severely dimmed in 1970, however, by Roger Penrose and Stephen Hawking's formulation of the singularity theorems which bear their names. The theorems disclosed that under very generalized conditions an initial cosmological singularity is inevitable. Since it's impossible to extend space-time through a singularity to a prior state, the Hawking-Penrose singularity theorems implied the absolute beginning of the universe. Reflecting on the impact of this discovery, Hawking notes that the Hawking-Penrose singularity theorems "led to the abandonment of attempts (mainly by the Russians) to argue that there was a previous contracting phase and a non-singular bounce into expansion. Instead almost everyone now believes that the universe, and time itself, had a beginning at the big bang."[19] Dawkins apparently labors under the delusion that a singularity does not form a boundary to space and time.

Moreover, the evidence of observational astronomy has been consistently against the hypothesis that the universe will someday recontract into a big crunch. Attempts to discover the mass density sufficient to generate the gravitational attraction required to halt and reverse the expansion continually came up short. In fact, recent observations of distant supernovae indicate that, far from slowing down, the cosmic expansion is actually speeding up! There is some sort of mysterious "dark energy" in the form of either a variable energy field (called "quintessence") or, more probably, a positive cosmological constant or vacuum energy causing the expansion to proceed more rapidly. If the dark energy does indicate the existence of a positive cosmological constant, as the evidence increasingly suggests, "the Universe will expand forever."[20]

Furthermore, wholly apart from the physical and observational difficulties confronting oscillatory models, the thermodynamic properties of such models imply the very beginning of the universe that their proponents sought to avoid. For entropy is conserved from cycle to cycle in such models, which has the effect of generating larger and longer oscillations with each successive cycle. Thus, as one traces the oscillations

---

[19]Stephen Hawking and Roger Penrose, *The Nature of Space and Time,* The Isaac Newton Institute Series of Lectures (Princeton, N.J.: Princeton University Press, 1996), p. 20.

[20]See the NASA website of the Wilkinson Microwave Anisotropy Probe <http://map.gsfc.nasa.gov/m_mm/mr_limits.html>.

back in time, they become progressively smaller until one reaches a first and smallest oscillation. Ya. B. Zeldovich and I. D. Novikov therefore conclude, "The multicycle model has an infinite future, but only a finite past."[21] In fact, astronomer Joseph Silk estimates on the basis of current entropy levels that the universe cannot have gone through more than one hundred previous oscillations.[22] This is far from sufficient to generate the sort of serial world ensemble imagined by Dawkins.

Finally, even if the universe could oscillate from eternity past, such a universe would require an infinitely precise fine-tuning of initial conditions in order to persist through an infinite number of successive bounces, so that the mechanism Dawkins envisions for generating his many worlds is not simple—in fact, quite the opposite! Moreover, such a universe involves fine-tuning of a very bizarre sort, since the initial conditions have to be set at minus infinity in the past. But how could that be done if there was no beginning?

Dawkins's second suggested mechanism for generating a world ensemble is Lee Smolin's evolutionary cosmology, according to which black holes are portals to baby universes being birthed by ours. Universes which produce lots of black holes therefore have an evolutionary advantage in producing more offspring. Since black holes are the result of star formation, and stars promote planets where life can evolve, the unintended effect of evolutionary cosmology is to make life-permitting universes more probable.

Dawkins acknowledges that "not all physicists" are enthusiastic about Smolin's scenario. Talk about an understatement! For Smolin's scenario, wholly apart from its ad hoc and even disconfirmed conjectures, encountered insuperable difficulties.

First, a fatal flaw in Smolin's scenario was his assumption that universes which produce lots of black holes would also produce lots of stable stars. In fact, the exact opposite is true: the most proficient producers of black holes would be universes which generate primordial black holes *prior* to star formation, so that life-permitting universes would actually be *weeded out* by Smolin's cosmic evolutionary scenario. Thus, it turns out that Smolin's scenario would actually make the existence of a

---

[21]I. D. Novikov and Ya. B. Zeldovich, "Physical Processes near Cosmological Singularities," *Annual Review of Astronomy and Astrophysics* 11 (1973): 401-2.

[22]Joseph Silk, *The Big Bang,* 2nd ed. (San Francisco: W. H. Freeman, 1989), pp. 311-12.

life-permitting universe even more improbable.

Second, speculations about the universe's begetting "baby universes" via black holes have been shown to contradict quantum physics. The conjecture that black holes may be portals of wormholes through which bubbles of false vacuum energy can tunnel to spawn new expanding baby universes was the subject of a bet between Stephen Hawking and James Preskill, which Hawking in 2004 finally admitted, in an event much publicized in the press, that he had lost. The conjecture would require that information locked up in a black hole could be utterly lost forever by escaping to another universe. One of the last holdouts, Hawking finally came to agree that quantum theory requires that information is preserved in black hole formation and evaporation. The implications? "There is no baby universe branching off, as I once thought. The information remains firmly in our universe. I'm sorry to disappoint science fiction fans, but if information is preserved, there is no possibility of using black holes to travel to other universes."[23] That means that Smolin's scenario is physically impossible.

Even if Hawking had won the bet, the question would remain whether such a scenario could be in any case successfully extrapolated into the past, such that our universe is one of the baby universes spawned by the mother universe or by an infinite series of ancestors. It seems not, for while such baby universes appear as black holes to observers in the mother universe, an observer in the baby universe itself will see the big bang as a white hole spewing out energy. But this is in sharp contrast to our observation of the big bang as a low-entropy event with a highly constrained geometrical structure. Thus, Smolin's scenario is also invalidated by the data of observational astronomy.

These are the only mechanisms Dawkins suggests for generating an ensemble of randomly ordered universes. Neither of them is even tenable, much less simple. Dawkins has therefore failed to turn back the objection that his postulation of a randomly ordered world ensemble is an unparsimonious extravagance.

But there are even more formidable objections to the postulate of a world ensemble of which Dawkins is apparently unaware. First, there's no independent evidence that such a world ensemble exists. Recall, moreover,

---

[23]Stephen W. Hawking, "Information Loss in Black Holes" at <http://arXiv:hep-th/0507171>. Accessed April 28, 2009.

Borde, Guth and Vilenkin proved that any universe in a state of overall cosmic expansion cannot be infinite in the past. Their theorem applies to the multiverse too. Since the multiverse's past is finite, only a finite number of other worlds may have been generated by now, so that there's no guarantee that a finely tuned world will have appeared in the ensemble.

Second, if our universe is just a random member of an infinite world ensemble, then it is overwhelmingly more probable that we should be observing a much different universe than what we in fact observe. Roger Penrose has calculated that it is inconceivably more probable that our solar system should suddenly form by the random collision of particles than that a finely tuned universe should exist. (Penrose calls it "utter chicken feed" by comparison.)[24] So if our universe were just a random member of a world ensemble, it is inconceivably more probable that we should be observing an orderly universe no larger than our solar system. Observable universes like that are simply much more plenteous in the world ensemble than worlds like ours and, therefore, ought to be observed by us. Since we do not have such observations, that fact strongly disconfirms the multiverse hypothesis. From a naturalistic point of view, according to which there is no designer, it is therefore highly probable that there is no world ensemble.

The fine-tuning of the universe is therefore plausibly due neither to physical necessity nor to chance. It follows that the fine-tuning is therefore due to design, *unless* the design hypothesis can be shown to be even more implausible than its competitors.

Dawkins contends that the alternative of design is, indeed, inferior to the many worlds hypothesis. Summarizing what he calls "the central argument of my book," Dawkins insists that even in the admitted absence of a "strongly satisfying" explanation for the fine-tuning in physics, still the "relatively weak" explanations we have at present are "self-evidently better than the self-defeating . . . hypothesis of an intelligent designer."[25] Really? What is this powerful objection to the design hypothesis?

Here it is: we're not justified in inferring design as the best explanation of the complex order of the universe because doing so gives rise to a new problem: who designed the designer? This question is apparently supposed to be so crushing that it outweighs all the problems

[24]See Roger Penrose, *The Road to Reality* (New York: Knopf, 2005), pp. 762-65.
[25]Dawkins, *God Delusion*, p. 158.

with the world ensemble hypothesis.[26]

Dawkins's objection, however, has no weight for at least two reasons. First, in order to recognize an explanation as the best, you don't need to have an explanation of the explanation. This is an elementary point in the philosophy of science. If archaeologists digging in the earth were to discover things looking like arrowheads and pottery shards, they would be justified in inferring that these artifacts are not the chance result of sedimentation and metamorphosis but products of some unknown group of people—even if they had no explanation of who these people were or where they came from. Similarly, if astronauts were to come upon a pile of machinery on the back side of the moon, they would be justified in inferring that it was the product of intelligent agents—even if they had no idea whatsoever who these agents were or how they got there. To repeat: in order to recognize an explanation as the best, you don't need to be able to explain the explanation. In fact, such a requirement would lead to an infinite regress of explanations, so that nothing could ever be explained and science would be destroyed. For before any explanation could be acceptable, you'd need an explanation of it, and then an explanation of the explanation of the explanation, and then . . . Nothing could ever be explained!

So in order to recognize that intelligent design is the best explanation of the appearance of design in the universe, you don't need to be able to explain the designer. Whether the designer has an explanation can simply be left an open question for future inquiry.

Second, Dawkins thinks that a divine designer of the universe would be just as complex as the thing to be explained, so that no explanatory advance is made. This objection raises all sorts of questions about the role played by simplicity in assessing competing explanations. There are many factors besides simplicity that scientists weigh in determining which explanation is the best: explanatory power, explanatory scope and so forth. An explanation which has broader explanatory scope may be less simple than a rival explanation but still preferred because it explains more things. Simplicity is not the only, or even most important, criterion for assessing theories.

But leave those questions aside. Dawkins's fundamental mistake lies

---

[26]Because Dawkins erroneously thinks that the world ensemble is simple, it never occurs to him to ask, who designed the world ensemble?

in his assumption that a divine designer is just as complex as the universe. That is plainly false. In contrast to the contingent and variegated universe with all its inexplicable constants and quantities, a divine mind, being an immaterial entity not composed of parts, is startlingly simple.

Dawkins protests, "A God capable of continuously monitoring and controlling the individual status of every particle in the universe *cannot* be simple."[27] Dawkins has evidently confused a mind's ideas and effects, which may indeed be complex, with a mind itself, which—having no parts—is an incredibly simple entity. Certainly a mind may have complex *ideas*—it may be thinking, for example, of the infinitesimal calculus—and may be capable of doing complex *tasks*—such as controlling the trajectory of every particle in the universe—but the mind *itself* remains a remarkably simple, nonphysical entity. Therefore, postulating a divine mind behind the universe most definitely does represent an advance in simplicity, for whatever that's worth.

Dawkins's central argument thus fails to show that the alternative of design is in any way inferior to the many worlds hypothesis. Indeed, his smug and self-congratulatory attitude for this pitiful argument, sustained even in the face of repeated correction by prominent philosophers and theologians like Richard Swinburne and Keith Ward, is marvelous.

Therefore, of the three alternatives before us—physical necessity, chance or design—the most plausible explanation of cosmic fine-tuning is design.

ONTOLOGICAL ARGUMENT

The next argument to be discussed by Dawkins, and the last I have space to review, is the famous ontological argument. The version below comes from Alvin Plantinga and is formulated in terms of possible-worlds semantics. By "a possible world" I don't mean a planet or even a universe, but rather a complete description of reality, or a way reality might be. To say that God exists in some possible world is just to say that there is a possible description of reality which includes the statement "God exists" as part of that description.

In his version of the argument, Plantinga conceives of God as a being which is "maximally excellent" in every possible world. Plantinga takes maximal excellence to include such properties as omniscience, omnipo-

---

[27]Dawkins, *God Delusion*, p. 149.

tence and moral perfection. A being which has maximal excellence in every possible world would have what Plantinga calls "maximal greatness." Now Plantinga argues:

(1) It is possible that a maximally great being exists.

(2) If it is possible that a maximally great being exists, then a maximally great being exists in some possible world.

(3) If a maximally great being exists in some possible world, then it exists in every possible world.

(4) If a maximally great being exists in every possible world, then it exists in the actual world.

(5) If a maximally great being exists in the actual world, then a maximally great being exists.

(6) Therefore, a maximally great being exists.

It might surprise you to learn that premises (2-5) of this argument are relatively uncontroversial. Most philosophers would agree that if God's existence is even possible, then he must exist. The principal issue to be settled with respect to Plantinga's ontological argument is what warrant exists for thinking the premise "It is possible that a maximally great being exists" is true.

In order for the ontological argument to fail, the concept of a maximally great being must be incoherent, like the concept of a married bachelor. But the concept of a maximally great being doesn't seem even remotely incoherent. The idea of a maximally great being is intuitively a coherent idea, and so there is some prima facie warrant for thinking that it is possible that a maximally great being exists.

Dawkins devotes six full pages, brimming with ridicule and invective, to the ontological argument without raising any serious objection to Plantinga's argument. He notes in passing Immanuel Kant's objection that existence is not a perfection; but since Plantinga's argument doesn't presuppose that it is, we can leave that irrelevance aside. Dawkins also reiterates a parody of the argument designed to show that God does not exist: a God "who created everything while not existing" is greater than one who created everything and exists.[28] Ironically, however, far from undermining the ontological argument, this parody reinforces it. For a being who creates everything while not existing is a logical incoherence

---

[28]Ibid., p. 83.

and is therefore impossible: there is no possible world which includes a nonexistent being which creates the world. If the atheist is to maintain—as he must—that God's existence is impossible, the concept of God would have to be similarly incoherent. But it's not. That supports the plausibility of premise (1).

Dawkins also chortles, "I've forgotten the details, but I once piqued a gathering of theologians and philosophers by adapting the ontological argument to prove that pigs can fly. They felt the need to resort to Modal Logic to prove that I was wrong."[29] But this is just embarrassing. The ontological argument *is* an exercise in modal logic—the logic of the possible and the necessary. I can just imagine Dawkins making a silly ass of himself at this professional conference with his spurious parody, just as he similarly embarrassed himself at the Templeton Foundation conference in Cambridge with his flyweight objection to the teleological argument.

I'm out of space. There are other arguments to be discussed. Doubtless you can think of substantive objections to the arguments I have presented here. But at least I hope to have shown that the objections raised by Richard Dawkins to these arguments are not even injurious, much less deadly.

FOR FURTHER READING

Introductory Works
Craig, William Lane, and Walter Sinnott-Armstrong. *God? A Debate Between a Christian and an Atheist.* New York: Oxford University Press, 2003.

Strobel, Lee. *The Case for a Creator.* Grand Rapids: Zondervan, 2004.

Advanced Works
Craig, William Lane, ed. *Philosophy of Religion: A Reader and Guide.* New Brunswick, N.J.: Rutgers University Press, 2002.

Craig, William Lane, and Antony Flew. *Does God Exist?* Edited by Stan Wallace. Aldershot, U.K.: Ashgate, 2003.

Davis, Stephen T. *God, Reason, and Theistic Proofs.* Grand Rapids: Eerdmans, 1997.

King, Nathan, and Robert Garcia, eds. *God and Ethics: A Contemporary Debate.* Lanham, Md.: Rowman & Littlefield, 2008.

---

[29]Ibid., p. 84.

Leslie, John. *Universes*. London: Routledge, 1989.

O'Connor, Timothy. *Theism and Ultimate Explanation: The Necessary Shape of Contingency*. Oxford: Blackwell, 2008.

Plantinga, Alvin. *The Nature of Necessity*. Oxford: Clarendon, 1974.

Pruss, Alexander. *The Principle of Sufficient Reason: A Reassessment*. Cambridge Studies in Philosophy. Cambridge: Cambridge University Press, 2006.

Stewart, Robert, ed. *The Future of Atheism: Alister McGrath and Daniel Dennett in Dialogue*. Minneapolis: Fortress Press, 2008.

2

The Image of God and the
Failure of Scientific Atheism

J. P. MORELAND

> *And God created man in his own image,*
> *in the image of God he created him;*
> *male and female he created them.*
>
> GENESIS 1:27

One of the roles of a worldview is to provide an explanation of facts, of reality the way it actually is. Indeed, it is incumbent on a worldview that it explain what does and does not exist in ways that follow naturally from the core explanatory commitments of that worldview. In this sense, we can call a worldview an explanatory hypothesis.

From worldview explanations of facts to scientific theorizing to explaining little things in everyday life, we all quite appropriately engage in if-then reasoning, or what philosophers call the hypothetico-deductive method: If the moon were in such and such a place, then the tide would be thus and so. But the tide isn't thus and so, so the moon must not be in that place. If my daughter did not come straight home from school, she would not have had time to clean her room. The room is messy, so it is likely she did not come straight home from school. And so on. And if the facts are as we deduce they should be, given our hypothesis, then this provides confirming evidence that our hypothesis is true—the best explanation for the facts.

A theory may explain some facts quite nicely, but there are recalcitrant facts that doggedly resist explanation by a theory. No matter what a theory's advocate does, the recalcitrant fact just sits there and is not easily incorporated into the theory. In this case, the recalcitrant fact provides falsifying evidence for the theory and some degree of confirmation for its rivals.

The Bible teaches that human beings are made in the image of God (Gen 1:27). This implies that there are things about our makeup that are like how God is. At the beginning of his *Institutes of the Christian Religion*, John Calvin observed:

> No man can survey himself without forthwith turning his thoughts towards the God in whom he lives and moves; because it is perfectly obvious, that the endowments which we possess cannot possibly be from ourselves.[1]

As image-bearers, human beings have all those endowments necessary to represent and be representative of God, and to accomplish the tasks and exhibit the relationality placed before them: endowments of reason, self-determination, moral action, personality and relational formation, and so on. In this sense, the image of God is straightforwardly rooted in God's nature, or *ontological.*

The ontological nature of the image of God, among other things, implies that the makeup of human beings should provide a set of recalcitrant facts for other worldviews. The reasoning behind this claim goes like this:

(1) If Christianity is true, then certain features should characterize human beings.

(2) Those features do, in fact, characterize human beings.

(3) Thus, these features provide a degree of confirmation for Christianity. These features characterize God and, moreover, come from him. He made us to have them.

The Christian, then, offers a challenge to other worldviews—partic-

---

[1]John Calvin *Institutes of the Christian Religion* 1.1.1.

ularly scientific naturalism: show that you have a better explanation for these features than Christianity does (with its doctrine of the image of God), or show that these features are not actually real, even though they seem to be.

The recalcitrant nature of human persons for scientific naturalism has been widely noticed. Thus, Berkeley philosopher John Searle recently noted,

> There is exactly one overriding question in contemporary philosophy. . . . How do we fit in? . . . How can we square this self-conception of ourselves as mindful, meaning-creating, free, rational, etc., agents with a universe that consists entirely of mindless, meaningless, unfree, nonrational, brute physical particles?"[2]

For the scientific naturalist, the answer is "Not very well." Notable atheists have failed to notice the difficulty for scientific naturalism in accounting for these commonsense features of human beings. In fact, the nature of human persons has led some to embrace theism. In the seismic book recounting the shift to theism by famous atheist Antony Flew—*There Is a God*—Roy Abraham Varghese notes that

> the rationality [consciousness, freedom of the will and unified self] that we unmistakably experience—ranging from the laws of nature to our capacity for rational thought—cannot be explained if it does not have an ultimate ground, which can be nothing less than an infinite mind.[3]

In what follows I shall first offer a brief sketch of contemporary scientific naturalism and then mention five features of human persons that provide evidence *against* naturalism and *for* biblical theism. I shall employ more direct quotations than is typical for a chapter like this, and it may make reading what follows a bit cumbersome. I do this to demonstrate that my depiction of these five features is acknowledged by top atheists themselves as serious problems for atheism and as grounds for believing in God. By quoting top atheists directly, it will be hard to accuse me of creating a strawman depiction of contemporary naturalism.

---

[2]John Searle, *Freedom & Neurobiology* (New York: Columbia University Press, 2007), pp. 4-5.
[3]Antony Flew and Roy Abraham Varghese, *There Is a God* (New York: HarperCollins, 2007), p. 167. In context, only rationality is mentioned, but in other parts of the book, reference is also made to consciousness, free will and the self.

THE NATURE OF SCIENTIFIC NATURALISM

To gain further insight into why consciousness is such a problem for naturalists, it may be wise to look briefly at the nature of naturalism as a worldview. Naturalism usually includes

- different aspects of a naturalist understanding of what constitutes knowledge (for example, a rejection of so-called first philosophy along with an acceptance of either weak or strong *scientism*—the view that science is the paradigm of truth and rationality);[4]

- a Grand Story which amounts to an etiological account of how all entities whatsoever have come to be, told in terms of an event-causal story described in natural scientific terms, with a central role given to the atomic theory of matter and evolutionary biology;

- a general ontology in which the only entities allowed are those that either (a) bear a relevant similarity to those thought to characterize a completed form of physics or (b) are dependent on and determined by the entities of physics and can be explained according to the causal necessitation requirement (that is, given a "suitable" arrangement of matter, the emergent entity *must* arise) in terms of the Grand Story and the naturalist epistemic attitude.

Scientism constitutes the core of the naturalistic understanding of what constitutes knowledge, its *epistemology*. Wilfrid Sellars says that "in the dimension of describing and explaining the world, science is the measure of all things, of what is that it is, and of what is not that it is not."[5] Contemporary naturalists embrace either weak or strong scientism. According to the former, nonscientific fields are not worthless nor do they offer no intellectual results, but they are vastly inferior to science in their epistemic standing and do not merit full credence. According to the latter, unqualified cognitive value resides in science and in nothing else. Either way, naturalists are extremely skeptical of claims about reality that are not justified by scientific methods in the hard sciences.

As I've been using the phrase, "the Grand Story" is the naturalist cre-

---

[4]The *strong* version of scientism maintains that science provides us with the *sole* basis of knowledge; the *weaker* version claims that science furnishes us with the *most certain* basis of knowledge, even if other disciplines provide more weakly justified beliefs or knowledge.

[5]Wilfrid Sellars, *Science, Perception, and Reality* (London: Routledge & Kegan Paul, 1963), p. 173.

ation account: All of reality—space, time and matter—came from the big bang. Various heavenly bodies developed as the universe expanded. On at least the earth, some sort of prebiotic soup scenario explains how living things came into being from nonliving chemicals. And the processes of evolution, understood in either neo-Darwinian or punctuated-equilibrium terms, gave rise to all the life forms we see, including human beings. Thus, all organisms and their parts exist and are what they are because they contributed to (or at least did not hinder) the struggle for reproductive advantage, more specifically, because they contributed to the tasks of feeding, fighting, fleeing and reproducing.

The Grand Story has three key features. First, at its core are two fundamental theories: the atomic theory of matter and evolutionary theory. If we take John Searle to be representative of naturalists here, this means that causal explanations are central to the (alleged) explanatory superiority of the Grand Story.[6]

Second, the Grand Story expresses a scientistic philosophical monism according to which everything that exists or happens in the world is susceptible to explanations by natural scientific methods. At first glance, the most consistent way to understand naturalism in this regard is to see it as entailing some version of strong physicalism: everything that exists is fundamentally matter, most likely, elementary "particles" (whether taken as points of potentiality, centers of mass/energy, units of spatially extended stuff/waves, or reduced to [or eliminated in favor of] fields), organized in various ways according to the laws of nature. No nonphysical entities exist, including emergent ones.[7]

Third, the history of the universe is a story of unfolding chains of events in which small particles constantly rearrange to form larger and more complicated wholes (for example, atoms, molecules, organisms, planets). The only sorts of causes in the universe are mechanical/efficient (that by means of which an effect is produced) and material (the stuff out of which something is made). There are no purposes, goals, final causes, irreducible teleology. And there are no free agents with the active power to be the real originating causes of their own actions without being determined to act by the laws of nature and external environmental factors.

---

[6]John Searle, *The Rediscovery of the Mind* (Cambridge: MIT Press, 1992), pp. 83-93.
[7]Even when naturalists venture away from strong physicalism, they still argue that additions to a strong physicalist ontology must be depicted as rooted in, emergent from, dependent on the physical states and events of the Grand Story.

Indeed, the Grand Story is deterministic in two senses. First, through time the state of the universe (and everything in it) at any particular moment, plus the laws of nature, are sufficient to determine or fix the chances of the state of the universe at the next moment. Second, at a point in time, the characteristics and behaviors of ordinary-sized objects like rocks and living organisms (including human persons) are determined by the characteristics and behaviors of their tiny parts at the level of microphysics.

In sum, there are three constraints for developing a naturalist ontology and locating entities within it:

- Entities should conform to the naturalist epistemology.

- Entities should conform to the naturalist Grand Story.

- Entities should bear a relevant similarity to those found in chemistry and physics or be shown to depend necessarily on entities in chemistry and physics.

FIVE RECALCITRANT FEATURES OF THE IMAGE OF GOD

Given that the metaphysical features of theism are fundamental in existence—God, the basic Being, is a unified, conscious self with rationality, free will and intrinsic value—it is hardly surprising that they appear elsewhere in the created order, especially in association with beings that are alleged to have been created to be like God. Thus, biblical theism predicts that these five features are irreducible, ineliminable aspects of human persons, and the fact that they seem to be such provides confirmation of biblical theism.

But things don't go so well for the scientific naturalist. He or she begins not with the Logos but with particles (strings, waves) that are brute, mechanical, unconscious, nonrational, nonteleological, slavishly subject to law and bereft of value. And then a story is told about how these continue to rearrange into larger and larger aggregates of the same stuff. On this view, living organisms—including human persons—are relational structures of parts held together by various forces, not unified, uncomposed substantial selves. For sixty years or so, naturalists have tried to reduce or eliminate these five features of human persons in order to depict them in ways natural to a scientific atheistic worldview and within the bounds of its constraints. Labeling these features "emergent phenomena" is just a placeholder for the problem to be solved, not a solution (e.g., consciousness simply emerges when matter reaches a suitable form of complexity). How, for example, could it be that they emerged in the first place? But human persons have resisted such efforts—they are *recalcitrant* facts for naturalists—and this is exactly what would be predicted if biblical theism were true. It is not what would be predicted from the Grand Story. Let's probe these issues more fully.

1. Consciousness and the mental. Many believe that finite minds provide evidence of a divine mind as their creator. If we limit our live options to theism and naturalism, it is hard to see how finite consciousness could result from the rearrangement of brute matter; it is easier to see how a conscious Being could produce finite consciousness.

This argument assumes a commonsense understanding of conscious states such as sensations, thoughts, beliefs, desires and volitions. So understood, mental states are in no sense physical since they possess four features not owned by physical states:

- There is a raw qualitative feel or a "what it is like" to have a mental state such as a pain.

- Many mental states have intentionality—*ofness* or *aboutness*—directed toward an object (e.g., a thought is *about* the moon).

- Mental states are inner, private and immediate to the subject having them.

- Mental states fail to have crucial features (e.g., spatial extension, location) that characterize physical states and, in general, cannot be described using physical language.

Given that conscious states are immaterial and not physical, at least two reasons have been offered for why there can be no natural scientific explanation for the existence of conscious states.

First, *something from nothing.* Before consciousness appeared, the universe contained nothing but aggregates of particles/waves standing in fields of forces. The naturalistic story of the cosmos's evolution involves the rearrangement of atomic parts into increasingly more complex structures according to natural law. Matter is brute mechanical, physical stuff. The emergence of consciousness seems to be a case of getting something from nothing.

In general, physico-chemical reactions do not generate consciousness.

Some say they do in the brain, yet brains seem similar to other parts of organisms' bodies (e.g., both are collections of cells totally describable in physical terms). How can like causes produce radically different effects? The appearance of mind is utterly unpredictable and inexplicable. This radical discontinuity seems like a rupture in the natural world.

Second, *the inadequacy of evolutionary explanations.* Naturalists claim that evolutionary explanations can be proffered for the appearance of all organisms and their parts. In principle, an evolutionary account could be given for increasingly complex physical structures that constitute different organisms. However, organisms are black boxes as far as evolution is concerned.

As long as an organism, when receiving certain inputs, generates the correct behavioral outputs under the demands of reproductive advantage, the organism will survive. What goes on inside the organism is irrelevant, becoming significant for the processes of evolution only when an output is produced. Strictly speaking, it is the output, not what caused it, that bears on the struggle for reproductive advantage. Moreover, the functions organisms carry out consciously *could just as well have been done unconsciously.* Thus, both the sheer existence of conscious states and the precise mental content that constitutes them are outside the pale of evolutionary explanation.

It will not do to claim that consciousness simply emerged from matter when it reached a certain level of complexity. "Emergence" is not an explanation of the phenomena to be explained. It's merely a label.

2. Free will. It is widely acknowledged that the commonsense, spontaneously formed understanding of human free will is what philosophers call libertarian freedom: one acts freely only if one's action was not determined—directly or indirectly—by forces outside his control, and one must be free to act or refrain from acting; one's choice is "spontaneous," it originates with and only with the actor.

It is not my purpose to argue for libertarianism. I simply offer two fairly obvious remarks.

For one thing, as John Searle has recently noted, the experience of libertarian free will is compelling—so compelling, in fact, that people cannot act as though that experience is an illusion, even if it is one.[8] He reminds us that when we are presented by the waiter with a choice be-

---

[8]John Searle, *Freedom & Neurobiology* (New York: Columbia University Press, 2007).

tween pork or veal, we cannot bring ourselves to reply, "Look, I'm a determinist. I'll just have to wait and see what order happens!"

According to a major understanding of Christianity, God has libertarian freedom and created his image-bearers to possess this freedom. By contrast, most philosophers are agreed that libertarian freedom and a theory of agency it entails are incompatible with the generally accepted depiction of naturalism presented earlier. John Searle says that "our conception of physical reality simply does not allow for radical [libertarian] freedom."[9] And if moral (and intellectual) responsibility has such freedom as a necessary condition, then reconciling the natural and ethical perspectives is impossible.

In what may be the best naturalist attempt to accomplish such a reconciliation, John Bishop frankly admits that

> the idea of a responsible agent, with the "originative" ability to initiate events in the natural world, does not sit easily with the idea of [an agent as] a natural organism. . . . Our scientific understanding of human behavior seems to be in tension with a presupposition of the ethical stance we adopt toward it.[10]

There are many reasons why atheists admit that free will is incompatible with scientific naturalism. But here's a major one. All the particular things and their behavior in the naturalist order are lawlike and, so, subsumable under laws of nature.[11] Further, a free act involves an exercise of active power by a first mover, an uncaused causer, an undetermined actor. By contrast, since all events in a naturalist ontology are passive happenings, they all are examples of moved movers. Something has to happen to an object first—an event that triggers and actualizes its passive causal powers—before it can cause something else to happen. In this sense, all naturalistic causation involves changed changers. But a first mover can actively produce change without having to change first to do so.

---

[9]John Searle, *Minds, Brains, and Science* (Cambridge, Mass.: Harvard University Press, 1984), p. 98.

[10]John Bishop, *Natural Agency* (Cambridge: Cambridge University Press, 1989), p. 1.

[11]In fact, all of them are subject to synchronic and diachronic determinism in this sense: Regarding synchronic determinism, at some time t, the physical conditions are sufficient to determine or fix the chances of the next event involving the object and its environment. Regarding diachronic determinism, at any time t, the object's states and movements are determined or have their chances fixed by the microphysical states of the object and its environment. This latter determination is bottom-up.

It should be obvious why such an agent is not an object that can be located in a natural ontology. Unmoved movers with active power are quintessentially unnatural! Indeed, in this regard they are exactly like the God of the Bible.

3. Rationality. According to Christianity, God—the fundamental being—is rational and created his image-bearers with the mental equipment to exhibit rationality and be apt for truth gathering in their various environments. But rationality is an odd entity in a scientific naturalist world. Christian philosopher Victor Reppert agrees: "The necessary conditions for rationality cannot exist in a naturalistic universe."[12] According to naturalist Thomas Nagel:

> The problem then will be not how, if we engage in it, reason can be valid, but how, if it is universally valid, we can engage in it. There are not many candidates to this question. Probably the most popular nonsubjectivist answer nowadays is an evolutionary naturalism: We can reason in these ways because it is a consequence of a more primitive capacity of belief formation that had survival value during the period when the human brain was evolving. This explanation has always seemed to me to be laughably inadequate. . . . The other well-known answer is the religious one. The universe is intelligible to us because it and our minds were made for each other.[13]

There are at least two reasons why human persons can't be rational agents in a scientific naturalist worldview but are predicted to be precisely such in a biblical worldview: (1) the necessity of the enduring, rational self and (2) the need for room for teleological (goal-directed) factors to play a role in thought processes.

There must be not only a unified self at each time in a deliberative sequence but also an identical self that endures through the rational act. Consider A. C. Ewing's argument:

> To realize the truth of any proposition or even entertain it as something meaningful the same being must be aware of its different constituents. To be aware of the validity of an argument the same being must entertain premises and conclusion; to compare two things the same being must, at least in memory, be aware of them simultaneously; and since all these

---

[12]Victor Reppert, *C. S. Lewis's Dangerous Idea* (Downers Grove, Ill.: InterVarsity Press, 2003), p. 70.

[13]Thomas Nagel, *The Last Word* (New York: Oxford University Press, 1997), p. 75.

processes take some time the continuous existence of literally the same entity is required. In these cases an event which consisted in the contemplating of A followed by another event which consisted in the contemplating of B is not sufficient. They must be events of contemplating that occur in the same being. If one being thought of wolves, another of eating, and another of lambs, it certainly would not mean that anybody contemplated the proposition "wolves eat lambs." . . . There must surely be a single being persisting through the process to grasp a proposition or inference as a whole.[14]

Rational deliberation and intellectual responsibility seem to presuppose an enduring I. But on the naturalist view, I am a collection of parts such that if I gain and lose parts, I am literally a different aggregate from one moment to the next. Thus, there is no such enduring I that could serve as the unifier of rational thought on a naturalist view.

But there's more. Consider the following argument:

(1) If naturalism is true, there is no irreducible teleology.

(2) Rational deliberation exhibits irreducible teleology.

(3) Therefore, naturalism is false.

Scientific naturalism completely eschews irreducible teleology. However, teleology is essential to reasons-explanations. To see this, look at these two sentences:

- The glass broke because the rock hit it.

- I raised my hand because I wanted to vote.

It seems clear that the first offers a reason-explanation and the second does not. "The glass broke because the rock hit it" cites an efficient (mechanical) cause after "because" (the rock hitting the glass). But "I raised my hand because I wanted to vote" is very different. It cites a teleological goal or end (to satisfy the desire to vote, to make a difference in the culture, etc.) for the sake of which the person raised his or her hand.

4. Unified selves. Naturalism cannot countenance a substantial, enduring mental self (what we could perhaps call a *mind* or *immaterial soul*). If one starts with separable physical parts, and simply rearranges them according to natural laws into new relational structures constituted by external relations, then in the category of "individual," one's

---

[14]A. C. Ewing, *Value and Reality* (London: George Allen and Unwin, 1973), p. 84.

ontology will have what are called atomic simples.

There are two basic reasons why a substantial, simple soul is not an option for a naturalist. First, the naturalist is committed to the closure of the physical. All physical events that have causes have entirely physical causes; when tracing the causal antecedents of a physical event, one need not—and, indeed, cannot—leave the physical realm. If by some sort of magic, a simple soul could be an emergent entity, then the soul would be an entity with no causal powers. However, most naturalists banish entities with no causal powers from their ontology, so a soul with no causal powers is tantamount to a nonexistent entity. Jaegwon Kim speaks for most naturalists when he says:

> If the immaterial mind is going to cause a neuron to emit a signal, . . . then it must somehow intervene in these electrochemical processes. But how could this happen? At the very interface between the mental and the physical where direct and unmediated mind-body interaction takes place, the nonphysical mind must somehow influence the state of some molecules, perhaps by electrically charging them or nudging them this way or that way. Is this really conceivable? . . . Even if the idea of a soul's influencing the motion of a molecule . . . were coherent, the postulation of such a causal agent would seem neither necessary nor helpful in understanding why and how our limbs move.[15]

Second, given the Grand Story, apart from atomic simples (if such there be), all larger wholes (such as brains and bodies) are aggregates composed of separable, substantial parts that stand in various external relations to each other. In such an ontology, macrosubstances are replaced with structures constituted by myriads of separable parts. There is no unified, substantial self or mind connected to a body. Daniel Dennett says, "We now understand that the mind is not . . . in *communication with* the brain some miraculous way; it *is* the brain, or, more specifically, a system or organization within the brain."[16] And Carl Sagan flatly asserts: "I am a collection of water, calcium and organic molecules called Carl Sagan. You are a collection of almost identical molecules

---

[15]Jaegwon Kim, *Philosophy of Mind* (Boulder, Co.: Westview, 1996), pp. 131-32. "Most physicalists . . . accept the causal closure of the physical not only as a fundamental metaphysical doctrine but as an indispensable methodological presupposition of the physical sciences" (pp. 147-48).

[16]Daniel C. Dennett, *Breaking the Spell: Religion as a Natural Phenomenon* (New York: Viking Press, 2006), p. 107.

with a different collective label."[17] The terms *configuration, system, organization* and *collection* capture nicely the nonsubstantial, relational nature of such aggregates. In contrast with scientific naturalism, Christianity's fundamental being is a substantial, unified spirit, and those made in his image are as well.

5. Intrinsic, equal value and rights. On a Christian view, God the fundamental being possesses intrinsic value, and his loving, just character is the source of objective moral obligation for human persons. Moreover, since all human beings share the image of God equally, they all have high, equal value and rights simply as such. Thus, a Christian worldview has a natural place for and provides an explanation of (1) the existence of intrinsic value, (2) the reality of objective moral obligation, and (3) high, equal value and rights for all humans. But these three cannot be accounted for adequately by scientific naturalism.

Let's look first at the existence of intrinsic value and an objective moral law. Evolutionary naturalist Michael Ruse notes that

> morality is a biological adaptation no less than are hands and feet and teeth. Considered as a rationally justifiable set of claims about an objective something, ethics is illusory. I appreciate that when somebody says "Love thy neighbor as thyself," they think they are referring above and beyond themselves. Nevertheless, such reference is truly without foundation. Morality is just an aid to survival and reproduction . . . and any deeper meaning is illusory.[18]

Given scientific naturalism, it is hard to see how there could be intrinsic value and an objective moral order or why that order would have anything to do with human persons. Moreover, the combinatorial processes of the Grand Story cannot account for the appearance of simple, intrinsic value; thus its existence counts against naturalism and for Christian theism. As atheist J. L. Mackie acknowledged: "Moral properties constitute so odd a cluster of properties and relations that they are most unlikely to have arisen in the ordinary course of events without an all-powerful god to create them."[19]

---

[17]Carl Sagan, *Cosmos* (New York: Random House, 1980), p. 105.

[18]Michael Ruse, "Evolutionary Theory and Christian Ethics," in *The Darwinian Paradigm* (London: Routledge, 1989), pp. 262-69.

[19]J. L. Mackie, *The Miracle of Theism* (Oxford: Clarendon, 1982), p. 115. Cf. J. P. Moreland and Kai Nielsen, *Does God Exist?* (Buffalo, N.Y.: Prometheus, 1993), chaps. 8-10.

In addition to intrinsic value and an objective moral order, scientific naturalism cannot account for the high, equal value and rights of human persons simply as such. Naturalists Peter Singer and Helga Kuhse acknowledge that the best, perhaps only, way to justify the belief that all humans have equal and unique value simply as such is in light of the metaphysical grounding of the Judeo-Christian doctrine of the image of God.[20] This claim by Singer and Kuhse has been acknowledged by a wide number of thinkers for some time. For example, in the early 1960s, Joel Feinberg, arguably the leading legal, political philosopher of that time, advanced the following argument.[21]

According to Feinberg, a natural right is a human right held unalterably, unconditionally, and possessing certain epistemological properties (e.g., perceivable by direct, rational intuition) and metaphysical groundings. If human rights are natural rights that apply to all human persons equally, then they presuppose equal human worth but not equal merit. Human merit (e.g., talents, skills, character, personality, various abilities) is graded, but human worth is not. Equal rights accrue to individuals quite apart from their graded merit.

The following skeptical question, Feinberg believes, has never been adequately answered: why should we treat all people equally in any respect in the face of manifest inequalities of merit among them? The simple response "Because we just have such worth" does not answer the skeptic's query. If "human worth" is real and generic, says Feinberg, then it must supervene on some subvenient base that (1) we all have equally in common and (2) is nontrivial and of supreme moral worth. Operating within a naturalist framework, Feinberg considers several attempts to delineate that base, and he judges them all to be a failure because they

- require an entity such as "pricelessness" for which we have no answer as to where it came from and with respect to which one must postulate a problematic, mysterious, intuitive faculty of direct awareness of such an entity;

- are grounded in a degreed property (one that is possessed to a greater or lesser degree) such as rationality (Feinberg takes the potential for

---

[20]Helga Kuhse and Peter Singer, *Should the Baby Live?* (Oxford: Oxford University Press, 1985), pp. 118-39.

[21]Joel Feinberg, *Social Philosophy* (Englewood Cliffs, N.J.: Prentice-Hall, 1973), pp. 84-97.

rationality to be degreed) which, therefore, cannot do the job of founding equal worth for all;

• simply name the problem to be solved and do not provide an explanation of the problem itself.

At the end of the day, Feinberg acknowledges that the notion of equal worth and equal rights for all human persons is groundless and may simply express a noncognitivist, unjustifiable pro-attitude of respect toward the humanity in each man's person.

My point in mentioning Feinberg is not to evaluate his claims, but to illustrate just how difficult it is to justify equal value and rights for all human persons if one has taken the naturalistic turn.

Evolutionary theory has also made equal human value and rights hard to justify. Thus, David Hull—perhaps the leading philosopher of evolutionary theory in the twentieth century—makes the following observation:

> The implications of moving species from the metaphysical category that can appropriately be characterized in terms of "natures" to a category for which such characterizations are inappropriate are extensive and fundamental. If species evolve in anything like the way that Darwin thought they did, then they cannot possibly have the sort of natures that traditional philosophers claimed they did. If species in general lack natures, then so does *Homo sapiens* as a biological species. If *Homo sapiens* lacks a nature, then no reference to biology can be made to support one's claims about "human nature." Perhaps all people are "persons," share the same "personhood," etc., but such claims must be explicated and defended *with no reference to biology*. Because so many moral, ethical, and political theories depend on some notion or other of human nature, Darwin's theory brought into question all these theories. The implications are not entailments. One can always dissociate "*Homo sapiens*" from "human being," but the result is a much less plausible position.[22]

Similarly, atheist James Rachels claims that a Darwinian approach to the origin of human beings, while not entailing the falsity of these notions, nevertheless provides an undercutting defeater for the idea that humans are made in the image of God and that humans have intrinsic dignity and worth as such. Indeed, according to Rachels, Darwinism is

---

[22]David Hull, *The Metaphysics of Evolution* (Albany: State University of New York, 1989), pp. 74-75.

the universal solvent that dissolves any attempt to defend the notion of intrinsic human dignity:

> The traditional supports for the idea of human dignity are gone. They have not survived the colossal shift of perspective brought about by Darwin's theory. It might be thought that this result need not be devastating for the idea of human dignity, because even if the traditional supports are gone, the idea might still be defended on some *other* grounds. Once again, though, an evolutionary perspective is bound to make one skeptical. The doctrine of human dignity says that humans merit a level of moral concern wholly different from that accorded to mere animals; for this to be true, there would have to be some big, morally significant difference between them. Therefore, any adequate defense of human dignity would require some conception of human beings as radically different from other animals. But that is precisely what evolutionary theory calls into question. It makes us suspicious of any doctrine that sees large gaps of any sort between humans and all other creatures. This being so, a Darwinian may conclude that a successful defense of human dignity is most unlikely.[23]

CONCLUSION

I have argued that on a Christian worldview, God the fundamental being possesses and shares with his image-bearers (1) consciousness, (2) libertarian free will, (3) rationality, (4) a unified self (and as a Trinity, three unified I's) and (5) intrinsic value. By contrast, given the epistemological and Grand Story constraints placed on the scientific naturalist ontology, not a single one of these five fits naturally in a non-ad-hoc way.

Naturalists can't appeal to emergence to solve their problems because (1) this is just a label for the problem to be solved and not a real solution and (2) it begs the question against Christian theism in a most egregious way. It would seem, then, that important features that characterize us human persons provide evidence that there is a Creator God who made us. And this is exactly what one would predict if biblical teaching about the image of God is true.

---

[23]James Rachels, *Created from Animals* (Oxford: Oxford University Press, 1990), pp. 171-72. Cf. pp. 93, 97, 171.

FOR FURTHER READING

Moreland, J. P. *Consciousness and the Existence of God*. London: Rout-
    ledge, 2008.

————. *The Recalcitrant Imago Dei: Human Persons and the Failure of
    Naturalism*. London: SCM Press, 2009.

Reppert, Victor. *C. S. Lewis's Dangerous Idea*. Downers Grove, Ill.: In-
    terVarsity Press, 2003.

Swinburne, Richard. *The Evolution of the Soul*, rev. ed. Oxford: Oxford
    University Press, 1996.

3

Evidence of a Morally Perfect God

PAUL K. MOSER

> *The one who does not love does not*
> *know God, for God is love.*
>
> 1 JOHN 4:8

The question of whether God exists is at least as old as the human race, if not the hills. But age has not yielded broad clarity in this case. In fact, this question—although obviously of first importance—has suffered from a certain widespread bias regarding how it should be approached. This essay uncovers the bias, challenges it and offers an alternative, more defensible approach to the question. We shall see that a morally robust version of theism is cognitively more resilient than contemporary critics have supposed.

THE KNOWLEDGE QUESTION

Many sane, educated and generally trustworthy people claim not only that God exists but also that they have genuine *knowledge*, including justified true belief, that God exists. Because claims are typically cheap and easy, however, the claim to know that God exists will prompt the following response, usually sooner rather than later: *How do they know?*

This common four-word question, although irksome at times, is perfectly intelligible and even valuable, as far as it goes. It seeks an explanation of how the belief that God exists exceeds *mere* belief, or opinion, and achieves the status of genuine knowledge. In particular, this question typically seeks an explanation of how, if at all, the belief that God exists is grounded, justified, reasonable or evidence-based regarding affirmation of its truth.

A plausible goal behind our four-word question is, at least for many inquirers, to acquire truth in a manner that includes an *adequate indication* of true belief. These truth-seeking inquirers aim not only to avoid false belief and lucky guesswork, but also to minimize the risk of error in their beliefs (at least in a way befitting to the acquisition of truth). We should aim for the same, as people who seek truth but who are faced sometimes with facts and other realities at odds with our opinions. In seeking truth about God's existence, in particular, we thus should seek truth based on evidence for God's reality. Such evidence, if available, would indicate that it is true that God exists, or (in other words) that God is real rather than fictional.

In treating any questions about God's existence, we do well to begin with some clarity regarding what (or whom) we are asking about: in this case, God's existence. Are we asking about a morally indefinite but strikingly powerful creator? Many academic writers on theism, "mere theism," deism, atheism, agnosticism and related philosophical positions inquire about the existence of such a creator, *whatever the creator's moral character may be*.[1] The creator in question may turn out to be an evil tyrant or at least a morally indifferent slouch. Such inquiry, however earnest and rigorous in its search for a creator, may rest on a misleading bias regarding God's character and would thus be significantly different from inquiry about the existence of a God who is *worthy of worship*, who is *morally perfect, including being perfectly loving toward all persons*. So let's clarify the latter kind of inquiry.

THE TITLE "GOD"

As suggested, we should approach the question about human knowl-

---

[1]For instance, in *Breaking the Spell: Religion as a Natural Phenomenon* (New York: Penguin, 2006), pp. 240-46, Daniel Dennett takes up the question Does God exist? without considering at all whether God's being perfectly loving would formatively influence the kind of evidence supplied by God to humans. Many other representatives of this misleading approach could be listed.

edge of God's existence by asking specifically what, or (better) whose, conceivable existence we are considering. Clearly, if the question of human knowledge of God's existence lacks value, then we should change the subject to something worthwhile.[2] Many people, however, will contend that this question actually has unsurpassed, life-or-death importance. The difference lies in what is meant by the term *God*. In this case, at least, one's meaning of a term matters significantly and thus deserves careful attention.

In keeping with a prominent traditional usage, we can fruitfully use the term *God* as a most exalted *title* rather than as a name. Part of the value of using the title thus is that it allows us to engage some central theological concerns of traditional monotheism (particularly of Judaism, Christianity and Islam) without arbitrarily dismissing atheists and agnostics by a naming fiat. For better or worse, people cannot name or postulate God into existence by refusing to imagine that God does not exist. Likewise, people cannot define or postulate God out of existence, as if a mere definition could block the actual existence of God. A God worthy of worship would not be at the linguistic mercy of people in any such way. The title *God,* on the proposed usage, signifies a being worthy of worship, even if such a being fails to exist and thus even if the title fails to refer to an actual thing.

Let's say that a being is worthy of worship if and only if that being, having inherent moral perfection, merits worship as unqualified adoration, love, trust and obedience. Of course, humans can worship a morally defective powerful being, perhaps out of human fear of harmful power, but the being in question would not be *worthy* of worship. Worthiness of worship requires inherent (or self-contained) moral perfection, including perfect moral righteousness, and such perfection in an agent demands, in turn, a perfectly loving character, including perfect love toward one's enemies (cf. Mt 5:38-48). An agent's selfish failure to love would block that agent from having a morally perfect character, however powerful and knowledgeable that selfish agent is. People, to their own detriment, often worship false gods, despite the unworthiness and unreliability of those gods. The results of such misguided worship

---

[2]Philosophical and theological questions about God often suffer from a seriously vague conception of God, resulting typically from undue abstractness in the assumed idea of God. Perhaps some humans use theological abstractness to divert attention from a divine moral challenge to humans.

do not include lasting human satisfaction, however, whatever else they include. Indeed, such worship is typically a recipe for frustration and other trouble.

Given the exalted moral standard for worthiness of worship, we can readily exclude most claimants to the title on the ground of moral deficiency. Moral defects bar a candidate from the status of God automatically and decisively. People sometimes casually use the term *God* in ways contrary to worthiness of worship, but this fact does not challenge the value of the current morally demanding usage.

INDICATIONS OF GOD

We can have an intelligible title such as *God* but have no ground whatever for acknowledging the reality of an actual titleholder. To avoid mere wishful thinking about God's existence we need some indication of the reality of an agent worthy of worship. In particular, given that worthiness of worship includes perfect love, we need evidence of the actual motivational power that is perfect love in an agent. This required power includes the agent's intention to bring about unselfishly what is good, and only what is good, for all affected persons, even those who are the agent's enemies. Perfect love thus underwrites the amazing phenomenon called "enemy-love" and hence does not settle for love just for one's friends or helpful associates. This accounts for its rare occurrence among humans.

Genuine, morally righteous love aims to culminate in beneficial intentional actions toward others, and thus it must be rooted in one's intentions to love in action. Because intentions to love, when real, operate at the very heart of an agent, particularly at the heart of agent motivation, perfect unselfish love would reside ultimately in an agent's motivational center, or "heart" (*kardia*, in ancient Greek). This position is assumed in the Jewish scriptures (Deut 6:4-6, for example) and in the Christian New Testament (Mk 12:29-30, for example). We humans, it is arguable, cannot create this rare power ourselves, but God as perfectly loving would seek uncoercively to introduce, proliferate and sustain this power among all humans, at their motivational centers (see 1 Jn 4:7-9, 19). Humans would thus depend on God for this unusual power, even if some humans mistakenly take credit for it themselves. Such mistaken self-credit, I suggest, is the typical root of failing to apprehend salient evidence of God's existence.

Ideally, by divine hope, all capable agents would willingly receive divine love from God and then manifest it from the heart toward all agents, even toward their worst enemies and critics. Mere human agents, as suggested, would manifest such love in a manner dependent on God, but God would do so inherently, as a matter of inherent moral character. This consideration suggests a distinctive kind of theology: *kardiatheology,* as theology aimed at one's motivational heart (including one's will) rather than just at one's mind or one's emotions. Such theology accommodates Henry Sidgwick's observation, in keeping with Jesus' Sermon on the Mount/Plain, that "inwardness, rightness of heart or spirit, is the special and pre-eminent characteristic of Christian goodness."[3]

Divine self-revelation or self-manifestation to humans, it is arguable, would fit with kardiatheology in aiming uncoercively to realize divine perfect love in human hearts rather than just to expand human reflection or information. A God worthy of worship would not be in the business of just expanding our databases. Divine self-revelation and its corresponding evidence would thus seek to transform humans *motivationally,* and not just intellectually, toward perfect love. In this respect, a God worthy of worship would have important practical interests regarding human intentions and actions, beyond merely theoretical interests regarding human judgments and beliefs. This widely neglected consideration, we shall see, underwrites a distinctive account of the evidence for God.

If divine self-revelation to humans would include a manifestation and an offering of divine perfect love, then we inquirers about God's existence should identify, at least in general, what an actual indication of such a manifestation and an offering would look like. Perhaps the indication will be subtle, elusive and puzzling, in order (a) to avoid intimidating, coercing or indulging humans, and (b) to offer a profound existential, motivational challenge to wayward humans. God would thus have definite purposes in offering evidence of divine reality, and these purposes would guide the kind of evidence offered and the way it is to be received. We shall call this *purposively available evidence of divine reality,* because it would be offered in accordance with definite divine purposes for humans.

---

[3]Henry Sidgwick, *Outlines of the History of Ethics,* 5th ed. (London: Macmillan, 1902), p. 114.

BIAS IN INQUIRY ABOUT GOD

A widespread bias in human expectations of God is, as previously noted, that God would be revealed to humans as a morally indefinite creator, in a way that sets aside or postpones moral issues regarding humans relative to God. In asking about a morally indefinite creator, however, inquirers might miss out on available salient evidence of an ethically robust God—no morally indefinite creator but rather inherently morally righteous and challenging, particularly toward wayward humans. They might miss out on such evidence because they are looking for God in all the wrong places, especially in the supposedly morally indefinite places. The bias invites this largely ignored issue: are we humans in a position on our own to answer the question of whether God exists, without our being morally challenged by God, if God exists?

Perhaps the true God, being morally perfect, is in fact intentionally elusive and even obscure regarding the ethically casual issue of whether there is a morally indefinite creator. One of God's aims with divine elusiveness would be to focus and highlight a more urgent question for humans: namely, who exactly is in charge here? Who is the proper moral authority over the universe, including over all humans? A related urgent question in need of focus may be: exactly how is God in charge over this morally troubled universe?

A morally *definite*, perfectly loving God could use such questions to prompt us to ask seriously: To whom are we humans, as responsible agents, ultimately morally accountable—even with regard to how we inquire about God? Will we let God be truly God (and thus morally robust) even in the area of human inquiry about God?

We harmfully jump the gun, philosophically speaking, when we pursue the question of God's existence as if God is morally indefinite and thus not intentionally elusive toward human pursuit of a morally indefinite creator. Indeed, our jumping the gun in this manner may involve a kind of cognitive idolatry, whereby we use cognitive standards that displace God's cognitive and moral supremacy, including God's authority over the manner of divine self-manifestation and corresponding evidence. Such idolatry would inevitably be harmful to inquirers in its distancing them from needed suitable knowledge and evidence of the true God.[4]

---

[4]For the details of and the solution to this widespread problem, see Paul K. Moser, *The Elusive*

Jesus may have had a challenge to cognitive idolatry in mind with this otherwise puzzling prayer of gratitude for divine hiding:

> At that time Jesus said, "I praise you, Father, Lord of heaven and earth, because you have *hidden* these things from the wise and learned, and revealed them to little children. Yes, Father, for this was your good pleasure. All things have been committed to me by my Father. No one knows the Son except the Father, and no one knows the Father except the Son and those to whom the Son chooses to reveal him." (Mt 11:25-27, italics added; cf. Lk 10:21-22; 1 Cor 2:4-14)

Jesus thus portrays his divine Father as hiding divine ways and means from people who are pridefully "wise and learned" in their own eyes. He suggests that God is intentionally elusive, even to the point of hiding, relative to people who oppose God's authority and morally righteous ways. This suggestion agrees with a long-standing teaching of the prophetic tradition in the Hebrew scriptures, including Isaiah 45:15: "Truly you are a God who hides himself, O God and Savior of Israel." If we take Jesus and the Hebrew prophetic tradition seriously, we should expect God to be morally righteous, perfectly loving and thus at times elusive toward wayward humans. God would then be anything but a morally indefinite creator.

People, however, are sometimes not ready and willing to receive God's self-manifestation aright, with due honor and gratitude. Accordingly, God would offer needed challenges of various sorts to humans, and some divine hiding is one such challenge (cf. Rom 1:18-23).[5] In this regard, we should expect God to be a moving target, and not an object for casual or convenient human inspection or speculation. God's morally profound character and aims would preclude God's joining in human intellectual games that shortchange serious human moral needs. We must be wary, then, of morally neutralizing or otherwise domesticating God in our inquiry about God's existence. Accordingly, we should steer clear of the aforementioned bias.

A perfectly loving God would have morally definite purposes toward humans, including the purpose to invite and encourage able-minded humans to enter into cooperative fellowship with God—and thereby to

---

God: Reorienting Religious Epistemology (Cambridge: Cambridge University Press, 2008).
[5]On the role of divine judgment and its cognitive effects in such challenges, see Edward Meadors, *Idolatry and the Hardening of the Heart* (London: T & T Clark, 2006).

become loving as God is loving, even toward resolute enemies. As suggested, therefore, God would make evidence of divine reality purposively available to humans, that is, available in a way that serves God's perfectly loving aims for humans.

These aims would include a call from God to humans to yield to and obey God as authoritative Lord, and this call would seek uncoercively to engage humans at a level of motivational depth, rather than at a superficial level. This God would thus contrast sharply with the relatively aloof creator postulated by deism or morally indefinite theism. Human inquiry about God should be prepared to follow suit, in agreement with its quarry.

COGNITIVE GRACE

On reflection, we should expect a perfectly loving God to offer any divine self-manifestation and accompanying evidence toward humans as a matter of *divine cognitive grace,* rather than human merit or even humanly controllable evidence. In other words, divine self-manifestation and its corresponding evidence, if they were to come at all, would come to humans as a humanly unearned gift. Humans would not be in charge or control how or when the gracious gift is offered to them.

Being anchored in such a gracious gift, human knowledge (and evidence) of a perfectly loving God would differ importantly from the kinds of human knowledge that have humanly controllable objects, such as lab specimens, kitchen appliances or patio-furniture pieces. Even so, the divine gracious gift in question, in its invitational call to humans, could and would make uncoercive demands on humans for the sake of reconciling humans to God.

Given divine moral perfection, an *obedient* human response to divine demands to receive and to practice divine love would be the suitable way for a human to receive the divine gift on offer. Accordingly, we should expect the availability of some evidence of divine reality to be sensitive to the will of its intended human recipients. Inquiry about divine reality would thus move to a new level, beyond mere reflection and inference, to human obedience and disobedience. The key question will thus become: who is inquiring about the existence of God? More specifically, what *kind* of person is inquiring about divine reality—a person willing or unwilling to yield to a perfectly loving God?

A perfectly loving God would thus turn the tables on human inquirers by asking about their own status, particularly their own moral position, before God. Inquiry about divine reality would no longer be a casual, morally indefinite matter akin to a spectator sport. Approached aright, it would become morally loaded and humanly humbling. Inquirers about God's existence typically overlook this important cognitive consideration about a God worthy of worship.

GIVING SERIOUS QUESTIONS DUE SERIOUSNESS

We are reorienting inquiry about God's existence by asking with due seriousness the following questions:

- What if God would be perfectly loving even in offering to humans any divine self-manifestation and corresponding evidence of divine reality?
- What would available evidence of God's existence then be like?
- How would it call us inquirers to account before God?
- How might one's lacking evidence of divine reality then concern primarily one's own moral character and attitudes before God rather than the actual availability of such evidence?

Philosophers and theologians have not given adequate attention to such important questions. As explanatory disciplines, philosophy and theology routinely introduce and explore what-if questions. We do well, accordingly, to extend the previous list of questions a bit in order to identify some areas in need of explanation:

- What if we humans, in our moral imperfection and our resistance to unselfish love, are typically not ready and willing to receive God *on God's terms*?
- What if human pride, including our desired self-sufficiency, obscures our apprehending (a) who God truly is, (b) the reality of God's call to us and (c) what God wants for us?
- What if divinely desired human knowledge of God is not a spectator sport but rather calls for obedient human knowledge of God *as authoritative Lord,* not as a morally indefinite creator?

In that case such knowledge would demand, at least to some extent, human volitional yielding to God as Lord. We would then have to consider an important distinction between *unavailable* spectator knowledge of God and *available* authoritative and invitational knowledge of God.

What would become of evidence of God if we set aside spectator knowledge of God as unavailable to humans? Could there still be salient evidence of God's reality available? There definitely could be, as long as the relevant evidence would fit with God's distinctive character and purposes. That is, the evidence in question would be purposively available to humans in keeping with God's perfectly loving purposes for humans. Its being apprehended by humans would thus be sensitive to the attitudes, including volitional attitudes, of humans toward God's character and purposes. It is no surprise, then, that in regard to the evidence of divine intervention through himself, Jesus speaks of the need for "eyes to see and ears to hear" (cf. Mk 4:22-23).

Many writers assume that God would have a magic cognitive bullet, whereby God guarantees that the divinely offered evidence of God's existence is actually willingly received by humans. This is a mistake. A sincere person's telling the truth to others does not guarantee that the intended audience actually willingly receives that truth. Intended recipients of evidence can fail to be actual willing recipients, owing to their unreceptive, resistant ways. For example, to acknowledge a humbling truth about themselves may seem too painful, and therefore they might opt not to acknowledge it. Similarly, love offered to a person clearly need not be received or valued at all by that person. Accordingly, unreceptive humans would be able to block any magic cognitive bullet on God's part.

WHOSE ARE WE?

As inquirers about God's existence, we should attend to various questions of the form "What if God wanted . . ." given that such questions can reliably guide and even correct human expectations about divine evidence. Our questions about the evidence for God would then be sensitive to what God would want to accomplish in offering the relevant evidence to humans. They would include, for instance, a question of this sort: if God desired to use divine self-manifestation uncoercively to challenge human selfishness and pride, including self-righteousness, and to transform humans toward unselfish, morally righteous love, then what generally would the relevant evidence of divine reality look like? Traditional philosophy of religion suffers from inadequate attention to such a question. A correct answer, however, would be invaluable to the inquiry.

A perfectly loving God would seek uncoercively to have others willingly receive and then manifest God's perfect love at the level of their motivational center (or heart) for the sake of building God's kingdom community. This would involve not just a theology of the mind or emotions but also the aforementioned kardiatheology. So, certain kinds of evidence expected or demanded by many humans would not fit at all with what a perfectly loving God seeks. Divine massive fireworks displays, for instance, however entertaining they may be for some humans, would not do the desired job. We should not expect God to offer such relatively superficial displays. Instead, we should expect something more profound, and more challenging too.

A perfectly loving God would desire, and uncoercively promote, that all people, both individually and collectively, willingly receive divine love and thereby worship God and live in loving fellowship with God from their heart, for their own good. The desired fellowship would include uncoerced human *volitional* (that is, will-based) *cooperation* with God, particularly cooperation with God's advancement of unselfish love toward all people, even toward God's enemies. To that end, God would want people to be related to God on perfectly loving terms that exclude selfishness and pride and advance unselfish love toward all agents.

Being related to God on these terms would include people in a morally transformative divine-human relationship that increasingly replaces human selfishness and pride with human reception and promotion of divine morally righteous love. These people would be individually in an I-Thou relationship and collectively in a we-Thou relationship with God. They would receive divine love, and on that basis they would adore, love, trust and obey God directly and, ideally, wholeheartedly. Evidence of divine reality, anchored in divine cognitive grace, would conform to such distinctive purposes.

The transformative relationship in question would include an initiating and sustaining divine call, via human conscience: specifically, a call away from human selfishness and pride, including self-righteousness, and toward (receiving and manifesting) divine perfect love and its morally righteous requirements. This follows from the fact that divine perfect love would be *invitational*. It would invite people into volitional fellowship with God and thereby with others who have similar aims. This invitational call would be directed at human conscience for the sake of existential personal depth, and it would thereby invite one to be sincerely disclosed, or revealed, before God. In particular, it would seek free disclosure of who one truly is morally, and who one morally ought to be by the exalted standard of a perfect loving God. God would thus seek a relationship of human transformation toward God's perfect love, in divine-human volitional fellowship. Being purposively available, evidence of divine reality for humans would emerge from, and fit with, the same divine desire for human transformation in divine-human cooperation.

The divine evidence in question would itself be invitational, including a call to humans to enter into volitional fellowship with God. This evidence would also be authoritative—an authoritative call to humans from an authoritative God. The divine authority thereby indicated would include God's being inherently worthy of human love, trust and obedience, in contrast to any kind of spectator evidence that makes no demand or call on the direction of a human will or life (such as either observational evidence from design or order in nature, or theoretical evidence concerning the need for a first cause of experienced contingent events). Let's acknowledge, then, a distinction between authoritative-invitational evidence and spectator evidence.

AGAPĒ

The ancient Greek term *agapē* refers to the divine morally righteous unselfish love that uncoercively seeks what is good for all people involved. *Agapē*-enhancing occasions are "*agapē*-enlightening" in that they bring *agapē* regarding God and others into human attention (at least for the willing humans involved) as worthy of being received or advanced. In contrast, *agapē*-resisting occasions are "*agapē*-dimming" in that they obscure or reduce for the relevant humans the value of *agapē* regarding God and others. An *agapē*-enhancing occasion, where a human is willingly receiving *agapē* from or advancing *agapē* toward God and other agents, is distinct from an *agapē*-resisting occasion, where a human is willingly neglecting *agapē* or opposing *agapē* toward God and other agents. God's desired transformation of humans would include a change from *agapē*-resisting to *agapē*-enhancing occasions.

If God's character is inherently a character of *agapē*, as some of the

Hebrew prophets and New Testament writers suggest, then *agapē*-resisting tendencies among humans could obscure the value of God's presence for those humans. In doing so, those tendencies could also obscure the reality of God's presence, because in neglecting the value of divine love we could easily fail to look for it at all. How we treat *agapē* toward people could be equivalent to how we treat God: with acceptance, indifference or rejection. To the extent that we take credit for unselfish love toward people, we obscure its real source and the evidence for that source. We also then fail to give credit where credit is due: to God.

What we may call "*agapē*-transformation" would aim for cooperative divine-human fellowship and thus would include a manifestation, if temporary and incomplete, of God's morally perfect character. This divine manifestation, in keeping with God's perfectly loving character, would seek to offer divine love to a wider audience or to a particular audience more deeply.

The question of evidence for God's existence should become for us humans the question of how we respond to the gift of *agapē* toward ourselves and others. In this connection, philosophy can only remove obstacles and clear a path for something ultimately nonphilosophical, because that "thing" is uncontrollable and more profound and transformative than any philosophy. It is irreducibly person-to-person: an I-Thou acquaintance of a person with the living God. At this sacred place, humans will be in the presence of the personal God of holy love whom Blaise Pascal met and memorialized as follows:

> God of Abraham, God of Isaac, God of Jacob, not of philosophers and scholars.
> Certainty, certainty, heartfelt, joy, peace.
> God of Jesus Christ. God of Jesus Christ.
> My God and your God.

We all now face not an abstract argument but a life-or-death question: are we sincerely attending to the divine call via conscience and experienced *agapē* in a way that leads us before the God of Abraham, Isaac, Jacob and Jesus, where we can become part of God's new creation? The evidence for God can then be clarified and deepened in a way that we ourselves become part of this evidence as newly recreated children of the living God (cf. Jn 3:1-8; 2 Cor 5:14-18). The best explanation of our new lives will be that God has indeed visited us, and that is evidence enough.

FOR FURTHER READING

Farmer, H. H. *The World and God.* 2nd ed. London: Nisbet, 1936.

————. *God and Men.* New York: Abingdon, 1947.

Moser, Paul K. *The Elusive God: Reorienting Religious Epistemology.* Cambridge: Cambridge University Press, 2008.

————. *The Evidence for God.* Cambridge: Cambridge University Press, 2010.

Oman, John. *Grace and Personality.* 4th ed. Cambridge: Cambridge University Press, 1931.

————. *Concerning the Ministry.* London: SCM Press, 1936.

Part **2**

GOD IS GREAT

4

God and Physics

JOHN POLKINGHORNE

Every worldview involves a commitment to a foundational belief, which is not itself to be explained but which will provide the basis on which all subsequent forms of explanation will ultimately have to rest. No worldview can be free from such an initial commitment, for nothing comes of nothing.

In Western thinking about the nature of reality there have been two particularly influential traditions: materialism and theism. They are both still very active today, and they differ in what they treat as their assumed foundation. The unexplained brute fact of the former is the existence of matter; for the latter, the existence of a divine Creator. Which is to be chosen depends upon how intellectually satisfying its brute-fact assumption is found to be.

My contention will be that the materialist starting point is unsatisfying. The laws of nature, as modern physics has discovered them to be, have a character which is not self-contained but rather seems to point beyond them to the need for a further and deeper level of intelligibility.

THE UNIVERSE POINTS BEYOND ITSELF

The universe that science explores has proved to be profoundly rationally transparent to our inquiry and endowed with a deep rational beauty. It is scarcely surprising that we are able to make good sense of the world at the level of everyday experience.

Evolutionary processes may be expected to have shaped our brains so that we can cope with survival necessities. If we could not figure out that it is a bad idea to step off the top of a high cliff, then life could prove short. That is one thing, but it is quite another thing when someone like Isaac Newton comes along and, in an astonishing creative leap of the human imagination, is able to see that the same force that makes the cliff dangerous is also the force that holds the moon in its orbit around the earth and the earth in its orbit around the sun, and, by discovering the mathematically beautiful universal inverse-square law of gravity, can explain the behavior of the whole solar system. That goes far beyond anything that we need for our survival or what might be considered to be a happy spinoff from such a necessity. As Sherlock Holmes once remarked to a shocked Dr. Watson, it did not matter at all for his daily work as a detective whether the earth went round the sun or the sun went round the earth!

The insights of modern science carry us far beyond the macroscopic realm of everyday events, downward into the microscopic realm of quantum physics and upward into the cosmic realm of curved space-time. Understanding these regimes remote from mundane experience calls for counterintuitive ways of thinking quite different from those of everyday, but physicists have proved equal to the challenge. Thus the universe has proved to be deeply intelligible and profoundly transparent to scientific inquiry. This is surely a significant fact about the world, too remarkable to be accepted simply as a happy accident or a brute fact. Albert Einstein once said that the only mystery of the universe is that it is comprehensible.

Things are more mysterious than that, for it has proved time and again that mathematics provides the key to unlock the secrets of the cosmos. It is an actual technique of discovery in fundamental physics to seek theories that are expressed in terms of beautiful equations.[1] This quest for mathematical beauty is no aesthetic indulgence on the part of the physicists; it has repeatedly proved to be the case that the theories found in this way establish their claim to be describing true aspects of nature by the long-term fruitfulness of explanation that they provide. Einstein used this kind of mathematical insight to guide his formulation

---

[1]Mathematical beauty involves qualities such as economy and elegance. Like all forms of beauty, it is easier to recognize than to describe, but mathematicians can agree about its presence, so that it is an intersubjectively recognized property.

of general relativity. Paul Dirac, one of the founding figures of quantum theory, made his many discoveries by a lifelong and highly successful quest for beautiful equations. His most celebrated discovery made in this way was the relativistic equation of the electron (engraved on his memorial tablet in Westminster Abbey). It immediately provided an unanticipated explanation of why the magnetic properties of the electron are twice as strong as classical physics would have led one to expect. Two years later it led to the discovery of the existence of antimatter.

When the abstract subject of mathematics leads to important physical discoveries in this way, something remarkable is happening. Why is it the case that some of the most beautiful patterns that the mathematicians can dream up in their minds are found actually to occur in the structure of the physical world around us? What links together the reason within (mathematical thinking) and the reason without (the laws of physics)? Dirac's brother-in-law Eugene Wigner, who himself won a Nobel Prize for physics, put the matter epigrammatically: "Why is mathematics so unreasonably effective?"

It would be intolerably intellectually lazy just to shrug one's shoulders and say, "That's just the way it is—and a bit of good luck for those who are good at math." Science has found that the universe is profoundly rationally transparent and beautiful. The feeling of wonder at the marvelous order of the world is a fundamental experience in physics and a fitting reward for all the labor involved in research. In a word, one could say that physics explores a universe that is shot through with signs of mind. Thus the laws of physics seem to point beyond themselves, calling for an explanation of why they have this rational character. It is intellectually unsatisfying simply to treat them as brute fact.

The deep intelligibility of the cosmos can itself be made intelligible if behind its marvelous order is indeed the mind of its Creator. The theist can say that science is possible precisely because the universe is a creation and scientists are creatures made in the image of their Creator, the God whose role is not simply to initiate the big bang but continuously to hold in being a world endowed with wonderful rational structure. Materialism just does not explain enough.

A FINELY TUNED UNIVERSE

The laws of physics have been found to point beyond themselves in another way as a result of an increasing understanding of the history of the cosmos. The observable universe started 13.7 billion years ago in an extremely simple form—just an almost uniform expanding ball of energy. Now it is very rich and varied, the home of saints and scientists. Cosmologists understand many of the processes by which this fertile evolution has occurred, and they have found that they were only possible because the laws of physics—the given physical fabric of the world—took a very precise, "finely tuned" form. Carbon-based life can evolve only in a universe that has a remarkably specific character. While life did not appear on the cosmic scene until the universe was about ten billion years old, fine-tuning meant that the cosmos was pregnant with the potentiality for life essentially from the big bang onward.

Many considerations have led to this conclusion; it is possible here to give only an illustrative sample of them. Let us start with the formation of the chemical elements essential for life. The very early universe, for the first three minutes of its life, was a kind of cosmic hydrogen bomb, sufficiently hot for nuclear reactions to be taking place everywhere. When expansion cooled it below the relevant temperature, these reactions ceased, having made only the two simplest elements, hydrogen and helium. They have too boring a chemistry to be able to produce anything as interesting as life. For that many more elements are needed, including especially carbon, which is essential for the formation of the long chain molecules that are the biochemical basis of life.

After about a billion years, when the first stars had condensed, nuclear reactions started up again, now confined to hot stellar cores. These are the sites where carbon was made; every atom of carbon in every living being was once inside a star. We are people of stardust, made of the ashes of dead stars. The processes by which the heavier elements are made from a beautiful and delicate chain of nuclear reactions—essentially successively compounding α-particles (helium nuclei) step by step to form the sequence beryllium, carbon, oxygen . . .

There is a problem about the second step, however, since beryllium is very unstable and in the ordinary way would not survive long enough to enable the next reaction (forming carbon) to take place. This process is possible only because there is a very large enhancement effect (resonance) at precisely the right energy to enable the addition of the next α-particle to take place anomalously rapidly, catching the beryllium before it disappears. If the laws of nuclear physics were a little different, this resonance would either not be there at all or it would be at the wrong energy.

This chain of reactions inside the star cannot get beyond iron, the most stable of the nuclear species. Thus two problems remain: to make the elements beyond iron—some of which, such as zinc and iodine, are needed for life—and to get the elements already made out of the star and into the environment where eventually they can form part of a life-bearing planet. It turns out that with the nuclear forces in the form that they actually take in our universe, both of these problems are solved by some stars exploding as supernovae.

Another essential condition for a life-bearing universe is that it should neither expand too rapidly, becoming too dilute for fertile processes to take place, nor expand too slowly so that gravity causes it to collapse long before life can evolve. Avoiding these twin disasters requires an extremely fine balance between expansive and gravitational effects in the very early universe. Almost all cosmologists believe that this balance was achieved in our universe by a speculative but very plausible process called inflation, a kind of extremely rapid "boiling" of space which over a very short period had the effect of producing the necessary balance. This is a natural process, but it requires that the laws of physics take a particular form to enable it (technically, that they incorporate certain scalar fields called inflatons).

We have already seen how getting the right sort of stars is essential for a life-bearing universe. The character of stars depends very sensitively on the balance between two of the basic forces of nature: electromagnetism and gravity. If that balance were different to only a tiny degree in one direction or another, all stars would be either blue giants or red dwarfs. The blue giants would be short-lived in comparison with the time-scales relevant to the evolution of life, and in any case, it is thought that they would be unlikely to form planets. The red dwarfs would probably be too feeble to support life on an encircling planet, and in any case, they would never explode as supernovae, an event whose indispensability we have already noted.

One final example of fine-tuning must suffice. It has recently been discovered that the expansion of the universe is accelerating, an effect which is attributed to a somewhat mysterious entity: dark energy, associated with space itself. Quantum physics can suggest a possible source of this energy: the vacuum is the lowest energy state of the system, but it is not an empty state in which nothing is happening. (Heisenberg's uncertainty principle does not permit a totally quiescent state in which one would know both what is happening—nothing—and where it is—here.) Instead there are continuous vacuum fluctuations in which entities appear and disappear in restless activity. This generates a vacuum energy that fills space. A reasonable estimate of the magnitude of this vacuum energy yields an enormously high figure; the observed dark energy is 10^{-120} smaller than this estimate. Were it not fine-tuned to this astonishing degree, the universe would have either blown apart or collapsed (depending upon the sign of the energy) with an incredible rapidity which would totally have eliminated any possibility of life forming.

Physicists agree that our universe is characterized by a precise quantitative specificity which has been necessary for its being able to evolve carbon-based life. This specificity refers to the physical fabric of the cosmos, the given ground rules which are the prior basis for the possibility of any actual events. The collection of insights on which this conclusion rests has often been given the name of the anthropic principle—a somewhat unfortunate term; the carbon principle would have been a better choice, since it is the potentiality for carbon-based life in general, rather than *homo sapiens* in particular, which is involved.

Fine-tuning came as a surprise to all physicists and as a shock to some. The inclination of scientists is toward the general rather than the particular. The natural prior expectation was that our universe would be just a typical specimen of what a universe might be like, with nothing too special about it. Fine-tuning seemed a counter-Copernican insight: humans do not live at the center of the universe, but the cosmos has been found to be intrinsically structured in a way that permits human presence within it. Of course, if that had not been the case, we would not be here to be astonished at fine-tuning. Yet the collection of anthropic insights seems altogether too remarkable and precise to be treated as just a happy accident. It seems to point beyond the brute fact of physical law and require to be set in a context of deeper intelligibility. Two metascientific possibilities have been extensively discussed.

THE MULTIVERSE

For the theist, the universe is not just "any old world." It is a creation which has no doubt been endowed by its Creator with just the finely tuned laws and circumstances which have enabled it to have the fruitful history which is the expression of the divine purpose.

Disliking the threat of theism, some scientists have sought an alternative explanation of apparent fine-tuning. This is provided by the conjecture of the multiverse, a grossly extended form of naturalism which supposes that this universe is just one member of a vast portfolio of separate worlds, each with its own different laws and circumstances. If this collection is sufficiently large and varied, it might be that one of these universes is fine-tuned for carbon-based life, and that is ours because we are carbon-based life. Our fertile universe is then simply a random winning ticket in some great multiversal lottery.

Of course, if this explanation is to have any force, there must be some independent reason for believing in the existence of the multiverse. Otherwise, any remarkable feature whatsoever could be explained away by incorporating it in some arbitrary assembly, a significant needle concealed in a meaningless haystack. The collateral arguments in support of the multiverse have relied mostly on speculative versions of quantum cosmology which may seem to suggest the generation of many different worlds. At present there is no fully worked out physical theory consistently combining quantum theory and gravity, but many believe that string theory represents the most promising candidate.

In evaluating this proposal, it is important to recognize how speculative much of contemporary fundamental physics has come to be, relying solely on mathematical possibility, without the complementary input of constraining empirical results. The string theorists purport to tell us how nature behaves on a scale sixteen orders of magnitude beyond anything of which we have direct knowledge. So great a change of scale would take one from the size of a town of a hundred thousand inhabitants to much less than the size of an atom, an immense extrapolation. For this reason, the multiverse must be classified as a metascientific approach to the issue of fine-tuning.

There are also many technical difficulties in evaluating the consistency and effectiveness of the multiverse theory as far as fine-tuning is concerned. For example, simply having an infinite collection of entities is no guarantee that it will contain one with any particular property. There are an infinite number of even integers, but one will never be found with the property of oddness. Materialism may be driven to the multiverse hypothesis in order to cope with fine-tuning, but theism finds an unforced explanation already available within its overall worldview.

GOD AND PHYSICS IN THE TWENTY-FIRST CENTURY

The twentieth century saw a significant change in the character of the account that physics gives of the processes of the universe. Classical physics of the Newtonian type visualized individual hard atoms (possibly with hooks), interacting in a determinate manner in the container of absolute space and in the course of the unfolding of absolute time. This picture was not substantially changed when the discoveries of Michael Faraday and James Clerk Maxwell led in the nineteenth century to the formulation of field theories. Classical fields are strictly deterministic in their behavior and, though not directly visible, they are clearly perceptible from their effects, as when iron filings line up along the lines of force of a magnetic field. In a word, the physical world was still thought to be clear and determinate, mechanical in its character.

All this changed in the first quarter of the twentieth century with the discoveries of relativity theory and quantum theory. Space and time were found to be intimately interrelated and their description to be dependent on the motion of the observer, while subatomic processes were found to be cloudy and fitful in their character. Mere mechanism had died with the discovery of intrinsic unpredictabilities present in the processes of nature.

Later in the century, the discovery of chaos theory showed that even the classical Newtonian world was not free of intrinsic unpredictability, for there are many systems in it which are so exquisitely sensitive to the slightest disturbance from their environment that their future behavior is beyond the possibility of detailed prediction. The word *intrinsic* is important here: these are not unpredictabilities that could be removed by more exact measurement or more precise calculation. Unpredictability is an epistemic property; it implies that we cannot know what future behavior will be. A fundamental problem in philosophy, and perhaps the central question in the philosophy of science, involves what connection there may be between epistemology (what we can know) and ontology (what is the case). The answer will not be determined by science alone, for it is a matter requiring metaphysical decision.

For example, quantum physics is certainly probabilistic, but does this feature arise from necessary ignorance of all the factors that actually fully determine what will happen, or is it due to an intrinsic indeterminacy in nature? In fact, it has turned out that, as far as science is concerned, either answer can be given. There are deterministic and indeterministic interpretations of quantum theory which lead to exactly the same empirical consequences. The choice between them has to be made on philosophical grounds, such as naturalness of explanation, rather than scientific criteria.

I claim that the same metaphysical options are open in the interpretation of chaotic unpredictabilities. The fact that mathematically chaos theory arose from studying the properties of deterministic nonlinear equations does not settle the issue, since these classical equations are known to be only approximations and not an exact and true account. Scientists are instinctively realists, believing that what we know is a reliable guide to what is the case—that is, that science is actually telling us what the world is like. For them it should be perfectly appropriate metaphysically to interpret the intrinsic unpredictabilities as signs of a degree of causal openness in nature. To do so is not to suppose that the future is some random lottery but that there are additional causal factors that bring it about, beyond the exchanges of energy between constituents that have been physics's traditional story.

Taking this view is encouraged further by a new development beginning to take place in science. Instead of decomposing systems into their component parts, it has become possible to investigate the detailed behavior of modestly complex systems, treated in their totalities. It has been found time and again that dissipative systems, held far from thermal equilibrium by the exchange of energy and entropy with their environment, prove capable of spontaneously generating astonishing patterns of large-scale orderly behavior of a kind that is wholly unforeseeable in terms of constituent properties. As someone once said, "More is different"; the whole exceeds the sum of its parts.

A new kind of physics, complexity theory, seems to be on the scientific horizon, though it has not yet been properly formulated in any general kind of way. Its outline character, however, seems clear. It will be holistic rather than constituent, and its focus will be not on localized inputs of energy but on the overall patterns in which energy flows. The latter could be described by what one might appropriately call "information." It seems reasonable to expect that by the end of the twenty-first century some well-defined concept of information will have become as central in physics as energy has been for the last 150 years. The causal concept of active information, a top-down influence of the whole upon the parts, is a strong candidate for one of the extra principles that serve to determine the future. This prospect is made more attractive by the faint but suggestive analogy between active information and the exercise of agency, a fundamental experience of human persons, who have surely always known as well as they have known anything that they are not mechanical automata. The duality of energy-information is not wholly unlike the much more profound duality of matter-mind.

Physics has certainly not proved the causal closure of the world in its own reductionist terms. This conclusion is further supported by recognition of the patchiness of much of physics's account, with connections between different regimes not at all well understood. For example, it is not possible to combine quantum theory and chaos theory in a consistent synthesis, since quantum theory has an intrinsic scale, set by Planck's constant, while the fractal character of chaotic dynamics implies that it is scale free, appearing the same on whatever scale it is sampled. One may take physics with all the due seriousness that it deserves without being driven to deny our human capacity to act as intentional agents. And the theist cannot be forbidden to believe that God has chosen to interact providentially with unfolding history, within the open grain of cosmic process that modern science has discerned.

GOD, EVOLUTION AND QUANTUM THEORY

The potentiality present in the laws of nature has been turned into actuality in the course of the 13.7 billion years of cosmic history by a variety of evolutionary processes. While the biological evolution of life on earth is the most familiar of these scenarios, evolutionary process has also been of great significance for the physical structure of the universe. In the course of the first billion years of cosmic history, the initial almost uniform ball of matter-energy turned into a world that became grainy and lumpy with stars and galaxies. Where there had been a little more matter than average, there was an additional gravitational attraction, which then drew in further matter in a kind of snowballing process. In this way the initial small inhomogeneities were enhanced to produce ultimately a starry universe.

The essence of any evolutionary process is an interplay between contingent variations (in this case, small fluctuations of matter density in the early universe) and lawful regularity (in this case, the force of gravity). A slogan way of expressing this is to talk about chance and necessity. It is important to recognize that in this phrase "chance" is by no means a sign of meaninglessness but stands for the contingent particularity of what actually happens. Even in the course of 13.7 billion years, only a tiny fraction of what could have happened has actually taken place. The formation of stars and galaxies illustrates the general scientific insight that regimes in which true novelty emerges are always "at the edge of chaos," where order and openness, chance and necessity are interwoven. Too far on the orderly side of that frontier, and things are too rigid for the emergence of anything really novel to be possible; too far on the haphazard side of the frontier, and no novelty that does emerge will be able to persist.

The theist has no need to be worried by the widespread role of evolutionary process. God is the ordainer of nature, and God acts as much through natural processes as in any other way. Commenting on Charles Darwin's great discovery of biological evolution, his contemporary Charles Kingsley said that we had been shown that God had not made a ready-made world but had done something cleverer than that, making a world in which creatures "could make themselves." Chance is simply creation's shuffling exploration of divinely given fertility, by means of which potentiality is made actual. The theist will see the twin roles of chance and necessity as the gifts to creation of both independence and reliability, by a God who is both loving and faithful.

The physicist may well see this interweaving of order and openness reflected in the character of quantum physics and speculate that at the subatomic level this has been an important property in allowing the universe to be biofertile. While quantum physics is only capable of assigning probabilities for a number of possible results of a measurement, the range of these possibilities is also constrained by the actual character of the wave function describing the system. It is certainly not the case that anything might happen. The wave function itself evolves in time according to the Schrödinger equation, which is a deterministic differential equation. According to the widely accepted indeterministic interpretation of quantum theory, it is only when the definite form of the wave function is used to calculate the consequences of a measurement that probabilities enter the theory. Most physicists understand measurement to be the irreversible macroscopic registration of a state of affairs in the subatomic system, and it is not necessarily associated with the direct influence of a conscious observer. In other words, surely quantum processes had actual outcomes over the many billion years of cosmic history in which there were no observers present in the universe.

The interpretation of quantum theory is still a contentious issue, with a variety of incompatible points of view being advocated, but the notion of "observer-created reality" is very much a minority position. At most, "observer-influenced reality" (in laboratory experiments affected by choices of what measurements to make) is as much as should be said.

Quantum theory has also contributed to a growing recognition that nature is deeply relational and that atomism is only part of the picture. Once two quantum entities have interacted with each other, they can retain a power of mutual influence that is not diminished by spatial separation. Acting on one here will have an immediate effect on the other, even if it is now "beyond the moon," as we conventionally say. Einstein was the first to recognize the possibility of quantum entanglement, but he thought it was "too spooky" to be true. He considered that its prediction must show that there was something wrong with conventional quantum mechanics. However, experiments have abundantly confirmed the phenomenon. The instantaneous character of the influence conveyed does not contradict special relativity, since it turns out that it cannot be used to transmit information faster than the velocity of light. Nature, it seems, rebels against a crass reductionism: even the subatomic world cannot be treated atomistically. The theist who is a trinitarian thinker will not be surprised to learn that created reality is relational.

Finally, physicists can not only peer into the universe's past but also foresee aspects of its future. The timescales are very long, but in the end the prediction is that it will all end badly. As far as the earth is concerned, in about five billion years the sun will have consumed all its hydrogen fuel. It will then turn into a red giant, burning to a frazzle any life then left on the earth. By then life might well have migrated elsewhere in the galaxy; that, however, would only be a temporary reprieve. Over immensely long timescales, the universe itself will die, most probably by continuing to expand and becoming ever colder and more dilute. Carbon-based life will certainly prove to have been a transient episode in the history of the universe.

Eventual futility lies at the end of science's "horizontal" story, extrapolating physical process into the distant future. However, theism has a different, "vertical" story to tell, based on the everlasting faithfulness of God. For the religious believer, the last word lies not with death but with God. That is a conviction that goes beyond anything that physics can speak about, either for or against.

FOR FURTHER READING

Holder, Rodney. *God, the Multiverse and Everything.* Aldershot, U.K.: Ashgate, 2004.

Polkinghorne, John. *Belief in God in an Age of Science.* New Haven: Yale University Press, 1998.

————. *Quantum Theory: A Very Short Introduction.* Oxford: Oxford University Press, 2002.

————. *Quantum Physics and Theology.* New Haven: Yale University Press, 2007.

Smolin, Lee. *The Trouble with Physics.* London: Allen Lane, 2006.

5

God and Evolution

Michael J. Behe

The earth is full of wonderful creatures with marvelous abilities. Huge whales swim the ocean's depths; delicate butterflies flitter by on a summer's day, sporting breathtaking colors. Majestic eagles soar through the skies, shy deer nibble foliage in the evening, bees dutifully gather nectar in the sunshine, fierce lions stalk their prey. And humans, in some ways the most dazzling of all creatures, build civilizations and cultures, accumulating wisdom through the ages, and reflecting on the world around them.

Even though humans are born into this world, it has struck very few of us as humdrum, as something to be taken for granted. Since antiquity poets and wise men have written paeans to the beauty and bounty of nature. The creatures that fill the earth have evoked a love of nature in many a breast. The apparent extraordinariness of the living world, the intuited contingency of nature, the felt knowledge that it didn't have to be like this, led from the earliest times of humans inexorably to the question, where did it all come from?

IN THE BEGINNING

For most of written history, the overwhelming answer to that question has been that a preexisting intelligence somehow fashioned it. The beauty and functionality of nature needed an explanation; it did not arise from nothing. The orderliness behind nature and the craft behind nature's creatures pointed strongly to a craftsman, a lawgiver, who could order something as vast as life. As the medieval philosopher Thomas Aquinas would say, by this we mean God.

There were a few naysayers among the ancients, who thought that the world and life had no intelligent cause. For example, the Greek Democritus speculated that perhaps matter sometimes, rarely, formed itself into heads, or arms, or other body parts, which quickly perished. But, he went on, if by chance matter arranged itself into a coherent animal or plant—one with all its parts in the right relationship to the whole—then that plant or animal might survive and prosper.

The ancients who first pondered these questions were at a distinct disadvantage to modern people in several respects. They knew very little about the animals they could see. In a sense, they didn't know how they "worked." For example, the great Roman physician Galen thought that blood was pumped out from the heart of an animal to feed and "irrigate" its tissues, sinking into the tissues as water from an irrigation ditch sinks into farmland. He had no conception of the circulation of the blood. Galen was held in such high regard that his ideas were taught for more than a thousand years after his death. Not until the Middle Ages did educated people escape from his mistaken notion and begin to learn the wonders of the workings of life.

In the early 1600s, in an extraordinary act of intellect that presaged the advent of modern science, an Englishman named William Harvey calculated that the great Galen must be wrong. Harvey reasoned that if each beat of the heart pumped two ounces of blood, and if there were 72 beats per minute, and 60 minutes in an hour, and 16 ounces in a pound, then in just one hour a normal man's heart would have pumped 540 pounds of blood! Clearly that much blood could not be produced by the body in such a short time; Harvey deduced that the blood had to recirculate.

IN THE MIDDLE

One major disadvantage that premodern people had to contend with was that, as we now know, many of the working parts of life are microscopic, invisible to the naked eye, simply too small to see. So when they tried to puzzle out how life worked, they did so with no knowledge of the nuts and bolts of life. That began to change in the 1600s, with the modern invention of the microscope by Anton van Leeuwenhoek. Even with the crude instruments that could be fashioned at the time, which used candles rather than bright electric lights to illuminate a specimen on a microscope stage, it was immediately apparent that life was much, much more complex than anyone had previously suspected.

Before the availability of the microscope, it was thought that insects had no internal organs. That's not because the people of the age were stupid but simply because the naked eye could not see to the required resolution. With the aid of the microscope, however, internal organs were seen aplenty. And even the external parts of familiar insects were seen to have very much more detail than had been known.

The perceived simplicity of insects and small animals had led many to think that small forms of life could arise spontaneously. For example, farmers who saw mice among their stored grain reasonably concluded that the grain had given rise to the mice. Meat left out in the open soon had maggots squirming on it, so decaying meat was thought to spontaneously give rise to insects. When the much greater complexity of insects and small animals was uncovered by the microscope, however, these ideas faded: although it may be easy to believe that relatively featureless insects could pop into existence from decaying meat, the complex bodies revealed by microscopes clearly could not. The more complex and functional life was discovered to be, the less plausible was the notion that it arose spontaneously, without guidance.

As microscopists studied life in more and more detail, cells were seen for the first time in plants, but their significance was unrecognized. It was not until the early nineteenth century that Schleiden and Schwann proposed the "cell theory" of life: living organisms are composed of cells and their secretions; and to a certain extent a cell has a life of its own.

The nineteenth century, of course, was also the time of Charles Darwin, who was born in 1809 and died in 1882. It was an age of great intellectual ferment, not only in biology but in geology as well. Excavations in the earth to build canals and railroad tracks unearthed fossil evidence of creatures that no longer appeared on earth; they were extinct. What's more, the creatures seemed in many cases to resemble modern animals, so that it seemed that the prehistoric creatures gave rise to the modern creatures over great spans of time.

Nonetheless, although much progress had been made since van Leeuwenhoek, Darwin's day was still quite ignorant of the foundation of life. In fact, in the nineteenth century many scientists such as the German Ernst Haeckel thought that the cell, the foundation of life, was "a simple little lump of albuminous combination of carbon,"[1] pretty much a piece of microscopic Jell-O. And like people in the middle ages who thought mice and flies could arise spontaneously because they were perceived as simple, many scientists of the nineteenth century thought cells might arise spontaneously—because they were then thought to be simple. In fact, Haeckel and Thomas Huxley, another friend and admirer of Darwin, thought that under the microscope some sea mud dredged up by an English exploring ship resembled cells they had seen from living tissue. So they concluded that the sea bottom could spontaneously give rise to cells. From there it was a short imaginative leap to simple creatures arising from the cells, and more complex creatures arising from the simpler ones.

This is the intellectual milieu, then, in which Darwin developed his theory of evolution by random variation and natural selection. The cellular and molecular foundation of life was a black box—a system that did marvelous things but whose workings were substantially unknown. And since they were unknown, many scientists thought they were simple. Darwin therefore concentrated his theory on how animal and plant forms might change but had no choice but to neglect the question of what mechanisms really undergirded those changes.

NOW

Since Darwin's day, although many mysteries remain, science has advanced relentlessly in our understanding of how life works. The intuition of nineteenth-century scientists that the cell is a simple glob of protoplasm has turned out to be spectacularly wrong. Rather, modern science now realizes that the cell is akin to an automated, nanoscale factory, filled with literal machines of great complexity which perform the necessary chores of life. We have found out that, much as the work of a computer takes place in tiny circuits invisible to the eye, so does the work of the cell take place with nanomachinery that can't be seen even with a microscope. And just as biology was stalled until the invention of the microscope, and then quickly advanced, a host of new techniques

---

[1]John Farley, *The Spontaneous Generation Controversy from Descartes to Oparin* (Baltimore: Johns Hopkins University Press, 1979), p. 73.

that were not available to earlier scientists have enabled modern science to advance in its understanding of life by leaps and bounds.

One technique called x-ray crystallography has advanced our modern understanding of life comparably to the microscope's advancement of medieval understanding. With x-ray crystallography (and related techniques) an investigator can "see" (or at least mathematically reconstruct) the shape of single molecules of life. Before the first x-ray picture of one of the cell's components (a protein called myoglobin), it was thought (again) that proteins—the workhorses of the cell—would turn out to be simple entities, perhaps little crystals that used magnetism or some simple force to do their jobs. The structure of myoglobin turned out to be anything but simple. Rather, its shape was as complex as the shape of any sophisticated machine, like, say, an air conditioner or fan. Other proteins whose shapes were discerned by crystallography were similarly shown to be complex, not simple. So the science of the 1950s and 1960s did away forever with the notion that life fundamentally is a simple phenomenon. Instead, we discovered that it's complexity and elegance all the way down.

That should have been the end of Darwinism's strong claim right there—to explain all of life as the product of random mutation and natural selection—but intellectual inertia and wishful thinking kept it going.

With a gathering head of steam, science marched on during the second half of the twentieth century. In the 1950s the elegant double-helical shape of DNA was discovered by James Watson and Francis Crick. Shortly thereafter the genetic code was deciphered, showing that DNA actually carried information in the form of a code to specify all the protein machinery that the cell contains. The discovery of the genetic code was the first instance where biologists found themselves unwittingly using the language of information and intelligence to describe life. After all, no chemist had found anything like a "code" in organic chemistry thus far. This was followed by discoveries that the information carried by the DNA code was "transcribed" into an intermediary language made up of RNA before it was "translated" into the language of protein.

In the late 1960s and early 1970s clever techniques were invented by several scientists to determine the exact sequence of "building blocks" (called nucleotides) in DNA. Initially just small pieces of longer DNA fragments had their sequences determined. But as techniques improved rapidly, we have reached the point where the entire genetic complement of hundreds of organisms is known exactly, including that of human, dog, chimp, fruit fly and many more. Our knowledge has allowed us to see at least some of the mysteries of DNA. It turns out that many genes are not contiguous pieces of DNA as was once thought. Rather, the genes occur in discrete pieces, interrupted by DNA fragments called introns that don't code for protein. The exact reason for this arrangement is still disputed.

In more recent years parts of the genome that were thought to have no function (and derided with the epithet "junk DNA") have been found to contain tiny regions that are transcribed into RNA but not translated into proteins. These have been dubbed micro-RNAs and are thought to regulate the activity of other parts of the genome, switching on and off other genes at the proper time and place. In the 1950s and early 1960s it was discovered that pieces of DNA that were near to genes could exert an effect on whether the genes were turned on or off. These are called regulatory elements, emphasizing the fact that DNA not only has to code for the proteins that make up the machinery of life; the construction program has to be regulated to an exquisite level of detail. In recent years, regulatory elements for genes have been discovered in sequences of DNA that are physically far removed from the genes they are supposed to regulate. The system has turned out to be so intricate that a writer for the journal *Nature* gushed that "the picture these studies paint is one of mind-boggling complexity."[2]

WHERE DARWINISM STANDS NOW

Darwin knew that his theory of gradual evolution by natural selection carried a heavy burden. "If it could be demonstrated," he wrote, "that any complex organ existed which could not possibly have been formed by numerous, successive, slight modifications, my theory would absolutely break down," adding "but I can find out no such case."[3] In this passage Darwin was emphasizing that evolution had to improve an organism slowly, in tiny steps, over long periods of time. He realized that if organisms improved rapidly, in large leaps, then it would look suspi-

---

[2]Helen Pearson, "What Is a Gene?" *Nature* 441 (2006): 398-401.
[3]Charles Darwin, *The Origin of Species*, 6th ed. (New York: New York University Press, 1988), p. 154.

ciously as if something other than random variation and selection were driving the unfolding of life.

Yet, if we concentrate on the "complex organs" that fill the cell—the molecular machinery of life—then the prerequisite for his theory is destroyed. Almost none of the molecular machines discovered in the cell lend themselves easily to being built by a slow, gradual process of improvement. Rather, like the comparatively simple machines of our everyday lives—mousetraps, ballpoint pens, electric lights and so forth—the machines of the cell contain separate components needed for them to work. I have termed this property "irreducible complexity," and it is a severe practical barrier to Darwinian explanations of life. The problem is that such systems don't work as the modern systems we have discovered do until they are pretty much all put together. So natural selection has little to select, or is stuck selecting a property that has little or nothing to do with the final system.

In response to my argument, Darwinists have offered more speculative scenarios where random mutation might get around the problem of irreducible complexity. However, I find the scenarios quite unconvincing, and I think anyone with a modicum of skepticism will too.

So has the argument reached an impasse, with the majority of biologists content to imagine what has never been seen and the legions of skeptics mired in their skepticism? For a while it seemed that way, but new data has become available, showing with some precision the limits of Darwin's theory. This new data has the power to settle the argument for anyone willing to consider it.

THE CRITICAL ROLE OF RANDOM MUTATION

Darwin's theory is not a simple one. It contains several different, independent ideas, some of which may be right, while others are wrong or are quite limited. The three most important ideas that are wrapped together under the name of "Darwin's theory of evolution" are (1) random variation, or mutation, (2) natural selection, and (3) common descent.

The idea of common descent usually gets the most attention. It is the contention that modern day organisms are descended from creatures that lived in the distant past, and that therefore all living creatures share a common ancestor. So, for example, dogs and ducks share an ancestor that lived in the misty past. From that ancestor, the theory goes, different lines of organisms arose which led to the two quite different modern organisms. More contentiously, humans are postulated to share a common ancestor with other animals too; our most recent ancestor with other animals is thought to have given rise to us and to chimpanzees.

While that's an interesting and publicly controversial contention about natural history, I take the position that, even if true (which I think it is) it is in a profound sense trivial. The reason I think common descent is trivial is because the bare fact of descent does not tell us what is driving this extraordinary process. It simply says that the ancestors lived in the past and gave rise to modern creatures. But the "how" of the process is missing.

Like common descent, I think Darwin's idea of natural selection is interesting but not that surprising. After all, who would dispute the contention that on average creatures who are more fit than their siblings would stand a better chance of survival in nature?

While common descent and natural selection are interesting but unsurprising ideas, the role of random mutation is different. Every important scientific and philosophical claim of Darwin's theory is packed into the too-neglected role of random mutation. In Darwin's theory, random mutation is the fuel that allows natural selection to operate, giving rise to different creatures in the process of common descent. Random mutation supplies the raw material, the theory goes, that when winnowed by selection gives rise to all of the intricate, elegant, complex machinery of the cell, which in turn gives rise to the more visible features of life— flight in birds, the strength of tigers and so on—that we so admire.

Well, that has been the theory. However, as I wrote above, in Darwin's day the underlying basis for the variation in creatures was unknown; the central role of DNA—even its structure—was unknown. In modern times we have unraveled those knotty problems, but it has still been a massive effort to track down which changes in which parts of DNA give rise to beneficial mutations.

It turns out that mutations in DNA can come in several "flavors." Perhaps the simplest kind of mutation is called a substitution mutation, because one nucleotide in DNA is switched for another. A second kind of mutation is called a deletion which, as the name implies, results from a chunk of DNA being accidentally left out when the double helix is replicated. There are also mutations called insertions, gene duplications, transversions and others which I will not describe here.

Since organisms contain much DNA (even "simple" bacteria have millions of building block nucleotides; large animals and plants can have billions), until recently it was a very difficult, nearly impossible problem to track down the change in an organism's DNA that gave it an advantage over its brother and sister organisms. Scientists could see that, for example, a bacterium could survive in the presence of an antibiotic where other bacteria died, but the difficulty of determining what change in the bacterium's DNA conferred that ability was daunting. Similarly, some humans are resistant to malaria, but it was only comparatively recently that science determined the molecular changes in DNA that were responsible for this benefit. It turns out that, when the changes were finally tracked down, they told a rather different story than many Darwinists expected. Rather than mutations building up molecular machinery, improving an organism relentlessly, many mutations actually destroyed parts of a creature's DNA, or rendered some of the molecular machinery it coded for ineffective. It turns out that mutations which break things can sometimes have a salutary effect.

MALARIA AND RANDOM MUTATION

To see the effect of random mutation on the human genome, how it can help and hurt, let's look at what science has learned about the battle between humans and malaria over the past ten thousand years. Many people in the Western world forget, since malaria has been substantially eliminated here, but the disease remains a major cause of death and morbidity in the world. Each year a million people, mostly children under the age of five, die from the mosquito-borne disease. Hundreds of millions of people yearly are sickened by it. During the ten millennia in which the most lethal form of malaria has plagued humankind, a number of mutations have cropped up in the human genome which give their lucky bearers a measure of immunity to malaria. Since these human mutants can survive in malarious areas of the world where their unmutated relatives die, the mutation increases in the population when the resistant people have children.

The most well-known of such mutations is the sickle cell mutation, which is mentioned in almost every biology textbook that discusses evolution. In the sickle cell mutation one DNA nucleotide is changed from what it normally would be. This causes a single change in the protein hemoglobin, which the DNA gene codes for. The change is the replacement of one kind of amino acid (called glutamic acid), which enjoys being in water, with another kind of amino acid (called valine), which would much rather be shielded from water. Because of this single change in the hundreds of amino acids that comprise hemoglobin, under certain circumstances the hemoglobin aggregates to shield the valine and bury it away from water. While for technical reasons this behavior helps protect against malaria's effects when a child has just one copy of the sickle gene from one parent (and a normal gene from the other parent), when a child inherits two copies of the mutated gene (one from each parent) the results are deadly. Two copies lead to sickle cell disease, which in underdeveloped areas of the world generally means death by the age of ten. So while the sickle mutation does help some people, it has a dark side, leading to the death of many others. Even more interesting, the sickle mutation is not a change in the body's immune system, whose role it is to protect us from infection. The sickle mutation is a random change in another system that by happenstance did a bit of good.

Other mutations have been discovered in recent decades which give a measure of resistance to malaria. One class of mutations is called thalassemia. In this class an entire gene coding for a part of hemoglobin is either deleted or rendered less- or nonfunctional. Here random mutation breaks functioning genes, which again are not part of the immune system but which by serendipity help in the fight against malaria. The story is similar for a handful of other human genes whose mutation helps fight malaria. The breakage or diminution of certain genes coding for proteins (namely, glucose-6-phosphate dehydrogenase, Duffy factor, pyruvate kinase, Band 3 protein and more) aids the fight against malaria. So we see from our new knowledge of the mutations underlying malaria resistance in humans that the mutations are all reductive—that is, they reduce the number of functioning features coded for by the normal human genome.

Our knowledge of the evolutionary battle between humans and malaria has shown us, for the first time in history, that random mutation is incoherent; that is, it makes changes in any genes that help, no matter whether the changes add up to any "system" or not. Such incoherent changes are, to say the least, unlikely to be responsible for the profoundly coherent, integrated, complex systems that fill the cell. Rather, something that has the ability to look forward—to see what an integrated system should be like when it is completed—is required for cellular systems.

Our experience with malaria also shows us that random mutation much more easily breaks genes than makes them. Like a bull in a china shop, random changes of delicate structures are unlikely to help, and if they do help they are likely to be crude, quick fixes for an urgent problem.

E. COLI AND RANDOM MUTATION

Is our experience with malaria backed up by experiments in other systems? Yes. I discuss several such systems in my recent book *The Edge of Evolution: The Search for the Limits of Darwinism*. Here I will discuss in a bit of detail just one other system, the common gut bacterium *Eschericia coli*. Almost all of the pertinent work that has been done on E. coli is from the laboratory of Richard Lenski of Michigan State University, who was recently honored with election to the National Academy of Sciences.

In the late 1980s Lenski began a long-term project to grow E. coli in his lab and watch how it evolved over time. The advantage of doing evolutionary experiments on bacteria is that they can be grown in enormous numbers and have very short generation times. Every day in his laboratory Lenski would grow six to seven generations of bacteria, in numbers approaching ten trillion. Over the decades his experiment has been in progress there have now been a total of over forty thousand generations of bacteria with a cumulative population size of one hundred trillion. The very large numbers of bacteria and many generations allow solid answers to many evolutionary questions.

Almost from the beginning of his experiment Lenski saw that the bacteria became better and better adapted to their environment, as beneficial mutations apparently accumulated. However, as discussed above, in the early days it was quite difficult to track down which mutations were responsible for the benefits. But over the past decade, as the result of laborious efforts, Lenski and colleagues have identified the mutations which have the greatest beneficial effects. The overarching pattern of the results is surprisingly similar to that seen in the human response to malaria—completely different organisms.

The first mutations to help were the breaking of genes. The bacteria rapidly lost the ability to make the sugar ribose (a component of RNA); for some reason that helped the mutant bacteria compete against non-mutants. A handful of other genes involved in metabolism were also deleted. Some bacteria had their ability to repair DNA badly damaged. Most bacteria lost the ability to metabolize the sugar maltose.

The mutations were incoherent, scattered in different genes, with no recognizable theme among them. They were not in the process of building any new system in the cell. They simply took advantage of opportunities that helped them grow faster in their current milieu. This is what random mutation does, even when it "helps."

THE DESIGN OF THE UNIVERSE AND LIFE

For most of written history, the overwhelming answer to the question of how life got here has been that a preexisting intelligence, God, somehow fashioned it. Yet for most of history humanity could see only the beauty and elegance of the external features of life. As science has advanced we now see that the hidden foundation of life is even more ingenious than its visible features. For a while, in our ignorance, we thought that chance might explain the overwhelming appearance of design in life, if it were filtered by natural selection. Now, after the hard work of many scientists, there is no longer any reason to think that. The complex and elegant molecular machinery of the cell strongly proclaims its design, and the incoherent breaking of genes by random mutation shows the pitiful limits of the ability of unguided processes to fashion life.

Our discovery of the design of life coincides with great progress in understanding the design of the universe as a whole. In the nineteenth century, not only was the cell thought to be relatively simple, so was the universe at large. It seemed to be eternal and largely unchanging, obeying a few simple rules. Now, through the work of many physicists and astronomers, we know the universe is balanced on a knife edge to allow for life. And not just the universe, but our solar system, our moon and our world are fashioned for life in ways that scientists of earlier centuries never recognized. With the help of science we reaffirm and extend the wisdom of antiquity in its affirmation of the purposeful design of life.

FOR FURTHER READING

Behe, Michael J. *Darwin's Black Box: The Biochemical Challenge to Evolution*. New York: Free Press, 1996.

————. *The Edge of Evolution: The Search for the Limits of Evolution*. New York: Free Press, 2007.

Denton, Michael J. *Nature's Destiny: How the Laws of Biology Reveal Purpose in the Universe*. New York: Free Press, 1998.

Gonzalez, Guillermo, and Jay Richards. *The Privileged Planet: How Our Place in the Cosmos Is Designed for Discovery*. Washington, D.C.: Regnery, 2004.

Witt, Jonathan, and Benjamin Wiker. *A Meaningful World: How the Arts and Sciences Reveal the Genius of Nature*. Downers Grove, Ill.: InterVarsity Press, 2006.

6

Evolutionary Explanations of Religion

Michael J. Murray

Over the last decade a small number of scientists working largely in obscurity began to ask themselves this question: is there any evidence that religion is hard-wired into the human mind? It is not hard to see why someone might ask this question. No matter where you travel around the globe, every human community, culture, tribe and nation has religion. Every human group, settled or nomadic, has religious leaders: priests, imams, monks, shamans, witch doctors and so on. And every human group that stays largely in one place has religious structures: churches, temples, pyramids, totems, shrines and the like. In light of the fact that religion is so pervasive—across both times and cultures—it is natural to think that there is something about the human mind that makes religion natural for us.

Applying the methods of their fields these scientists began to propose and test answers to this question, with some striking results. Psychologists and neuroscientists have now begun to amass some powerful evidence that human minds are in fact, if not exactly hard-wired, at least strongly predisposed to religious belief and behavior. And isn't that just what we would expect to find, given the widespread nature of religion?

As a philosopher who does research on issues at the intersection of science and religion I have been paying close attention to this scientific research and found the results to be both fascinating and energizing. Perhaps these scientists are discovering the God-shaped vacuum that Augustine and Pascal saw in the human heart. Or perhaps they are giving empirical support for the "sense of the divine" that, Calvin argued, wells up within each of us. In any case, it seems that the evidence is lining up in favor of the claim that we have a mental gravitational attraction toward God.

As a result I was surprised—indeed shocked—to crack open the works of New Atheists like Richard Dawkins and Daniel Dennett to find them arguing that scientific accounts of the origin of religious belief show us that religious belief is false, unjustified or in some other way intellectually disreputable. How could showing that we have a natural disposition toward such beliefs show that?

That is the question I would like to get to by the time we reach the end of this essay. I will begin by providing some background concerning attempts by scientists to explain the origins of beliefs more generally and religious beliefs in particular. That sort of thing seems initially puzzling to some because we typically think of beliefs as *explained by reasons* rather than as *generated by causes*. So what is it that scientists engaged in this task are trying to do anyway? Second, I will describe the different types of explanations that are currently on offer when it comes to scientific accounts of religious belief. Some of these accounts argue that religion is something that evolved—that is, evolved through Darwinian process. But other scientific accounts don't have much to say about evolution at all. It will be important to clarify this, since Christians and other theists who are resistant to evolution might be tempted to throw all of these scientific accounts of religion into the drink because of the Darwinian affiliation, and that would be a mistake. We will then turn to the central question of the essay: if one or more of these accounts is correct, what does that mean for religious belief?

BACKGROUND

Since genuinely scientific psychology is a relatively new intellectual enterprise, one might be tempted to think that scientific accounts of belief are a fairly new business. That would be a mistake. In one sense, scientific accounts of the origin of beliefs go back at least as far as the philosophical writings of Plato and Aristotle in the fourth century B.C. And scientific accounts of the origin of *religious* belief extend back at least as far as the works of the first-century B.C. Roman philosopher Cicero. In what is arguably his most famous philosophical treatise, *On the Nature of the Gods,* Cicero writes as follows:

> As infinite kinds of almost identical images arise continually from the innumerable atoms and flow out to us from the gods, so we should take the keenest pleasure in turning and bending our mind and reason to grasp these images, in order to understand the nature of these blessed and eternal beings.[1]

Here Cicero (parroting the thought of the even older third-century B.C. philosopher Epicurus) argued that belief in the gods was caused by a sort of divine atomic bombardment. While Cicero saw this process as arising from the activity of the gods themselves, he nonetheless conceived of the formation of religious belief as a natural process involving detectable causal pathways.

Scientific accounts of the origin of belief were a source of continuing discussion through the medieval period and into the era of the rise of modern science. Scientists gave what now appear to us to be fairly crude accounts of the workings of perception, memory, imagination, theoretical reasoning and other cognitive operations. Although they had the tools of modern experimental science at their disposal, these scientists' explanations were often little more sophisticated than accounts offered in the premodern period. However, during this period one issue was of central importance, and it left a legacy that is crucial for understanding what is happening in contemporary psychological theorizing about the origin of religion and religious belief.

In the seventeenth century all of the major "scientists of the minds" were engaged by the question of whether any of our beliefs are hard-wired into our minds. Well, almost. The phrase "hard-wired" connotes something that arises out of the physical structures of the brain; most of these scientists still conceived of the mind as at least one aspect of an immaterial soul possessed by each human being. As a result, they cast the debate not in terms of hard-wiring but rather in terms of whether beliefs are sometimes innate or instead entirely learned by way of experience. Roughly, the English-speaking world favored the notion that all ideas were learned via experience, while those on the continent of Europe were more inclined to think that some ideas are innate.

---

[1]Cicero, *On the Nature of the Gods,* trans. Horace C. P. McGregor (New York: Viking Penguin, 1986), pp. 87, 90.

When psychology was beginning to emerge as a genuine scientific discipline in the late nineteenth and early twentieth centuries, the debate about innate ideas was largely regarded as settled. In part because of the work and influence of Swiss developmental psychologist Jean Piaget, scientists concluded that the evidence was squarely against the claim that we are born with any innate cognitive structures or content. However, in the last forty years or so psychologists have amassed a body of data that thoroughly refutes Piaget. Research shows that, from birth, infants possess an amazing array of both ideas and dispositions to form ideas that far outstrip the evidence available to them. These innate beliefs and dispositions make up what psychologists now call "folk beliefs," and it appears that we have many of them—in the domains of mathematics (that one and one equal exactly two, for example), physics (that objects move continuously through space), biology (that organisms give birth to organisms of the same species), psychology (that human beings have minds) and so on. Indeed developmental psychology is an area of active scientific research in part because those working in this area are actively plumbing the extent of our native cognitive endowments.

Where do these native cognitive endowments come from? Some psychologists and evolutionary theorists think that they can explain the origin of these innate structures by appeal to the evolutionary forces of natural selection. On this view, if some of our human ancestors were born "hard-wired" with certain cognitive contents, and those contents helped them get to the place of having true and useful beliefs before others (who were forced to learn them from scratch), this may have provided an adaptive advantage which explains why these innate beliefs were selected for.

But not all scientists endorse evolutionary explanations of this sort. Many of them think that evolutionary explanations in this vein amount to unscientific, armchair speculations about our ancestral past that can never be properly tested. Critics of this sort are happy to continue to look for innate cognitive structures, but they don't think we can say much of interest about exactly how human beings came to have those capacities.

As we will see, something similar is true when it comes to contemporary attempts to explain the origin of religious belief. Some theorists are interested in showing only that there are certain cognitive dispositions and neural structures built into us that make believing in God easy and natural for us. They take no stance on the question of whether, or how, evolutionary forces might have shaped our minds in this way. Others want to go further and argue that these dispositions and structures arose because they provided (or are connected with traits that provide) our ancestors with certain competitive advantages.

Before we go further, let me explain the parenthetical remark in the last sentence. Evolutionary scientists are interested in explaining how the forces of natural selection work on varying traits of organisms in order to explain why organisms are the way they are (and why they were the way they were). You might be tempted to think that these scientists would then reason as follows: every widespread trait in some species of organism exists and can be explained because it provided some advantage to its ancestors. That advantage was selected for, and now lots of organisms have it.

If you are tempted to think that, you should resist the temptation. Evolutionary theorists are insistent that widespread traits can have a few different sorts of causes. Some traits are explained just as described—they are widespread because they increase fitness (i.e., the ability to survive and reproduce). These traits are called "adaptations." However, other traits might be mere *byproducts* of adaptations; such traits would exist even if they have no fitness benefits at all.

For example, the ability to dance is found in just about everyone (every human, that is). But even if you accept Darwinism in its entirety, no one would claim that our ability to dance evolved because it increased our fitness. It exists simply because it is adaptive for us to be able to walk gingerly on two legs, and any organism that can do that can also dance. The ability to dance is an inevitable byproduct of having the adaptive trait of gingerly two-legged walking. In evolutionary biology, such byproduct traits are called "spandrels."

As byproducts, spandrels are not explained in terms of their fitness advantages. Some spandrels might start out as simply neutral—neither helping nor harming our fitness—but later come to have some valuable purpose (perhaps dancing evolves into a complex ritual that makes it easier to find mating partners); such traits are called "exaptations." Some spandrels might start out as neutral and stay that way (perhaps armpit hair is an example of that). And other spandrels might actually be harmful to our fitness. If evolution is right, the fact that we eat, drink and breathe through the same hole in our heads is an evolutionary accident—but it is not ideal. If you have ever had the Heimlich maneuver performed on you, you know what I mean. That trait is a spandrel, but not an especially helpful one. Still, it is not so bad that those who have it have been weeded out of the population. So it persists.

In light of these distinctions it will not be surprising to learn that scientific accounts of religion fall into different categories. Some explanations claim that religion arises from natural cognitive dispositions, while remaining silent on the evolutionary significance of religion itself. Others argue that religion exists because it is an adaptation, that is, because engaging in religious belief and behavior increases the likelihood that one will survive and reproduce. Finally, others argue that religion is a spandrel, a byproduct of other adaptive traits. The latter camp divides into those who think that religion started out as a mere byproduct and then came to have a useful function later (an exaptation), those who think it is entirely neutral, and those who think that it is downright harmful. Readers will not be surprised to learn that Richard Dawkins and most of the New Atheists fall into the last category.

SCIENTIFIC ACCOUNTS OF RELIGION

There are, roughly speaking, five major scientific accounts of the origin of religion currently being defended. Three of those are adaptationist accounts; two are spandrel accounts.

One of the spandrel accounts, the cognitive model, is by far the most widely known and discussed. In fact, in popular treatments of scientific accounts of religion like those we find in the work of the likes of Dawkins and Dennett, it is the only one discussed. This could be because the New Atheists find spandrel accounts most plausible, but the more likely reason is that they have not done their homework in the field. Indeed, adaptationist accounts are rapidly gaining ascendancy among the specialists.

Before we turn to that most widely discussed account, I will provide a summary of the alternatives. Let's first consider adaptationist accounts: *supernatural punishment theories, costly signaling theories* and *group selection theories.*

Adaptationist theories of religion tend to focus on one aspect that (a) they take to be characteristic of religion generally and (b) can be shown to have particular fitness benefits. In particular, all such explanations of religion—supernatural punishment theories (Johnson and Bering), costly signaling theories (Bulbulia) and group selection theories (Wilson)—argue that the adaptive character of religion arises because of its capacity to sustain cooperation among groups of individuals in the face of forces that threaten their unity.

It is uncontroversial that living in cooperative groups brings significant adaptive benefits both to the individuals in the group as well as to the group as a whole. Social organization allows groups of organisms to interact with their local environment in ways that allow them to extract greater benefits from it, and to do so with greater efficiency. Cooperating groups can work together to harvest more resources from their environments, groups of hunters can bring down more and larger game, and groups of farmers can divide their labor in order to make efficient agriculture production possible. Large cooperating groups can ward off predators and other threats. Furthermore, groups permit members to develop technical and intellectual specializations that allow specific individuals to develop unique adaptive talents that address narrow needs of the group, while leaving other needs to be handled by other members of the group. The result is that groups can have doctors, soldiers, scientists and so on, each bringing specialized and valuable assets to the group that would not be possible without the contributions of others.

However, while the potential benefits of group life are substantial, these benefits are hard to get and sustain in the face of threats of defection. For example, you and I both benefit if I agree to protect your property in return for your growing my food. But if I can get away with having you grow my food without having to spend my time protecting you, so much the better for me. The prospect of defection without loss of reward provides powerful incentives for members of the group to free-ride on the efforts of others, and this prospect constitutes the central problem of group life: it must be solved if groups of organisms are going to enjoy the adaptive power of their numbers.

So how can we sustain cooperation and scare off potential cheaters? One answer is: threaten to punish the cheaters. We set up police forces, courts, prisons and so on expressly for the purpose of providing disincentives for those who contemplate breaking the law. Of course, all of those things are very expensive, so if there were a cheaper way of sustaining group cooperation, natural selection would, in general, tend to select for it. An ideal system of punishment would be one which costs nothing, was not liable to corruption and could not be evaded.

Supernatural punishment theories argue that religions tend to give us exactly this. Gods and ancestors are able to monitor our every move (and sometimes our every thought), holding us accountable when we deviate from the demands of morality or cooperation by threats of punishment in this life or the next. As a result, on these views, religion is an adaptation which tends to "keep us in line."

Costly signaling theories focus on the fact that religions tend to exact substantial costs on their members. Religions require people to forego not just pleasures but evolutionary necessities (through fasting, abstaining from potential sources of nutrition—cows for Hindus, pork for Jews—avoiding sex and so on), while also requiring substantial expenditures of resources (for building temples, churches and shrines, giving tithes and offerings, sacrificing children, abstaining from work on certain holy days, devoting long stretches of time to religious ritual or learning, etc.). What could be the point?

Costly signaling theorists argue that these evolutionary sacrifices are meant to serve as signs to others that individuals are indeed fully committed to the group, and thus to cooperation with its members. These costly displays thus allow those who are genuinely likely to cooperate to find one another and to affiliate. Those who are tempted to cheat would not be truly committed to the group and would thus be unwilling to put up these costly down payments. As a result, religions are adaptations that sustain cooperation by getting groups of cooperators together.

Finally, group selection theories focus on the tendency of religious groups to promote altruistic acts by group members. From an evolutionary standpoint, sacrificing my well-being for the sake of others makes no sense. The Darwinian motto is "survival of the fittest," and that means looking out for number one. So how can religions, which promote looking out for others, survive, never mind prosper?

Group selection theories argue that we should think about groups of individuals in the same way we think about groups of cells that make up an organism. In our bodies we have certain immune cells that sacrifice themselves in order to promote the survival of the organism as a whole.

Without their "willing sacrifice" we wouldn't last long. What is true for cells and organisms, group selectionists argue, is true for organisms and groups. While the soldier who loses his life on the front line will not survive and reproduce, his sacrifice might, like that of the immune cell, advance the fortunes of his society. As a result, if societies are set up or programmed to have a certain subgroup that routinely sacrifices its interests for the larger group, this might be adaptive at a higher level of organization—the group level.

Each of these theories faces formidable difficulties, none of which I have the space to discuss here.[2] Instead, we will turn our attention to the more popular nonadaptationist explanations. For the most part these theories fall into one of two categories: cognitive theories and meme theories. Cognitive theories are predominant; meme theories of religion are vastly underdeveloped. Indeed, it would be fair to say that no one has really laid out a full blown memetic theory. What would it look like if they did?

Something like this. "Memes," a term coined by Richard Dawkins, are "units of cultural information." These can be songs, recipes, stories, moral platitudes, technological innovations and so on. Very crudely, memes are ideas that can be transmitted from mind to mind. Like genes, memes are susceptible to variation as they pass from mind to mind, and like genes they can be more or less successful in passing themselves on. Some recipes, songs, poems and the like "catch on" and others don't. Those that do, spread, and those that don't, don't.

Once we see this we can also see that memes, like genes, can evolve and be selected for. Recipes, architectural designs, clothing fashion, sitcoms and so on vary in ways aimed at making them "catch on" even more than their predecessors. And those that are successful become the Betty Crockers, Frank Lloyd Wrights, Ralph Laurens and Seinfelds of culture. Meme theorists argue that religions exist and spread because they are good at exploiting belief-acquisition tendencies that we naturally have. Richard Dawkins, for example, argues that one mode of meme transmission involves "parental instruction"; that is, children

---

[2]For more on this, see Michael Murray's "Scientific Explanations of Religion and the Justification of Religious Belief" and, with Andrew Goldberg, "Evolutionary Accounts of Religion: Explaining and Explaining Away," in *The Believing Primate: Scientific, Philosophical, and Theological Reflections on the Origin of Religion,* ed. Jeffrey Schloss and Michael Murray (Oxford: Oxford University Press, 2009).

have an innate tendency to believe what parents tell them and to do what their parents say. (This theory, of course, makes you wonder if Dawkins has children; the answer is yes, a daughter by his second marriage.) So on this view, religion exists and spreads because religions instruct parents to pass along religious teachings to children, who internalize them and pass them along to their children.

Meme theories suffer from numerous problems, many of which are immediately obvious, but none of which we can touch here.[3] Instead we will move on to consider the most widely held view, one that some have taken to calling the "standard model" of the origin of religion. The cognitive model contends that human beings have specific and identifiable mental tools that make religious belief easy and natural.[4] For example, we have a mental tool that makes us think there are agents around when we detect certain seemingly unnatural sounds (rustling in the bushes), motions (clothes blowing on the line at dusk) or configurations (crop circles) in nature.

This "hypersensitive agency detection device" (or HADD, as it is known in the field) leads us to hypothesize agents that, for example, control the forces of nature. In addition, our minds are naturally disposed to remember and transmit ideas that violate certain innate expectations we have about the workings of the world. Earlier I noted that psychologists are discovering all sorts of folk beliefs that we have hardwired into us. For example, we are born (they claim) thinking that agents are physical things. When we (via HADD) are led to hypothesize agents causing the lightning or the wind, we are led to think that there are invisible agents. But invisible agents are counterintuitive and strange. As a result, we easily remember them and talk about them, thus making such concepts (including religious concepts) spread rapidly.

In addition, there is very strong evidence that we are naturally disposed, from an early age, to see goal-directedness in everything, including the natural world. This tendency has come to be called "intuitive theism" by developmental psychologists, since it is a tendency to see purposiveness throughout our world.[5] This naturally disposes us to be-

---

[3]For more on this, see Michael J. Murray, "The Evolution of Religion: Nonadaptationist Accounts," in *Science and Religion*, ed. Melville Stewart (Oxford: Wiley-Blackwell, 2009).

[4]Justin L. Barrett, *Why Would Anyone Believe in God?* (Walnut Creek, Calif.: AltaMira Press, 2004).

[5]Deborah Kelemen, "Why Are Rocks Pointy? Children's Preferences for Teleological Expla-

lieve in an invisible, counterintuitive, purpose-giving force in the universe: gods or a God.

I have not done much (or really anything) in the way of providing evidence for these views. Doing that would require more space than I have. But let's be clear: there is a good deal of evidence in favor of them (some more than others). Given the evidence we have, it seems reasonable to think that, in fact, human minds, for whatever reason, have some strong natural affinities for religion.

WHAT ARE THE IMPLICATIONS
IF SUCH ACCOUNTS ARE TRUE?

What does all of this evidence show us? Does it show, for example, that religion is just a trick that our minds play on us? Some scientists and philosophers have answered with a resounding yes. Michael Persinger, professor of behavioral neuroscience at Laurentian University, argues that this work shows us that "God is an artifact of the brain."[6] Dawkins concludes that "the irrationality of religion is a by-product of the built in irrationality mechanism in the brain."[7] Matthew Alper, author of *The God Part of the Brain*, argues as follows:

> If belief in God is produced by a genetically inherited trait, if the human species is "hardwired" to believe in a spirit world, this could suggest that God doesn't exist as something "out there," beyond and independent of us, but rather as the product of an inherited perception, the manifestation of an evolutionary adaptation that exists exclusively within the human brain. If true, this would imply that there is no actual spiritual reality, no God or gods, no soul, or afterlife. Consequently, humankind can no longer be viewed as a product of God but rather God must be viewed as a product of human cognition.[8]

Even less subtle is Jesse Bering who is quoted as saying that with such research, "we've got God by the throat and I'm not going to stop until

---

nations of the Natural World," *Developmental Psychology* 35 (1999): 1440-53.

[6]J. K. Chu, B. Liston, M. Sieger and D. Williams, "Is God in Our Genes?" *Time*, October 25, 2004.

[7]Richard Dawkins, "Viruses of the Mind," posted on Center for the Study of Complex Systems (September 2001) <www.cscs.umich.edu/~crshalizi/Dawkins/viruses-of-the-mind.html>.

[8]Matthew Alper, *The God Part of the Brain: A Scientific Interpretation of Human Spirituality and God* (New York: Rogue Press, 2000), p. 79.

one of us is dead." For Bering, the deliverances of the psychology of religion are "not going to remain in the privileged chapels of scientists and other scholars. It is going to dry up even the most verdant suburban landscapes, and leave spiritual leaders with their tongues out, dying for a drop of faith."[9]

What makes these scientists think that scientific accounts of the origin of religion make religious belief disreputable? I could suggest that we now turn to the arguments these critics offer on behalf of this conclusion. Unfortunately, they don't offer any. They take it to be fairly obvious that these accounts have such consequences, but this is not obvious at all. To see why, just consider the fact that developmental psychologists have tried to explain why human beings believe (from birth), among other things, that one and one equal two, that animals give birth to offspring of the same species and that certain unnatural events are caused by agents. No one thinks those beliefs are disreputable simply because they immediately spring to mind through our innate cognitive dispositions.

In fact, in some cases, the only thing that commends a belief to us is that it spontaneously arises through the natural workings of our minds. Beliefs of this sort, which philosophers call "basic beliefs," are those bedrock beliefs which act as evidence for all of our other beliefs, even though they themselves do not rest on any evidence. For example, the belief that other human beings have minds (that is, that they have centers of consciousness with beliefs and desires and such) is a basic belief that we all have, despite having no evidence for it. Of course we have evidence that people behave *as if* they had minds—the issue here is whether those behaviors that we *think* are caused by minds really *are*. We have no evidence one way or the other on that question, and yet we all spontaneously assume, and firmly believe, that others do in fact have minds.

So the mere fact (if it is a fact) that we are naturally disposed to form, for example, belief in God is no evidence that such belief is disreputable. But if that is not the problem, what do these scientists think the problem is?

At this point we need to engage in a little reverse engineering of our own, trying to reconstruct what it is that might have or could motivate

---

[9]Jesse Bering, quoted in Julia Reischel, "The God Fossil," *Broward-Palm Beach New Times,* March 9, 2006.

such a conclusion. Here is another line of reasoning that might be at work. In some cases when we form beliefs, the cause of that belief is the target of the belief itself. I believe, for example, there is a computer in front of me *because there really is,* or I believe my feet are propped up on the desk *because they really are.* What these accounts of religion show us, then, is that we have no good reason to think that our belief in God is due to the fact that God *is really there.* Instead, the God belief seems to be caused by purely natural mechanisms that don't involve God at all. As a result, God beliefs come about in a very different way than our beliefs in more ordinary things come about. It is this difference which explains why, if these scientific accounts are right, religious beliefs are disreputable.

The problem with this line of argument is that it is, well, just plain mistaken. I believe there is a deer in the neighborhood because I can see its tracks in the mud in my yard. I don't see it directly, but I see things that are causal consequences of the deer's presence, and this triggers in me a belief that it is around. What this line of argument does not see or even acknowledge is the possibility that the mechanisms that lead us toward belief in God might be, like the deer tracks, causal consequences of God's activity. If that is right, then it would not be true that God is not at all involved in the origin of religious belief. God would be the (remote) cause of them.[10] Thus, in order for this line of reasoning to work, the defender would have to claim that human beings would exist and have minds that form God beliefs *whether or not* there were a God. If our minds were insensitive to reality in this way (and we knew it) then we should at least be agnostic about whether or not there is a God.

Here an example might prove helpful. I am holding my hand in front of my face and have the belief "there is a hand in front of my face." What if, however, someone were to tell me that a scientist is pointing a special ray gun at my head right now which makes people (a) go blind and (b) believe that their hand is in front of their face? If that were to happen I would be left to think that, if the gun really exists, I would believe my hand was in front of my face *whether or not* it really was. In such a case, until I can be sure that there really is a hand there, I should be agnostic about the matter.

---

[10]Of course there is still a difference here. In the case of the deer track, we infer the presence of the deer from the causal evidence, and in the divine case the beliefs are directly caused in us by the remote causal activity of God. But in both cases, the beliefs—in the deer and in God—are caused by the target of the belief acting in ways that cause the belief.

But notice that the God case and the hand case are not analogous at all. I *do not* know that I would have the religious beliefs I do whether or not there really is a God. And the reason for that is simple: I think that there would be no universe, no earth, no life, no humans, no minds, no beliefs and no religion *unless* there were a God who created those things. The atheist might disagree. And then we would have something that we could intelligently discuss. But the question we would be discussing is not one that is settled by considering scientific accounts of the origin of religion, as we have seen. Thinking about scientific accounts of religion might lead us to think about this question—but they won't answer it. They can't.

Is that the end of the matter? Not exactly. There are other issues that are raised by scientific accounts of religion that are worth discussing. And perhaps "Newer Atheists" will come up with better (or even *some*) arguments that show that religious belief is disreputable in light of these accounts. But so far they haven't done so. Thus, for the moment, it seems perfectly acceptable for the Christian to hold that God created the world, human beings and human minds in such a way that when they are functioning properly, they form beliefs in the existence of rocks, rainbows, human minds and . . . God. For now, what we should conclude is that contemporary psychology has shown us the rather unsurprising fact that, in the words of Oxford psychologist Justin Barrett, "belief in gods and God particularly arises through the natural, ordinary operation of human minds in natural ordinary environments."[11] This discovery echoes the claim made four hundred plus years earlier by John Calvin that "there is within the human mind, and indeed by natural instinct, an awareness of divinity."[12]

FOR FURTHER READING

Barrett, J. *Why Would Anyone Believe in God?* Walnut Creek, Calif.: AltaMira Press, 2004.

Schloss, Jeffrey, and Michael J. Murray, eds. *The Believing Primate: Scientific, Philosophical and Theological Reflections on the Origin of Religion.* Oxford: Oxford University Press, 2009.

---

[11]Barrett, *Why Would Anyone Believe in God?*
[12]John Calvin *Institutes of the Christian Religion* 1.3.1.

Part **3**

GOD IS GOOD

7

God, Evil and Morality

Chad Meister

O ne of the most significant objections to belief in God—an objection which has transcended the ages—is called the "problem of evil." Perhaps one of the first persons to succinctly delineate the problem was Epicurus, a Greek philosopher from the third century B.C.:

> Either God wants to abolish evil, and cannot; or he can, but does not want to. If he wants to, but cannot, he is impotent. If he can, but does not want to, he is wicked. If God can abolish evil, and God really wants to do it, why is there evil in the world?[1]

More recently, Sam Harris restates the objection:

> Of course, people of all faiths regularly assure one another that God is not responsible for human suffering. But how else can we understand the claim that God is both omniscient and omnipotent? This is the age-old problem of theodicy, of course, and we should consider it solved. If God exists, either He can do nothing to stop the most egregious calamities, or He does not care to. God, therefore, is either impotent or evil.[2]

There is more than one problem latent in these words; in fact, there are various kinds of problems related to evil for those who believe in God. One is called the "logical problem of evil." It claims that the fol-

---

[1]Epicurus, according to Lactantius (ca. A.D. 240-320) in *De Ira Dei (On the Wrath of God),* trans. Philip Schaff <www.documentacatholicaomnia.eu/03d/0240-0320,_Lactantius,_ De_Ira_Dei_%5BSchaff%5D,_EN.pdf>.
[2]Sam Harris, *Letter to a Christian Nation* (New York: Knopf, 2006), p. 55.

lowing two statements contradict one another:

(1) God exists as an all-powerful, all-knowing and perfectly good being.

(2) Evil exists.

Since premise (2) is obviously true, premise (1) must be false. So God (defined as an all-powerful, all-knowing, perfectly good being—as most Christians, Muslims and Jews believe) must not exist.

Most people writing at the popular level aren't aware that professional philosophers of religion, theists and atheists alike have agreed in recent years that this version of the problem of evil has been decisively rebutted and is therefore unsuccessful.[3] That kind of consensus doesn't come very often in philosophy! There is no logical contradiction between the two claims, for it could be the case that an all-powerful, all-knowing and omnibenevolent God has good reasons for allowing evil to exist and persist—perhaps, for example, for the greater good of one or more persons.[4]

There are other versions of the problem which have not been so successfully rebutted;[5] much recent work has been done on them as well, and there are persuasive responses to each of them.[6] The New Atheists, however, are apparently unaware of the different forms of the problem and the various responses offered—or if they are aware of them, they tend to ignore them and continue to rehash "the problem" as though no responses even exist.

I think it's time the tables are turned, for it's not just the believer in God who has an apparent problem regarding evil. Everyone must provide an account of the evil which exists in the world, and of the various worldview options it seems clear to me that the atheistic account is the least successful. As a matter of fact, when it comes to the existence of evil in our world it's the atheists who should be on the defensive!

---

[3]Agnostic Paul Draper, considered to be one of the leading philosophers of religion currently writing on arguments from evil, makes the following comment: "I do not see how it is possible to construct a convincing logical argument from evil against theism." See Paul Draper, "The Argument from Evil," in *Philosophy of Religion: Classic and Contemporary Issues,* ed. Paul Copan and Chad Meister (Oxford: Blackwell, 2008), p. 146.

[4]For more on this argument, see Alvin Plantinga, *God, Freedom, and Evil* (Grand Rapids: Eerdmans, 1977), pt. 1.

[5]For an excellent delineation of various problems of evil, see Michael L. Peterson, *God and Evil: An Introduction to the Issues* (Boulder, Colo.: Westview Press, 1998).

[6]For some of these responses, see my *Evil: A Guide for the Perplexed* (London: Continuum, forthcoming).

If evil truly exists, what we could call "objective evil"—then there also exist objective moral values, moral values which are binding on all people, whether they acknowledge them as such or not. If rape, racism, torture, murder, government-sanctioned genocide and so forth are objectively evil, what makes them so? What makes them truly evil, rather than simply activities we dislike? What made the atrocities of the Nazis evil, even though Hitler and his thugs maintained otherwise? One cannot consistently affirm both that there are no objective moral values, on the one hand, and that rape, torture and the like are objectively morally evil on the other. If there are objective moral values, then there must be some basis—some metaphysical foundation—for their being so.

Interestingly, the New Atheists, including Richard Dawkins, appear to affirm some form of moral objectivism; they believe that some things (such as racism) are really evil and some things (such as generosity) are really good. But what grounds their moral positions? On what basis is it right and good to care about one's neighbor rather than to steal from her? What justification is there for affirming that it is better to help the poor and marginalized than to take advantage of them?

Dawkins, Harris and others routinely denounce the God of the Bible as morally monstrous and Christianity as morally pernicious and evil. What substantiates the claim of an atheist that the God of Christianity is evil and unjust? What basis do they have for making such judgments?

THE FOUNDATION OF MORALITY

William James once claimed, "If your heart does not want a world of moral reality, your head will assuredly never make you believe in one."[7] There may well be some atheists who do not want a world of moral reality; thankfully, the New Atheists are not in that category—they do want such a world. And yet they maintain that a person can live a good moral life without God in the picture. Christopher Hitchens, for example, says that it is "insulting" and "appalling" to claim that one does not know right and wrong without a God. He bemoans the "irritating mantle of righteousness" allegedly put forth by the religious faithful in their claim that only they (and not atheists) can make moral assessments. He puts forth the challenge to "name one ethical statement made, or one ethical

---

[7]William James, *The Will to Believe*, sect. 9 <http://falcon.jmu.edu/~omearawm/ph101will tobelieve.html>.

action performed, by a believer that could not have been uttered or done by a nonbeliever."[8]

But no one is arguing that atheists cannot utter ethical statements or live good, moral lives. Of course they can. This should be an obvious fact for Christians. In the New Testament book of Romans, the apostle Paul says:

> When the Gentiles, who do not possess the law, do instinctively what the law requires . . . [t]hey show that what the law requires is written on their hearts, to which their own conscience also bears witness; and their conflicting thoughts will accuse or perhaps excuse them. (Rom 2:14-15 NRSV)

Whether people believe in God's existence or know much if anything about God or the Bible is irrelevant to the issue at hand. When a person is functioning properly—and not censoring, repressing or ignoring her conscience—she knows right from wrong, good from evil. But *believing* that something is right or wrong and *justifying* one's belief that something is right or wrong are two very different matters.

In believing in morality without justifying morality, the New Atheists are confusing an epistemic (knowledge) issue with an ontological (foundational existence) one.[9] Believing something is one thing—having a foundation for that belief is quite another. For example, someone could believe that extraterrestrial beings exist and continually monitor happenings on the earth. Perhaps they do. But such a belief would be based on grounds which are suspect, to say the least. Similarly, the New Atheists can believe in right and wrong, good and evil. But what grounds their moral positions? What makes them more than mere subjective opinions?

Richard Dawkins maintains that we know right from wrong. Daniel Dennett affirms moral realism; he believes that moral values are objective features of the world. Christopher Hitchens uses the terms "good and evil," "right and wrong," and "moral and immoral" with dynamism and verve.[10] And Sam Harris claims that the golden rule is a "wonderful

[8]Christopher Hitchens, "An Atheist Responds," *Washington Post*, July 14, 2007, A17.
[9]For more on this, see Paul Copan, "The Moral Argument," in *Philosophy of Religion: Classic and Contemporary Issues*, ed. Paul Copan and Chad Meister (Oxford: Blackwell, 2008), pp. 127-41.
[10]See, for example, Hitchens's debates with Al Sharpton at <http://fora.tv/2007/05/07/Al_Sharpton_and_Christopher_Hitchens> and with Alister McGrath at <http://

moral precept."[11] But what moral theory do they advance to justify these beliefs and assertions?

Atheistic moral theories are relatively few. An atheist could, for example, affirm cultural or individual moral relativism.[12] But the New Atheists deny this. In a recent debate with Rick Warren—pastor of Saddleback Church—for example, Sam Harris made the following point about moral relativism:

> I'm not at all a moral relativist. I think it's quite common among religious people to believe that atheism entails moral relativism. *I think there is an absolute right and wrong.* I think honor killing, for example, is unambiguously wrong—you can use the word evil. A society that kills women and girls for sexual indiscretion, even the indiscretion of being raped, is a society that has killed compassion, that has failed to teach men to value women and has eradicated empathy. Empathy and compassion are our most basic moral impulses, and we can even teach the golden rule without lying to ourselves or our children about the origin of certain books or the virgin birth of certain people.[13]

Harris recognizes the dangers of moral relativism and argues against it in his book *The End of Faith*. He asserts that "questions of right and wrong are really questions about the happiness and suffering of sentient creatures."[14] So at first glance it appears that he is espousing a form of utilitarianism—the moral theory that right action is one that maximizes utility, such as pleasure or happiness. But no, he says, he is not doing so, because he doesn't think categories like that are useful.[15] So he doesn't want to be a moral relativist; he wants to equate right and wrong with happiness and suffering. But he doesn't want to be labeled a utilitarian either. So what is his moral theory? He doesn't tell us.

Daniel Dennett wants to avoid what he calls "imperialist

richarddawkins.net/article,1752,Debate-between-Christopher-Hitchens-and-Alister-McGrath,Christopher-Hitchens-Alister-McGrath>; see also Christopher Hitchens, *God Is Not Great: How Religion Poisons Everything* (New York: Twelve, 2007).

[11]Harris, *Letter to a Christian Nation*, p. 11.

[12]Sam Harris, however, argues that moral relativism is "nonsensical" in his book *The End of Faith: Religion, Terror, and the Future of Reason* (New York: W. W. Norton, 2004), pp. 178-82.

[13]"God Debate: Sam Harris Versus Rick Warren," *Newsweek,* April 9, 2007 <www.msnbc .msn.com/id/17889148/site/newsweek/print/1/displaymode/1098/> (emphasis added).

[14]Harris, *End of Faith*, pp. 170-71.

[15]Ibid., p. 171, n. 2.

universalism"—the idea that there are universal concrete standards of justice and human rights that apply to all societies. But he also affirms moral realism and wants to avoid moral relativism. A scientific stance toward morality should be taken, he argues, but within that stance we must presuppose the *"transcendent* values of truth and justice." It's hard to understand the existence of a *transcendent anything*, given an atheistic view of the world—why presuppose the transcendent values of truth and justice? His response is that we should "accept that these [transcendent] values are inescapably presupposed by human projects that *we all* participate in, simply by being alive: *staying* alive, and staying *secure*."[16] Even aliens (if they exist) could agree with this point, he suggests, and nothing more "parochial" (read "narrow minded and unreasonable, such as belief in God) needs to be considered in presupposing these values.

Certainly this bald proclamation needs some justifying. Did the big bang somehow spew forth moral platitudes like "Be compassionate to others," "Care for those in need" and "Love your enemies"? If not, where did they come from? What makes them something more than mere subjective opinions?

An atheist could put forth a consequentialist or perhaps even a deontological moral theory.[17] But the New Atheists don't take these options either. So what do they do? In terms of a moral theory, nothing. To his credit, Dawkins attempts to tackle this issue by rooting moral action in biological evolution. In the preface to his *Selfish Gene* he argues that "we are survival machines—robot vehicles blindly programmed to preserve the selfish molecules known as genes."[18] On his view of things, our moral aspirations and beliefs are predetermined posits of our genetic machinery, selfishly programmed to advance the gene pool. In his later work *The God Delusion*, he clarifies his position:

> On the face of it, the Darwinian idea that evolution is driven by natural selection seems ill-suited to explain such goodness as we possess, or our

---

[16]Daniel C. Dennett, *Breaking the Spell: Religion and a Natural Phenomenon* (New York: Viking Press, 2006), p. 376.

[17]Consequentialism is a kind of moral view that evaluates actions with respect to their consequences. Utilitarianism is a consequentialist theory. Deontological ethics considers certain features in a moral action to have intrinsic value, regardless of its consequences.

[18]Richard Dawkins, preface to *The Selfish Gene* (1976; reprint, New York: Oxford University Press, 1989), p. v.

feelings of morality, decency, empathy, and pity. Natural selection can easily explain hunger, fear, and sexual lust, all of which straightforwardly contribute to our survival or the preservation of our genes. But what about the wrenching compassion we feel when we see an orphaned child weeping, an old widow in despair from loneliness, or an animal whimpering in pain? What gives us the powerful urge to send an anonymous gift of money or clothes to tsunami victims on the other side of the world whom we shall never meet, and who are highly unlikely to return the favor? Where does the Good Samaritan in us come from? Isn't goodness incompatible with the theory of the "selfish gene"? No. This is a common misunderstanding of the theory—a distressing (and, with hindsight, foreseeable) misunderstanding. It is necessary to put the stress on the right word. The selfish *gene* is the correct emphasis, for it makes the contrast with the selfish organism, say, or the selfish species. Let me explain.

The logic of Darwinism concludes that the unit in the hierarchy of life which survives and passes through the filter of natural selection will tend to be selfish. The units that survive in the world will be the ones that succeeded in surviving at the expense of their rivals at their own level in the hierarchy. That, precisely, is what selfish means in this context.[19]

Dawkins agrees that "the most obvious way in which genes ensure their own 'selfish' survival relative to other genes is by programming individual organisms to be selfish." However, he argues, sometimes selfish genes "ensure their own selfish survival by influencing organisms to behave altruistically" or "morally." This happens especially with an organism's kin—brothers, sisters and children: "A gene that programs individual organisms to favour their genetic kin is statistically likely to benefit copies of itself."[20]

But it also happens through another means, he argues: "reciprocal altruism." This is the "you scratch my back and I'll scratch yours" idea, and it takes place not just with one's kin but also between various members of the species and even among members of different species. Also referred to as "symbiosis," this kind of relationship is one in which "both sides benefit from the transaction."[21]

---

[19]Richard Dawkins, *The God Delusion* (New York: Houghton Mifflin, 2006), pp. 214-15.
[20]Ibid., p. 216.
[21]In his debate with Al Sharpton, Christopher Hitchens seemed to base his moral position on this: "Why do I care? . . . Why do I mind about other primates [i.e., other human beings]? . . . Because I hope they mind about me in return." Is this a basis for right and wrong? Is this the kind of moral position we want to affirm? What about those people who can never return

To these "twin pillars" Dawkins adds two further elements which rest atop them: "reputation for generosity" (i.e., one acts altruistically so others will form the belief that you are generous) and "buying authentic advertising" (one acts altruistically or morally in order to prove that he has *more* than another—that he is dominant and superior—and thus can afford to be altruistic and moral).

So we have four components of an attempt to provide justification for acting morally:[22]

- *genetic kinship* (helping one's family members even at one's own expense)

- *reciprocation* (beyond one's kin, the repayment of favors given where both sides benefit from the transaction)

- *acquiring a reputation for generosity and kindness* (convincing others you are a moral altruist)

- *buying authentic advertising* (strutting your good deeds before others to impress them and so they infer your dominance and superiority).

In sum, Dawkins seems to be saying that our genes are preprogrammed to selfishly replicate themselves. Even so, individuals don't always act selfishly because our genes—working at the level of the *organism*—sometimes act in altruistic and moral ways, as this offers better gene propagation.

Now an obvious and glaring problem here is that this has very little to do with what we generally understand to be morality—with real right and wrong, good and evil. On Dawkins's schema, one is kind to his neighbor *because* he's been preprogrammed by his genes to do so (at least some individuals have been so preprogrammed; others perhaps not), and he's been so programmed *because* acting this way confers evolutionary advantage. It's not that it is a universally binding moral value to be kind. We simply call it "morally good" because our genes have, through eons of evolutionary struggle, gotten us to believe that it is so. Furthermore, on this account there is nothing *really* or *objectively* wrong with an individ-

---

the scratch? Is goodness based merely on tit-for-tat—I'll help you if (and only if) you'll help me? Reciprocal altruism may well be an important and perhaps even essential characteristic of morality, but a moral stance certainly includes much more than this. And Dawkins's additions are simply not enough to give us a moral foundation needed to provide us with a justification for objective good and evil.

[22]Dawkins summarizes these himself in *God Delusion*, pp. 219-20.

ual being selfish at the level of the organism, for example, or with an individual harming another for her own gain, or even with someone raping others for his own pleasure. It's just that acting in these ways does not generally confer an overall evolutionary advantage on an organism's genes and so has become socially prohibited over time.

But do Dawkins and Harris and the other New Atheists really believe that rape, murder and the like are not truly and universally evil? Are good and evil just illusions conjured up by our genes to get us to behave in certain ways? At times it seems that Dawkins and the others do not want this conclusion, but yet they don't want an absolutist morality either.[23] So what do they want? It's not clear. Dawkins realizes that he has not provided a moral theory with his account and hints that there are other types of moral theory besides relativism and absolutism that one could affirm. But he holds back from embracing any of them and just leaves the reader hanging.

But he can't have his cake and eat it too. If good and evil are objectively real, they need an objective foundation. No atheist has provided one, and it's doubtful that one will be forthcoming. We can put the problem concisely:

(1) If moral notions such as good and evil exist objectively, then there must be an objective foundation for their existence.

(2) Atheism offers no objective basis for the existence of moral notions such as good and evil.

(3) Therefore, for the atheist, moral notions such as good and evil must not objectively exist.

MORALITY AS ILLUSION

Evolutionary ethicist and atheist philosopher of science Michael Ruse (an atheist but not a New Atheist), along with his colleague Edward Wilson, are much more honest and consistent in recognizing that morality cannot be grounded in terms of naturalistic, biological evolution. They put it this way:

> Morality, or more strictly our belief in morality, is merely an adaptation put in place to further our reproductive ends. Hence the basis of ethics

---

[23]Dawkins states clearly that "morals do not have to be absolute" in *God Delusion*, p. 232.

does not lie in God's will—or in the metaphorical roots of evolution or any other part of the framework of the Universe. In an important sense, ethics as we understand it is an illusion fobbed off on us by our genes to get us to cooperate. It is without external grounding. Ethics is produced by evolution but is not justified by it because, like Macbeth's dagger, it serves a powerful purpose without existing in substance. . . . Unlike Macbeth's dagger, ethics is a *shared* illusion of the human race.[24]

So morality is something most of us believe in, but it doesn't exist in reality. This is really where the New Atheists' moral position ends up, whether they realize it or not.[25] He also refers to such moral values as kindness, altruism, generosity, empathy and pity as evolutionary "mistakes" or "misfiring."

What natural selection favors is rules of thumb, which work in practice to promote the genes that built them. Rules of thumb, by their nature, sometimes misfire. In a bird's brain, the rule "Look after small squawking things in your nest, and drop food into their red gapes" typically has the effect of preserving the genes that built the rule, because the squawking, gaping objects in an adult bird's nest are normally its own offspring. The rule misfires if another baby bird somehow gets into the nest, a circumstance that is positively engineered by cuckoos. Could it be that our Good Samaritan urges are misfiring, analogous to the misfiring of a reed warbler's parental instincts when it works itself to the bone for a young cuckoo? An even closer analogy is the human urge to adopt a child.[26]

Do we really believe that the moral urge to adopt a child is an evolutionary misfiring? I have several friends who have adopted children, and I don't suspect they would agree at all with Dawkins's explanation for why they did so. It was their kindness, love and moral concern for disenfranchised children that motivated them.

Knowing that his misfiring theory is more than most readers could swallow, Dawkins adds that even though moral notions are mistakes or

---

[24]Michael Ruse and Edward O. Wilson, "The Evolution of Ethics," in *Philosophy of Biology*, ed. Michael Ruse (New York: Macmillan, 1989), p. 316. In Shakespeare's tragedy, when Macbeth is about to kill King Duncan, he has a hallucination of a dagger floating in the air.

[25]Actually, I think Dawkins does realize it, for in an earlier work he says this: "The universe that we observe has precisely the properties we should expect if there is, at bottom, no design, no purpose, *no evil, no good*, nothing but pitiless indifference." Richard Dawkins, "God's Utility Function," *Scientific American*, November 1995, p. 85 (emphasis added).

[26]Dawkins, *God Delusion*, pp. 220-21.

misfirings, they are "precious mistakes"; they are misfirings of a "good" sort. But what in the world does that mean? Are they good in a moral sense? To claim this would be inconsistent, for it would be using the term *good* when the claim is now that there is no good, no evil. The attempt to offer a view of morality in which good and evil are not ultimately illusory on the one hand, and yet are not grounded in a transcendent reality on the other hand, is perhaps the most confused characteristic of the writings of Dawkins and the New Atheists.

In order to have a consistent and reasonable objective moral stance—a moral view in which you can substantiate a claim that *this* is right and *that* is wrong, *this* is good and *that* is evil—you need to have an objective moral basis. As C. S. Lewis argued so well, moral laws require a moral lawgiver,[27] and I don't see how one can have an objective lawgiver with anything other than a transcendent God. Surely from the physical perturbations of the big bang, moral values didn't spew forth. At most the illusion of moral values was eventually spawned. Certainly objective moral values didn't simply pop into existence ex nihilo (out of nothing) one lucky day in the ancient past. And indeed nothing in biological evolution, most especially the alleged selfish-gene phenomenon, is capable of providing the foundation necessary to ground unconditionally binding moral values.

Some years ago actress Katherine Hepburn made the following statement: "I'm an atheist, and that's it. I believe there's nothing we can know except that we should be kind to each other and do what we can for each other."[28] I'm glad she knew these things, but I wonder by what basis she could affirm her moral beliefs? No doubt atheists like her or Dawkins can believe such things. They can win Emmys and write first-rate books on the importance of acting morally, of treating people with compassion, dignity and respect. They can even spend their lives fighting evil and injustice. But what they cannot do, from within their atheistic worldview, is provide a reasonable justification for the existence of non-subjective, universally binding moral values such as compassion, dignity and respect or moral vices such as evil and injustice. For that task, they would need to include God in their inventory of what exists.[29]

---

[27]C. S. Lewis, *Mere Christianity* (New York: Macmillan, 1953), chaps. 1-5.

[28]Katherine Hepburn in *Ladies' Home Journal* (October 1991) as quoted in David Mills, *Atheist Universe* (Berkeley, Calif.: Ulysses Press, 2006), p. 33.

[29]Thanks to James Stump, David Cramer and William Lane Craig for helpful comments on an earlier draft of this essay.

FOR FURTHER READING

Adams, Robert M. *Finite and Infinite Goods: A Framework for Ethics.* Oxford: Oxford University Press, 1999.

Copan, Paul. "The Moral Argument." In *The Routledge Companion to Philosophy of Religion,* edited by Chad Meister and Paul Copan, pp. 362-72. London: Routledge, 2007.

Lewis, C. S. *Mere Christianity.* New York: Macmillan, 1953.

McGrath, Alister. *Suffering and God.* Grand Rapids: Zondervan, 1995.

Meister, Chad. *Evil: A Guide for the Perplexed.* London: Continuum, forthcoming.

Rist, John. *Real Ethics: Rethinking the Foundations of Morality.* Cambridge: Cambridge University Press, 2003.

8

Is Religion Evil?

ALISTER MCGRATH

In October 2005, the World Congress of the International Academy of Humanism took place in upstate New York. Its theme: "Toward a New Enlightenment." To judge from the conference publicity, its organizers had no doubt of the urgency of their theme. Religion is regaining the ascendancy! We are facing a new dark ages, a new evil empire! Only a return to the Enlightenment can save us! Yet perhaps quite contrary to the intentions of its organizers, the conference offered a fascinating glimpse of the crisis of confidence which is gripping atheism.

Belief in God was meant to have died out years ago. When I was an atheist myself, back in the late 1960s, everything seemed so simple. A bright new dawn lay just around the corner. Religion would be relegated to the past, a grim and dusty relic of a bygone age. God was just a cozy illusion for losers, best left to very inadequate and sad people. It was just a matter of waiting for nature to take its course. I was in good company in believing this sort of thing. It was the smug, foolish and fashionable wisdom of the age. Like flared jeans, it was accepted enthusiastically, if just a little uncritically.

NEW ENLIGHTENMENT—NEW ATHEISM

Since then, the ideas of the "New Enlightenment" conference have been aggressively promoted by the group of writers now linked together as the "New Atheism." One of its central themes is the simplistic soundbite ideally attuned to a media-driven culture which prefers breezy slogans to serious analysis: *Religion is evil.*

It resonates deeply, perhaps at a subrational level, with the fears of many in Western culture. The 2001 suicide attacks by Islamic fanatics on the World Trade Center in New York and elsewhere are seen as sure-fire demonstrations of the intrinsic evil of religion. Lurking within every religious believer lies a potential terrorist; get rid of religion, and the world will be a safer place.

Generalizations like this are found throughout Richard Dawkins's *God Delusion*, Christopher Hitchens's *God Is Not Great* and Sam Harris's *End of Reason.* Harris offers his own readings of central religious texts such as the Bible and the Qur'an to demonstrate that they possess an innate propensity to generate violence. Yet there is no attempt to analyze how these texts are interpreted and applied within their respective religious communities. Dawkins tells us that to take the Bible seriously is to "strictly observe the sabbath and think it just and proper to execute anyone who chose not to" or to "execute disobedient children."[1] Dawkins seems to assume that his readers know so little about Christianity that they are willing to believe that Christians are inclined to stone people to death.

A reality check is clearly in order. As the cultural and literary critic Terry Eagleton pointed out in his withering review of *The God Delusion,* "Such is Dawkins's unruffled scientific impartiality that in a book of almost four hundred pages, he can scarcely bring himself to concede that a single human benefit has flowed from religious faith, a view which is as *a priori* improbable as it is empirically false."[2] Harris assumes, without any serious argumentation or appeal to evidence, that the naturalistic worldview he proposes as a replacement for religion will generate more happiness, compassion or peace than religion can. His work bristles with the curious and highly problematic idea that scientists have a keener or deeper appreciation than religious people of how to deal with personal or moral problems. Yet such is the force of his rhetoric that such evidential deficits are airbrushed out of the picture. The New Atheism wants to take us back to the rationalism and sanity of the Enlightenment.

---

[1]Richard Dawkins, *The God Delusion* (Boston: Houghton Mifflin, 2006), pp. 249-50.
[2]Terry Eagleton, "Lunging, Flailing, Mispunching: A Review of Richard Dawkins' *The God Delusion," London Review of Books,* October 19, 2006. For Eagleton's subsequent magisterial demolition of the views of Dawkins and Hitchens, see Terry Eagleton, *Reason, Faith, and Revolution: Reflections on the God Debate* (New Haven: Yale University Press, 2009).

So what is "new" about the New Atheism? An innocent reader might assume that this movement had discovered new scientific evidence or new philosophical arguments that demonstrated that God was the arbitrary and meaningless construction of the human mind. Yet it soon becomes clear that there are no new arguments here. The old, familiar and somewhat tired arguments of the past are recycled and rehashed. What is new is the aggressiveness of the rhetoric, which often seems to degenerate into bullying and hectoring. It serves a convenient purpose, by papering over the obvious evidential gaps and argumentative lapses that are so characteristic of this movement. But it does little to encourage anyone to take atheism with intellectual seriousness.

In this essay, I want to look more closely at this core claim that religion is evil. Such is its cultural power that it tends to be assumed, rather than demonstrated, by those who advocate it. In fact, it turns out to be an article of faith, a belief which can be sustained only by highly selective use of evidence and what comes close to manipulation of history.

When I was an atheist myself, things seemed admirably clear. I grew up in Northern Ireland, infamous back in the late 1960s for its religious tensions and violence. It seemed obvious to me that if there were no religion, there would be no religious violence. I bought into the now outdated Enlightenment view that humanity was innocent and disinclined to violence until religion came along, a view which I find charmingly yet not a little uncritically echoed in the manifestos of the New Atheism. Get rid of religion, and humanity could rediscover a golden age of reason and toleration.[3]

It's a neat idea, which makes for great rhetoric. Yet it is indefensible in the face of the evidence, rather like believing in Santa Claus or the tooth fairy. A core belief of the New Atheism, which it persistently tries to represent as scientific fact, is that religion is the cause of the ills of humanity. But what is the evidence for this atheist revision of the idea of original sin?

---

[3]This theme is particularly evident in the string of soundbites, implausibly passed off as an argument, in Christopher Hitchens, *God Is Not Great: How Religion Poisons Everything* (New York: Twelve, 2007). In this chapter I shall focus particularly on Dawkins's *God Delusion*, as it is widely seen as the most influential and intellectually sophisticated of the recent writings from the New Atheist school.

RELIGION: A FALSE UNIVERSAL

The first point to make is simple: individual religions exist; "religion" doesn't. The Enlightenment was characterized by a love of universals, most famously stated in the idea of a universal human reason, whose fundamental characteristics were independent of history and culture. For the Enlightenment, this universal human reason could be the basis of a true, global ethic and philosophy, which would sweep aside irrational superstitions as relics of a barbarous past. In the end, this noble idea proved to be unworkable, in that human patterns of reasoning turned out to be much more culturally conditioned than had been realized.

The key point here is that the Enlightenment understandably yet wrongly regarded "religion" as a universal category. During the period of colonial expansion, many Europeans came across worldviews that differed from their own and chose to label them as "religions," when in fact many of these, such as Confucianism, were better regarded as philosophies of life. Some were explicitly nontheistic, yet the Enlightenment belief in a universal notion called "religion" led to these being forced into the same mold.

In recent years, there has been concerted criticism of this unhelpful and deeply problematic approach. It is increasingly agreed that definitions of religion tend to reflect the agendas and bias of those who propose them. There is still no definition of "religion" which commands scholarly assent.

So what is the relevance of this for the New Atheism? Let's take a statement by cultural commentator Carolyn Marvin, of the University of Pennsylvania. "Nationalism is the most powerful religion in the United States." Marvin's comment makes the point that there are many belief and value systems which can achieve religious status. Indeed, the noted English philosopher Mary Midgely argued that evolution, as developed by Richard Dawkins and others, had itself become a religious belief system. The porous and imprecise concept of "religion" extends far beyond those who believe in God, embracing a wide range of beliefs and values.

As Richard Wentz points out, the real issue is absolutism. People create and sustain absolutes out of fear of their own limitations, and people react with violence when others do not accept them. Religion may have a tendency toward absolutism, but the same tendency is innate in any human attempt to find or create meaning, especially when it is challenged. The key thing here, it seems, is not the ideas or values, but the dedication, even fanaticism, of those who follow them.

This leads into a central theme of many postmodern critiques of modernity—that it creates an intellectual context which legitimates suppression of what it regards as aberrant or "irrational" beliefs. The New Atheism is a superb example of a modern metanarrative—a totalizing view of things, locked into the worldview of the Enlightenment. As many have suggested, atheism is the natural religion of modernity. (Or should we say "worldview"?) So what happens when the Enlightenment is charged by its postmodern critics with having fostered oppression and violence, and having colluded with totalitarianism? When a new interest in spirituality surges through Western culture? When the cultural pressures that once made atheism seem attractive are displaced by others that make it seem intolerant, unimaginative and disconnected from spiritual realities? It is a point that postmodern critics of modernity would wish to press home.

It is vitally important to make a distinction between "religion" and "worldview." Yet it is a distinction that the New Atheism singularly fails to make or defend. Both religions (such as Christianity) and worldviews (such as Marxism) demand allegiance from their followers. The most successful worldviews incorporate religious elements, even if they are fundamentally secular in their outlook—as in the Soviet Union's use of quasi-religious rituals to mark essentially secular events. The historian Martin Marty, noting the lack of any viable definition of *religion,* offers five "features" that he holds to be characteristic of religion; all five, he notes, are also characteristic of political movements. It is not unreasonable to point out that, if religion is dangerous on this count, then so are politics. There can be (and are) political fanatics, just as there can be (and are) religious fanatics. The problem is fanaticism, not religion itself. In fact, the tone of the New Atheism critique of religion suggests that fanaticism may not be limited to the ranks of those who defend religion.

The New Atheism, of course, argues that religious worldviews offer motivations for violence that are not paralleled elsewhere—for example, the thought of entering paradise after a suicidal attack. Yet this conclusion is premature, and needs very careful nuancing. For Dawkins and Harris, it is obvious that it is religious belief that leads directly to suicide bombings. It's a view that his less-critical secular readers will applaud, provided they haven't read the empirical studies of why people are driven to suicide bombings in the first place.

As Robert Pape showed in his definitive account of the motivations of such attacks, based on surveys of every known case of suicide bombing since 1980, religious belief of any kind does not appear to be either a necessary or a sufficient condition to create suicide bombers. The infamous "suicide vest," for example, was invented by Tamil Tigers in 1991, leading to a large number of suicide attacks from this ethnic group. Pape's analysis of the evidence suggests that the fundamental motivation for suicide bombings appears to be political, not religious—namely, the desire to force the withdrawal of foreign forces occupying land believed to belong to an oppressed people who have seriously limited military resources at their disposal.

The New Atheism offers a superficial explanation for suicide bombings, designed to resonate with cultural anxieties about the heightened profile of religion in the United States and many parts of the world. Yet it is not a sustainable analysis, which does little to help us understand why these bombings arise and what can be done to prevent them. They have simply been hijacked as part of a crude atheist apologetic, rather than taken seriously as a cultural and social phenomenon. Happily, there are many serious studies, particularly from an anthropological perspective (including the important work of Scott Atran of the University of Michigan), which point in more realistic and informed directions. For Atran, the solution to suicide bombings is not the excoriation of religion, still less its suppression, but the empowerment of religious moderates.

SO WHAT "GOD" ARE WE ACTUALLY TALKING ABOUT?

If there is a serious point to be made by the New Atheism, it is that religion—or at least, certain forms of religion—can transcendentalize normal human conflicts and disagreements, transforming them into cosmic battles of good and evil, in which the authority and will of a transcendent reality is implicated. If God tells you to kill someone, who can argue with that? Although this point is often made in a muddled and overstated manner, there is a serious point that needs to be considered: why might someone think that God would order them to kill someone?

I must make two points clear here. First, I am a Christian, and write and think from that perspective. Second, I regard the idea that all religions teach pretty much the same thing as fatuous, lacking any empirical support. It is an idea that is curiously favored both by theological liberals (anxious to elevate the generic concept of "religion" above any specific religious system) and atheists (anxious to show that religion is evil, by singling out a single religion as representative of all—witness Sam Harris's stereotypical account of Islam).

As a Christian, I hold that the face, will and character of God are fully disclosed in Jesus of Nazareth. And Jesus of Nazareth did no violence to anyone. He was the object, not the agent, of violence. Instead of meeting violence with violence, rage with rage, Christians are asked to "turn the other cheek" (see Mt 5:39; Lk 6:29) and not to let the sun go down on their anger (Eph 4:26). This is about the elimination of the roots of violence—no, more than that: it is about its *transfiguration*. Does the God and Father of our Lord Jesus Christ command anyone to kill in his name? Certainly some Christians have argued so, especially during the age of the Crusades. But that belief is deeply problematic when confronted with the person of Christ. Christ commanded the sword to be put down, not to be taken up, in his defense. (The contrast with Islam is particularly instructive at this point.)

The importance of the witness of Christ on this matter can be seen in a tragic event in North America which took place in October 2006, within a week of the publication of Dawkins's *God Delusion*. A gunman broke into an Amish school in Pennsylvania and gunned down a group of schoolgirls. Five of the young girls died. The Amish are a Protestant religious group who repudiate any form of violence on account of their understanding of the absolute moral authority of the person and teaching of Jesus of Nazareth. When those unfortunate schoolchildren were murdered, the Amish community urged forgiveness. There would be no violence, no revenge—only the offering of forgiveness. The gunman's widow spoke, gratefully and movingly, of how this provided the "healing" that she and her three children "so desperately need."[4]

Richard Dawkins is nauseatingly condescending about the Amish in his *God Delusion*. Yet I cannot help but feel that he misses something

---

[4]Damien McElroy, "Amish Killer's Widow Thanks Families of Victims for Forgiveness," *Daily Telegraph* (London), October 16, 2006 <www.telegraph.co.uk/news/worldnews/1531570/ Amish-killers-widow-thanks-families-of-victims-for-forgiveness.html>.

rather important in his blanket dismissal of their significance. If the world were more like Jesus of Nazareth, violence might indeed be a thing of the past. But that does not appear to be an answer that Dawkins feels comfortable with.

WHAT ABOUT ATHEIST VIOLENCE AGAINST RELIGION?

As someone who grew up in Northern Ireland, I know about religious violence only too well. There is no doubt that religion can generate violence. But it's not alone in this. The history of the twentieth century has given us a frightening awareness of how political extremism can equally cause violence. In Latin America, millions of people seem to have "disappeared" as a result of ruthless campaigns of violence by right-wing politicians and their militias. In Cambodia, Pol Pot eliminated his millions in the name of socialism.

The rise of the Soviet Union was of particular significance. Lenin regarded the elimination of religion as central to the socialist revolution, and put in place measures designed to eradicate religious beliefs through the "protracted use of violence." One of the greatest tragedies of this dark era in human history was that those who sought to eliminate religious belief through violence and oppression believed they were justified in doing so. They were accountable to no higher authority than the state. It's a problem that was anticipated by Dostoyevsky in his great novel *The Possessed*. The most important character in the novel is Kirillov, who argues that the nonexistence of God legitimates all forms of actions. The importance of this theme for Dostoyevsky is best appreciated from his 1878 letter to N. L. Ozmidov, in which he sets out the implications of atheism for morality:

> Now assume that there is no God, or immortality of the soul. Now tell me, why should I live righteously and do good deeds, if I am to die entirely on earth? . . . And if that is so, why shouldn't I (as long as I can rely on my cleverness and agility to avoid being caught by the law) cut another man's throat, rob and steal?[5]

In *The Possessed* Kirillov adopts a related line of argument: if there is no God, it follows that he, Kirillov, is God. This puzzles Stephanovich,

---

[5]Letter to N. L. Ozmidov in *Selected Letters of Fyodor Dostoyevsky*, trans. Andrew R. MacAndrew, ed. Joseph Frank and David I. Goldstein (New Brunswick, N.J.: Rutgers University Press, 1987), p. 446.

who asks him to explain what he means. Kirillov responds as follows:

> If God exists, then everything is His will, and I can do nothing of my own apart from His will. If there's no God, then everything is my will, and I'm bound to express my self-will.

Since the idea of God is a pure human invention, Kirillov reasons that he is free to do as he pleases. There is no higher authority to whom he is ultimately accountable or who is able to negate his totalitarian moral self-assertion.[6]

In one of his more bizarre creedal statements as an atheist, Dawkins insists that there is "not the smallest evidence" that atheism systematically influences people to do bad things. It's an astonishing, naive and somewhat sad statement. Dawkins is clearly an ivory tower atheist, disconnected from the real and brutal world of the twentieth century. The facts are otherwise. In their efforts to enforce their atheist ideology, the Soviet authorities systematically destroyed and eliminated the vast majority of churches and priests during the period 1918–1941. The statistics make for dreadful reading. This violence, repression and bloodshed were undertaken in pursuit of an atheist agenda—the elimination of religion. Atheists can be just as repressive, brutal and bloodthirsty as any other human ideology. Atheism is just fine when it remains nothing more than ideas, discussed in university seminar rooms. But when it grasps political power, it turns out to be just as bad as anything else.

This hardly fits in with another of Dawkins's spuzzling creedal statements: "I do not believe there is an atheist in the world who would bulldoze Mecca—or Chartres, York Minster, or Notre Dame."[7] This noble sentiment is a statement about his personal credulity, not the reality of things. The history of the Soviet Union is replete with the burning and dynamiting of huge numbers of churches. So is the postwar history of the German Democratic Republic. Dawkins's special pleading that atheism is innocent of the violence and oppression that he associates with religion is simply untenable and suggests a significant blind spot.

Dawkins's childishly naive view that atheists would never carry out crimes in the name of atheism simply founders on the cruel rocks of reality. Let me give an example from the pen of another Oxford scholar who

---

[6]Fyodor Dostoyevsky, *Devils*, trans. Michael R. Katz (Oxford: Oxford University Press, 1992), p. 691.
[7]Dawkins, *God Delusion*, p. 249.

comes to very different conclusions from those asserted (not argued) by Dawkins. In his outstanding study of the Romanian Christian dissident-intellectual Petre Tutea (1902-1991), the Oxford scholar Alexandru Popescu documents the physical and mental degradation Tutea suffered as part of the systematic persecution of religion in Romania during the Soviet era until the downfall and execution of Nicolae Ceaucescu. During this period, Tutea spent thirteen years as a prisoner of conscience and twenty-eight years under house arrest. His story is enormously illuminating for those who want to understand the power of religious faith to console and maintain personal identity under precisely the forms of persecution that Dawkins believes do not exist.

Dawkins gives every impression of being in denial about the darker side of atheism, making him a less-than-credible critic of religion. He has a fervent, unquestioning faith in the universal goodness of atheism which he refuses to subject to critical examination. Yes, there is much that is wrong with contemporary religion, and much that needs to be reformed. Yet the same is also true of atheism, which still needs to subject itself to the self-searching intellectual and moral criticisms that religious systems are willing to direct against themselves. Why is it that so many atheists apply moral standards to their critique of religion which they seem reluctant to apply to atheism itself?

The reality of the situation is that human beings are capable of both violence and moral excellence—and that both these may be provoked by worldviews, whether religious or otherwise. It is not a comfortable insight, but one that alerts us to the shortcomings and dangers of identifying any one people group as the source of violence and the ills of humanity. It may facilitate scapegoating; it hardly advances the cause of civilization.

Furthermore, Dawkins fails to appreciate that when a society rejects the idea of God, it tends to transcendentalize alternatives—such as the ideals of liberty or equality. These now become quasi-divine authorities, which none are permitted to challenge.

Perhaps the most familiar example of this dates from the French Revolution, at a time when traditional notions of God were discarded as obsolete and replaced by transcendentalized human values. In 1792 Madame Rolande was brought to the guillotine to face execution on trumped-up charges. As she prepared to die, she bowed mockingly toward the statue of liberty in the Place de la Révolution and uttered the words for which she is now remembered: "Liberty, what crimes are committed in your name." Her point is simple, and I believe it to be irrefutable. All ideals—divine, transcendent, human or invented—are capable of being abused. That's just the way human nature is. And knowing this, rather than lashing out uncritically at religion, we need to work out what to do about it. The problem lies in human nature. The Christian doctrine of original sin has a lot to say about this significant failure of humanity to live up to its ideals.

BINARY OPPOSITIONS, "IN-GROUPS" AND "OUT-GROUPS"

Let's take this line of thought a stage further. Suppose Dawkins's dream were to come true, and religion were to disappear. Would that end the divisions within humanity and the violence that ensues from them? Certainly not. Such divisions are ultimately social constructs which reflect the fundamental sociological need for communities to self-define and identify those who are "in" and those who are "out," those who are "friends," and those who are "foes." The importance of "binary opposition" in shaping perceptions of identity has been highlighted in recent years, not least on account of the major debate between different schools of critical thought over whether such "oppositions" determine and shape human thought or are the outcome of human thought.

A series of significant binary oppositions are held to have shaped Western thought—such as "male-female" and "white-black." Binary opposition leads to the construction of the category of "the other"—the devalued half of a binary opposition—when applied to groups of people. Group identity is often fostered by defining "the other"—as, for example, in Nazi Germany with its opposition "Aryan-Jew." At times, binary opposition is defined in religious terms, as in "Catholic-Protestant" or "believer-infidel."

As is well known, the binary opposition "Catholic-Protestant" came to be perceived as normative within Northern Ireland. Each side saw its opponent as "the other," a perception that was relentlessly reinforced by novelists and other shapers of public opinion. Media reporting of the social unrest in Northern Ireland from 1970 to about 1995 reinforced the plausibility of this judgment. Yet this is a historically conditioned oppositionalism, shaped and determined by complex social forces. *It is not a specifically religious phenomenon.* Religion was merely the social demarcator that dominated in this situation. In others, the demarcators would have to do with ethnic or cultural origins, language, gender, age, social class, sexual orientation, wealth, tribal allegiance, ethical values or political views.

This clearly points to religion, at least in theory, as a potential catalyst for rage and violence in some contexts. In concurring, Dawkins makes a significant concession in recognizing the *sociological* origins of division and exclusion. "Religion is a label of in-group/out-group enmity and vendetta, not necessarily worse than other labels such as skin colour, language, or preferred football team, but often available when other labels are not."[8] Yet even here, his antireligious animus leads him to some problematic judgments.

The simplistic belief that the elimination of religion would lead to the ending of violence, social tension or discrimination is thus sociologically naive. It fails to take account of the way in which human beings create values and norms, and make sense of their identity and their surroundings. If religion were to cease to exist, other social demarcators would emerge as decisive, some of which would in due course become transcendentalized. Dawkins has no interest in sociology, as might be expected. Yet the study of how individuals and societies function casts serious doubt on one of the most fundamental assertions of his analysis.

Furthermore, one may legitimately wonder whether Dawkins and others, such as Daniel Dennett, have given rise to precisely the same "in-groups" and "out-groups" by their unwise endorsement of the notion of "brights" in 2003. For those who missed this diverting episode in American cultural history, a "bright" was defined as someone who holds "a naturalistic worldview" which is "free of supernatural and mystical elements." Just as "gays" was seen as a better word to designate homosexuals, "brights" was coined as a term for atheists.

When launching the "bright" movement in the *New York Times* back in 2003, Dennett insisted that telling people that he was "a bright" was "not a boast but a proud avowal of an inquisitive world view." Well, that's not how anyone else saw it. The opposite of "bright" is "dim," a mildly offensive word that translates as "stupid." By choosing to use the label "bright," atheists were widely seen to be claiming to be smarter

---

[8]Dawkins, *God Delusion*, p. 259.

than everyone else. As ABC's commentator John Allen Paulos remarked, "I don't think a degree in public relations is needed to expect that many people will construe the term as smug, ridiculous, and arrogant."[9]

The choice of the term turned out to be a public relations disaster, reeking of intellectual and cultural arrogance. The problem lay not simply in the field of public relations. The use of the label immediately created a mindset leading to precisely the "in-groups" and "out-groups," mimicking what Dawkins and Dennett had declared to be one of the cardinal sins of religion. If atheists were really so smart, how could two of their leading representatives fail to see that their chosen label would backfire so spectacularly?

My concern, however, is not the arrogance or foolishness of the New Atheism at this point but its fundamentally divisive nature. This crude belief system divides the world between the "brights" and the "dims," creating a damaging polarity which the New Atheism asserts is the characteristic of religion. Atheism, it seems, is just as bad, having now added intellectual snobbery to its vices and nothing obvious to its virtues.

CONCLUSION: ON BEING REALISTIC

Michael Shermer, president of the Skeptics Society, has made the significant point that religions were implicated in some human tragedies such as holy wars. While rightly castigating these—a criticism which I gladly endorse—Shermer goes on to emphasize that there is clearly a significant positive side to religion:

> For every one of these grand tragedies there are ten thousand acts of personal kindness and social good that go unreported. . . . Religion, like all social institutions of such historical depth and cultural impact, cannot be reduced to an unambiguous good or evil.[10]

Yet the pejorative and hostile spin relentlessly placed upon religion by the New Atheism asserts that it is a universal, unambiguous evil, which is a dangerous threat to civilization. Yet just where is the balanced and judicious analysis that Shermer rightly demands? Why is it so conspicuously absent? I fear the answer is simple: because it doesn't make for the slick and simple soundbites that will reassure the godless

---

[9]Chris Mooney, "Not Too Bright," *Skeptical Inquirer*, March-April 2004.
[10]Michael Shermer, *How We Believe: Science, Skepticism, and the Search for God* (New York: Freeman, 2000), p. 71.

faithful at a time of religious resurgence. Sure, religion can lead to violence and evil. But so can politics, race, and ethnicity . . . and an atheist worldview.

All of us who are concerned for the creation and preservation of a human civil society want to put an end to violence and oppression. Yet the New Atheist attempt to demonstrate that religion is intrinsically and necessarily evil has proved to be a damp squib, simply leading its critics to conclude that it is capable of resorting to the kind of intellectual somersaults and doublespeak that most had hitherto associated only with the worst forms of scholastic theology. It's time to stop this implausible discriminatory stereotyping and deal with the real problems faced by the world.

FOR FURTHER READING

Atran, Scott. *In Gods We Trust: The Evolutionary Landscape of Religion.* Oxford: Oxford University Press, 2004.

———. "The Moral Logic and Growth of Suicide Terrorism." *The Washington Quarterly* 29, no. 2 (2006): 127-47.

Dawkins, Richard. *The God Delusion.* Boston: Houghton Mifflin, 2006.

Dickinson, Anna. "Quantifying Religious Oppression: Russian Orthodox Church Closures and Repression of Priests 1917-41." *Religion, State & Society* 28 (2000): 327-35.

Eagleton, Terry. *Holy Terror.* New York: Oxford University Press, 2005.

———. *Reason, Faith, and Revolution: Reflections on the God Debate.* New Haven: Yale University Press, 2009.

Fitzgerald, Timothy. *The Ideology of Religious Studies.* New York: Oxford University Press, 2000.

Gambetta, Diego, ed. *Making Sense of Suicide Missions.* Oxford: Oxford University Press, 2005.

Harris, Sam. *The End of Faith: Religion, Terror, and the Future of Reason.* New York: W. W. Norton, 2004.

Hitchens, Christopher. *God Is Not Great: How Religion Poisons Everything.* New York: Twelve, 2007.

Kakar, Sudhir. *The Colors of Violence: Cultural Identities, Religion, and Conflict.* Chicago: University of Chicago Press, 1996.

Martin, David. *Does Christianity Cause War?* Oxford: Clarendon Press, 1997.

Marty, Martin, with Jonathan Moore. *Politics, Religion, and the Common Good: Advancing a Distinctly American Conversation About Religion's Role in Our Shared Life.* San Francisco: Jossey-Bass, 2000.

Marvin, Carolyn, with David W. Ingle. *Blood Sacrifice and the Nation: Totem Rituals and the American Flag.* Cambridge: Cambridge University Press, 1999.

McGrath, Alister E. *Dawkins's God: Genes, Memes and the Meaning of Life.* Oxford: Blackwell, 2004.

Midgley, Mary. *Evolution as a Religion: Strange Hopes and Stranger Fears.* 2nd ed. London: Routledge, 2002.

Pape, Robert A. *Dying to Win: The Strategic Logic of Suicide Terrorism.* New York: Random House, 2005.

Popescu, Alexandru D. *Petre Tutea: Between Sacrifice and Suicide.* Williston, Vt.: Ashgate, 2004.

Rosenbaum, Ron. *Explaining Hitler: The Search for the Origins of His Evil.* New York: Random House, 1998.

Shermer, Michael. *How We Believe: Science, Skepticism, and the Search for God.* New York: Freeman, 2000.

Stark, Rodney. *For the Glory of God: How Monotheism Led to Reformations, Science, Witchhunts, and the End of Slavery.* Princeton, N.J.: Princeton University Press, 2003.

Ward, Keith. *Is Religion Dangerous?* Oxford: Lion, 2006.

Wentz, Richard E. *Why People Do Bad Things in the Name of Religion.* Macon, Ga.: Mercer University Press, 1993.

9

Are Old Testament Laws Evil?

PAUL COPAN

The New Atheists raise abundant complaints about Old Testament ethics.[1] Richard Dawkins thinks that Yahweh is a moral monster:

> What makes my jaw drop is that people today should base their lives on such an appalling role model as Yahweh—and even worse, that they should bossily try to force the same evil monster (whether fact or fiction) on the rest of us.[2]

Yahweh's commanding Abraham to sacrifice Isaac is both "disgraceful" and tantamount to "child abuse and bullying." Yahweh breaks into a "monumental rage whenever his chosen people flirted with a rival god," resembling "nothing so much as sexual jealousy of the worst kind." Add to this the killing of the Canaanites—an "ethnic cleansing" in which "bloodthirsty massacres" were carried out with "xenophobic relish." Joshua's destruction of Jericho is "morally indistinguishable from Hitler's invasion of Poland" or "Saddam Hussein's massacres of the Kurds and the Marsh Arabs." Besides all this, we have to contend with the "ubiquitous weirdness of the Bible" as well as the moral failures and hypocrisies of biblical characters: a drunken Lot seduced by and engaging in sexual relations with his daughters (Gen 19:31-36), Abraham's twice lying about his wife Sarah (Gen 12:18-19; 20:18-19), Jephthah's foolish vow that resulted

---

[1]This essay summarizes some of the themes found in Paul Copan, "Is Yahweh a Moral Monster? The New Atheists and Old Testament Ethics," *Philosophia Christi* 10, no. 1 (2008): 7-37.

[2]Richard Dawkins, *The God Delusion* (Boston: Houghton Mifflin, 2006), p. 248.

in sacrificing his daughter as a burnt offering (Judg 11).[3]

Daniel Dennett considers the "Old Testament Jehovah" to be a super-*man* who "could take sides in battles, and be both jealous and wrathful." Though Dennett concedes that God happens to be more forgiving and loving in the New Testament, he goes on to say, "Part of what makes Jehovah such a fascinating participant in stories of the Old Testament is His kinglike jealousy and pride, and His great appetite for praise and sacrifices. But we have moved beyond this God (haven't we?)." He thanks heaven that those thinking that blasphemy or adultery deserves capital punishment are a "dwindling minority."[4]

According to Christopher Hitchens, the now-forgotten Canaanites were "pitilessly driven out of their homes to make room for the ungrateful and mutinous children of Israel." Moreoever, the Old Testament contains

> a warrant for trafficking in humans, for ethnic cleansing, for slavery, for bride-price, and for indiscriminate massacre, but we are not bound by any of it because it was put together by crude, uncultured human animals.[5]

Sam Harris boldly asserts that if the Bible is true, we should be stoning people to death for heresy, adultery, homosexuality, worshiping graven images and "other imaginary crimes." Putting to death idolaters in our midst (Deut 13:6, 8-15) reflects "God's timeless wisdom."[6] Referring to Deuteronomy 13:7-11, Harris claims that the consistent Bible believer should stone his daughter if she comes home from a yoga class a devotee of Krishna. Harris wryly quips that one of the Old Testament's "barbarisms"—stoning children for heresy—"has fallen out of fashion in our country."[7] Furthermore, once we recognize that slaves are human beings who are equally capable of suffering and happiness, we'll understand that it is "patently evil to own them and treat them like farm equipment."[8] Indeed, we can be good and recognize right and wrong

---

[3]Ibid., pp. 242, 243, 247, 241.
[4]Daniel C. Dennett, *Breaking the Spell: Religion as a Natural Phenomenon* (New York: Viking, 2006), pp. 206, 265, 267.
[5]Christopher Hitchens, *God Is Not Great: How Religion Poisons Everything* (New York: Twelve, 2007), pp. 101-2.
[6]Sam Harris, *Letter to a Christian Nation* (New York: Knopf, 2006), p. 8.
[7]Sam Harris, *The End of Faith* (New York: W. W. Norton, 2004), p. 18.
[8]Harris, *Letter*, pp. 18-19.

without God or the Bible: we can know objective moral truths without "the existence of a lawgiving God"[9] and can judge Hitler to be morally reprehensible "without reference to scripture."[10]

These charges made by the New Atheists are a distorted representation of Old Testament ethics. They fail to consider issues such as the earliest creational ideals (Gen 1—2), the warm moral ethos of the Old Testament, the context of the ancient Near East, the broader biblical canon and the metaphysical context to undergird objective morality. I have attempted elsewhere to address at both scholarly and popular levels the various Old Testament ethical questions—slavery, the Canaanite issue, killing Canaanites versus Islamic jihad, "harsh" moral codes and "strange" levitical laws, Abraham's offering Isaac, the imprecatory psalms, divine jealousy, divine egotism, and so forth.[11] I'll only offer a broad overview here.

A RESPONSE TO THE NEW ATHEISTS

Biblical scholar John Barton warns that there can be no "simple route" to dealing with Old Testament ethics,[12] a topic that has been described as a kind of "patchwork quilt."[13] For example, John Goldingay correctly sees Israel's unfolding history as broken up into five distinct stages or contexts—wandering clan, theocratic nation, monarchy, afflicted remnant and postexilic community of promise—and each one of these requires distinct rather than uniform moral responses.[14] Thus, a proper response calls for greater attention to a range of relevant factors completely ignored by the New Atheists' somewhat crass hermeneutic and left-wing fundamentalism.

---

[9]Ibid., p. 23.

[10]Ibid., p. 24.

[11]See Paul Copan, *That's Just Your Interpretation* (Grand Rapids: Baker, 2001); *How Do You Know You're Not Wrong?* (Grand Rapids: Baker, 2006); *When God Goes to Starbucks: A Guide to Practical Apologetics* (Grand Rapids: Baker, 2008); and "Is Yahweh a Moral Monster? The New Atheists and Old Testament Ethics."

[12]John Barton, *Ethics and the Old Testament* (Harrisburg, Penn.: Trinity Press International, 1998), p. 7. See Brevard S. Childs, *Biblical Theology in Crisis* (Philadelphia: Westminster Press, 1970), p. 125, where he notes that there is no "clear-cut answer" on how to do biblical ethics.

[13]Bruce C. Birch, *Let Justice Roll Down: The Old Testament, Ethics, and Christian Life* (Louisville: Westminster John Knox, 1991), p. 36.

[14]See John Goldingay, *Theological Diversity and the Authority of the Old Testament* (Grand Rapids: Eerdmans, 1987), chap. 3.

1. *Mosaic law and historical narratives.* The Law of Moses (Ex 20—Num 10) isn't a self-contained moral code, but it is sandwiched between a larger narrative framework that provides a wider moral context to consider. A plain reading of Israel's priestly/legal codes reveals that they are embedded within a broader historical narrative. Unlike other ancient Near East cuneiform legislation, God ultimately instructs Israel not by laying down laws or principles but by telling stories of real people as they relate to their Creator and Covenant Maker. Ideally, God's moral character and his activity in Israel's history give the nation a necessary ethical framework to shape its way of life:

> I am the LORD your God, who brought you out of the land of Egypt, out of the land of slavery. You shall have no other gods before me. (Ex 20:2-3)

This is in contrast to, say, the prologue/epilogue to Hammurabi's Code, which, rather than offering historical narrative, contains lofty language about Hammurabi's being endowed by the gods as a benevolent earthly sovereign to be a just ruler on earth.

Brevard Childs observes that the Torah's legal material is consistently intertwined with narrative, thus providing "a major commentary within scripture as to how these commands are seen to function."[15] As we'll see below, the critics' assumption that Israel's holiness code offers an ultimate, universal ethic (compare Harris's comment about "God's timeless wisdom") is misguided.

Dawkins's claims that biblical characters are often deeply flawed may win him points in the rhetoric category, but he isn't saying anything with which Christians disagree. Such moral blackballing loses him points when he ignores many moral, noble actions of the biblical characters—Abraham's magnanimity toward Lot; Joseph's moral integrity; David's refusal to touch king Saul, despite the opportunities; Nathan's courage to confront David the adulterer. Indeed, many biblical narratives tend to confirm our moral intuitions, which reveal how biblical characters are often a mixed moral bag. As Barton wisely observes, "The reader [of these narratives] is obliged to look [human anger, lust, ambition and disloyalty] in the face and to recognise his or her affinity with the characters in whom they are exemplified."[16]

---

[15]Brevard S. Childs, *Biblical Theology of the Old and New Testaments: Theological Reflection on the Christian Bible* (Minneapolis: Fortress, 1993), p. 680.
[16]John Barton, *Understanding Old Testament Ethics: Approaches and Explorations* (Louis-

Thus, Christopher Hitchens's remarks about "the ungrateful and mutinous children of Israel" are accurate. St. Paul observes as much in
1 Corinthians 10: many of Israel's stories involving stubbornness,
treachery and ingratitude are vivid *negative* role models—ones to be
avoided. The Old Testament's descriptions ("is") do not necessarily
amount to prescriptions ("ought").

   2. The Mosaic law, human sin and divine ideals. The Mosaic law
reflects a meeting point between divine/creational ideals and the reality
of human sin and evil social structures. Birch observes that the ancient
Near Eastern world—its slavery, polygamy, war, patriarchal structures,
kingship and ethnocentrism—is "totally alien" and "utterly unlike" our
own social setting. He advises us to acknowledge this impediment:
"These texts are rooted in a cultural context utterly unlike our own,
with moral presuppositions and categories that are alien and in some
cases repugnant to our modern sensibilities."[17] The New Atheism ignores what Christians most likely affirm—that Mosaic legislation isn't
the Bible's moral pinnacle but rather a springboard anticipating further
development or, perhaps more accurately, a pointer back to the loftier
moral ideals of Genesis 1—2; 12:1-3. These ideals affirm the image of
God in each person (regardless of gender, ethnicity or social class), lifelong monogamous marriage and God's concern for the nations. The
moral implications from these foundational texts are monumental,
though Israel's history reveals a profound departure from these ideals.

   Consequently, the believer need not justify all aspects of the Sinaitic
legal code. After all, God begins with an ancient people who have im-
bibed dehumanizing customs and social structures from their ancient
Near Eastern context. Yet Yahweh desires to treat them as morally responsible agents who, it is hoped, *gradually* come to discover a better
way; he does this rather than risk their repudiating a loftier ethic—a
moral overhaul—that they cannot even understand and for which they
are not culturally or morally prepared.[18]

   Imagine a culture's strong resistance toward radical challenges to racial and social attitudes (e.g., Western nations' pressing for democracy

---

ville: Westminster John Knox, 2003), p. 73.
[17]Bruce C. Birch, "Old Testament Ethics," in *The Blackwell Companion to the Hebrew Bible*,
   ed. Leo G. Purdue (Oxford: Blackwell, 2001), p. 297.
[18]Alden Thompson, *Who's Afraid of the Old Testament God?* (Grand Rapids: Zondervan,
   1988), p. 33.

and equal human rights where tribal, social and religious structures do not readily assimilate such ideals). As Goldingay puts it: "God starts with his people where they are; if they cannot cope with his highest way, he carves out a lower one."[19] This kind of progression, as we shall see, is not biblical relativism, as some allege.[20] Indeed, we see unchangeable biblical ideals highlighted from the very beginning of the Scriptures (Gen 1:26-27; 2:24), which are reaffirmed throughout. As Birch observes, none of these inferior moral practices and attitudes (e.g., slavery, patriarchy, tribalism) is "without contrary witness" elsewhere in the Old Testament—a crucial point the New Atheists gloss over.[21]

3. Mosaic law, cuneiform law and moral improvements. Mosaic legislation reflects a revolutionary moral improvement over the existing ancient Near Eastern cuneiform laws—even if this is ethically inferior and less than ideal. Collections of cuneiform law include the laws of Ur-Nammu (c. 2100 B.C., during the Third Dynasty of Ur); the laws of Lipit-Ishtar (c. 1925 B.C.), who ruled the Sumerian city of Isin; the (Akkadian) laws of Eshnunna (c. 1800 B.C.), a city one hundred miles north of Babylon; the laws of Hammurabi (1750 B.C.); and the Hittite laws (1650-1200 B.C.) of Asia Minor.[22]

Despite parallels between these and Mosaic law codes and even certain improvements in ancient Near Eastern codes over time, some significant differences also exist. We have in the Mosaic law some genuine,

---

[19]Goldingay, *Theological Diversity*, p. 86.

[20]Hector Avalos makes this faulty claim, along with a number of outrageous distortions, in "Paul Copan's Moral Relativism: A Response from a Biblical Scholar of New Atheism," Debunking Christianity (August 1, 2008) <http://debunkingchristianity.blogspot .com/2008/07/paul-copans-moral-relativism-response.html>. I cannot here address them except in passing. For example, he essentially accuses me of holding that the killing of the Canaanites was good ("Killing women and children is sometimes good") and presumably should be applauded. No, this was, as John Stott said, "a ghastly business; one shrinks from it in horror" (John Stott and David Edwards, *Evangelical Essentials* [Downers Grove, Ill.: InterVarsity Press, 1988], p. 263). Punishment or the taking of life, even if just, is far from good and pleasant. (Consider, at a much lesser level, removing life support from a dying loved one; here we have a measure of last resort that is still far from "good.") Also, in the context of slavery (e.g., 1 Pet 2:18-20), Avalos claims that biblical writers believed it was "good to be treated in a dehumanizing way" and that, according to New Testament writers, it "is deemed good to suffer pain and injustice." This is a distortion. No, it is better to suffer for doing what is right than for wrongdoing; in the former case, such suffering is still unjust and thus not good. Nor is it virtuous to seek after suffering as good.

[21]Birch, *Let Justice Roll Down*, p. 43.

[22]See Joe M. Sprinkle, *Biblical Law and Its Relevance* (Lanham, Md.: University Press of America, 2004), chap. 3.

previously unheard-of improvements. Slaves in Israel, unlike their ancient Near Eastern contemporaries, were given radical, unprecedented
legal and human rights—even if not equaling that of free persons.[23] As
the *Anchor Bible Dictionary*'s essay "Slavery" observes, "We have in the
Bible the first appeals in world literature to treat slaves as human beings
for their own sake and not just in the interests of their masters."[24] By
comparison, "the idea of a slave as exclusively the object of rights and as
a person outside regular society was apparently alien to the laws of the
ANE," where slaves were forcibly branded or tattooed for identification
(contrast this with Ex 21:5-6). Indeed, in "contrast to many ancient doctrines, the Hebrew law was relatively mild toward the slaves and recognized them as human beings subject to defense from intolerable acts,
although not to the same extent as free persons."[25]

Another unique feature of the Mosaic law is its condemnation of kid-
napping a person to sell as a slave—an act punishable by death (Ex
21:16; cf. 1 Tim 1:10); this is a point lost on, or ignored by, those who
compare slavery in Israel to that in the antebellum American South.
While Israel was commanded to offer safe harbor to foreign runaway
slaves (Deut 23:15-16), Hammurabi demanded the death penalty for
those helping runaway slaves (sect. 16). In other less-severe cases—in
the Lipit-Ishtar (para. 12) and Eshunna (paras. 49-50) laws—fines were
demanded for sheltering fugitive slaves, who were still required to be
returned to their masters.[26]

As an aside, it has been alleged that Paul's returning the runaway
Onesimus to his owner Philemon is a step backward toward Hammurabi.[27] This is a false charge. Paul knows Philemon well and thus en-
courages this brother in Christ to receive Onesimus back as a "dear
brother" and "no longer as a slave" (Philem 16). Paul, who had

[23]Christopher J. H. Wright, *Walking in the Ways of the Lord* (Downers Grove, Ill.: InterVarsity Press, 1995), p. 124.
[24]Muhammad A. Dandamayev, "Slavery (Old Testament)," in *Anchor Bible Dictionary*, vol. 6,
ed. David Noel Freedman (New York: Doubleday, 1992).
[25]Ibid.
[26]All references to ancient Near Eastern legal texts are taken from William W. Hallo, ed., *The
Context of Scripture: Volume II: Monumental Inscriptions from the Biblical World* (Leiden:
Brill, 2003); Martha T. Roth, *Law Collections from Mesopotamia and Asia Minor*, 2nd ed.
(Atlanta: Scholars Press, 1997). A fine summary about crimes and punishments related
to women is Elisabeth Meier Tetlow, *Women, Crime, and Punishment in Ancient Law and
Society: Volume 1: The Ancient Near East* (New York: Continuum 2004).
[27]Contra Avalos, "Paul Copan's Moral Relativism."

declared that in Christ there is "neither slave nor free" (Gal 3:28), could appeal to Philemon based on (a) Paul's personal knowledge of Philemon (who wasn't a physical threat to Onesimus—which Exodus 21:16 presumes), (b) the spiritual debt Philemon himself owed Paul, and (c) the new brotherly relationship in Christ between Onesimus and Philemon. Thus Paul elsewhere can appeal to Christian masters—who have their own heavenly Master—to treat their slaves justly, impartially and without threatening (Eph 6:9; Col 4:1). And if slaves can gain their freedom (1 Cor 7:21), Paul encouraged this. Surely, this is dramatic departure from Hammurabi.

Hebrew (debt) slaves—which could be compared to indentured servanthood during the founding of America—were to be granted eventual release in the seventh year (Lev 29:35-43)—a notable improvement over other ancient Near Eastern law codes.[28] This release was to be accompanied with generous provisions and a gracious spirit (Deut 15:9). The motivating reason? "You were a slave in the land of Egypt, and the LORD your God redeemed you; therefore I command you this today" (Deut 15:15 NASB). Even if the poverty could not be eradicated, Deuteronomy 15's overriding, "revolutionary" goal was that there be no debt slavery in the land at all (Deut 15:4, 11).[29]

Another marked improvement is the release of injured slaves themselves (Ex 21:20-21)—in contrast to their masters merely being compensated (typical of ancient Near Eastern codes). The Mosaic law holds masters to legal account for their treatment of their own slaves (not simply another's slaves). This too is unparalleled in comparable codes.[30] Elsewhere in the Old Testament, Job recognizes that he and his slaves have the same Maker and come from the same place—the wombs of their mothers (Job 31:15). Thus, Christopher Hitchens and Sam Harris

---

[28]Some of my discussion here is taken from William J. Webb, "A Redemptive-Movement Hermeneutic," in *Discovering Biblical Equality*, ed. Ronald W. Pierce and Rebecca Merrill Groothuis (Downers Grove, Ill.: InterVarsity Press, 2005).

[29]Gordon McConville, *Grace in the End: A Study in Deuteronomic Theology* (Grand Rapids: Zondervan, 1993), p. 148.

[30]Avalos ("Paul Copan's Moral Relativism") mentions Exodus 21:21-22 as an indication of slaves being mere chattel. Actually, if a slave is killed by a master, the *master* is to be punished (following on the heels of this passage is mentioned "life for life"). This is quite remarkable and unique in the ancient Near East (on this unique feature, see Christopher J. H. Wright, *Old Testament Ethics for the People of God* [Downers Grove, Ill.: InterVarsity Press, 2004], p. 292). The debt slave is referred to as a master's "money," suggesting that the master harms himself if he harms his servant.

notwithstanding, such improvements—or pointers back to Genesis 1:26-27—can hardly be called "a warrant for trafficking in humans" or for treating them "like farm equipment."

Concerning the ancient Near East's inferior sexual morality, we're familiar with the condemnation of the Canaanite female and male cult prostitutes (see Gen 38:15, 22-23; Deut 23:18-19; Hos 4:14). Many ancient Near Eastern cuneiform laws, however, permitted activities that undermined family integrity and stability by, for example, allowing men to engage in adulterous relations with slaves and prostitutes. The laws of Lipit-Ishtar of lower Mesopotamia (1930 B.C.) take for granted the practice of prostitution (e.g., paras. 27, 30). In Hittite law (1650-1500 B.C.), "if a father and son sleep with the same female slave or prostitute, it is not an offence" (para. 194). Hittite law even permitted bestiality: "If a man has sexual relations with either a horse or a mule, it is not an offence" (para. 200a).[31]

Alongside morally inferior cuneiform legislation we find attendant harsh, ruthless punishments. Historian Paul Johnson observes: "These dreadful laws [of Hammurabi] are notable for the ferocity of their physical punishments, in contrast to the restraint of the Mosaic Code and the enactments of Deuteronomy and Leviticus."[32] Indeed, Hammurabi stresses the centrality of property whereas the laws in the "Book of the Covenant" (Ex 21—23) consider crimes against persons to be far more weighty.[33]

For certain crimes, Hammurabi mandated that the tongue, breast, hand or ear be cut off (sects. 192, 194, 195, 205).[34] One punishment in-

---

[31]Hittite law did not, however, permit sexual relations with a cow or sheep or pig or dog (paras. 187, 188, 199). These references are taken from Hallo, *The Context of Scripture;* Roth, *Law Collections from Mesopotamia and Asia Minor.*

[32]Paul Johnson, *Art: A New History* (New York: HarperCollins, 2003), p. 33.

[33]Robin Parry, *Old Testament Story and Christian Ethics* (Carlisle, U.K.: Paternoster, 2005), p. 68.

[34]Although Deuteronomy 25:11-12 appears to suggest that a woman's hand must be cut off if she seizes the genitals of the man who is in a fight with her husband (and if so, this would be the only biblical instance of punishment by mutilation), Jerome T. Walsh offers a more plausible interpretation—namely, *depilation* ("you shall shave [the hair of] her groin") rather than *mutilation*. The word translated "hand" here is *kaph*—the "palm" of a hand or some rounded concavity such as a dish, bowl, or spoon or even the arch of a foot—rather than the commonly used *yad* ("hand"). To "cut off" a "palm"—as opposed to a hand—would be quite odd. Furthermore, the verb *qasas* in the intensified *piel* form (ten occurrences) is rightly translated "cut off" or "[physically] sever." However, here *qasas* appears in the milder *qal* form. Three other Old Testament occurrences of *qasas* in the *qal* form mean

volved the accused being dragged around a field by cattle. Babylon and Assyria (and, earlier, Sumer) practiced the river ordeal:[35] when criminal evidence was inconclusive, the accused would be thrown into the river; if he drowned, he was guilty (the river god's judgment), but if he survived, he was innocent and the accuser was guilty of false accusation.[36] Besides punishments such as cutting off noses and ears, ancient Egyptian law permitted the beating of criminals (for, say, perjury or libel) with between one hundred and two hundred strokes.[37] In fact, a one-hundred-stroke beating was the "mildest form of punishment."[38] Contrast this with Deuteronomy 25:1-3 (NASB), which sets a limit of forty strokes for a criminal: "He may beat him forty times but no more, so that he does not beat him with many more stripes than these" so that "your brother is not degraded in your eyes." Furthermore, in Babylonian or Hittite law, status or social rank determined the kind of sanctions for a particular crime, whereas biblical law holds kings and priests and those of social rank to the same standards as the common person.[39] The informed inhabitant of the ancient Near East would have thought, *Quick, get me to Israel!*

What of Scripture's emphasis on *lex talionis*—an eye for an eye and a tooth for a tooth? First, except for capital punishment ("life for life"), these

---

"cut/shave [hair]." This would be the open concave region of the groin, and thus a shaving of pubic hair—a punishment of public humiliation not unusual in the ancient Near East. Thus, the talionic punishment is public sexual humiliation (of the woman) for public sexual humiliation (of the man). See Jerome T. Walsh, "You Shall Cut Off Her . . . Palm? A Reexamination of Deuteronomy 25:11-12," *Journal of Semitic Studies* 49 (2004): 47-48; also, Richard M. Davidson, *Flame of Yahweh: Sexuality in the Old Testament* (Peabody, Mass.: Hendrickson, 2007), pp. 476-80.

[35]Avalos ("Paul Copan's Moral Relativism") mentions an alleged biblical parallel with the river ordeal—the "water" (Num 5:16-22). But the difference here in this symbolic act is that the water itself is harmless (the ink is not toxic)—as opposed to the ancient Near Eastern punishment that ends up being the result of someone's not being able to swim! Furthermore, any physical judgment in Numbers 5 is quite evidently supernatural and miraculous. Avalos adds that this practice in modern days would be indefensible. I would agree, but that's a point I repeatedly make in my "Is Yahweh a Moral Monster?": such practices aren't the ideal morality—even if there is improvement.

[36]Tetlow, *Women, Crime, and Punishment in Ancient Law and Society*, pp. 12-13, 96-97, 136.

[37]David Lorton, "The Treatment of Criminals in Ancient Egypt," in *The Treatment of Criminals in the Ancient Near East*, ed. Jack M. Sasson (Leiden: Brill, 1977), pp. 1-64; see, e.g., p. 25.

[38]"Crime and Punishment," *The Oxford Encyclopedia of Ancient Egypt*, ed. Donald B. Redford (Oxford: Oxford University Press, 2001), 1:318.

[39]Johannes Renger, "Wrongdoing and Its Sanctions: On 'Criminal' and 'Civil' Law in the Old Babylonian Period," in *The Treatment of Criminals in the Ancient Near East*, ed. Jack M. Sasson (Leiden: Brill, 1977), p. 72; see also Wright, *Old Testament Ethics for the People of God*, p. 310.

texts (Ex 21:23-25; Lev 24:17-22; Deut 19:16-21) are not taken literally. Each example calls for (monetary) compensation, not bodily mutilation. Later in the New Testament, referring to this language that was being used as a pretext for personal vengeance outside the law courts, Jesus himself did not take such language literally (Mt 5:38-39)—no more than he took literally the language of plucking out eyes and cutting off hands if they lead to sin (Mt 5:29-30).[40] Childs comments: "The principle of *lex talionis* marked an important advance and was far from being a vestige from a primitive age."[41] Second, this principle served as a useful guide for exacting proportional punishment and compensation; this was designed to prevent blood feuds and disproportionate retaliatory acts.

Additionally, the increased complexity and stringency of Mosaic regulations are divine responses to Israel's disobedience. From the beginning, the earliest legislation (Ex 21—23) was intended to be simple and much less harsh comparable to patriarchal religion (cf. Jer 7:2; Gal 3:19, 22). However, the greater stringency of the ensuing laws is the result of three things: (a) Israel's refusal to approach God at the mountain as a "kingdom of priests" (Ex 19:6), instead sending Moses as their mediator; (b) Aaron's failure as high priest in the golden-calf incident (Ex 32), resulting in a tightening of priestly restrictions (Ex 35—Lev 16); and (c) the people's worship of the goat idols (Lev 17:1-9), resulting in more severe laws for the community (Lev 17:10—26:46).[42] Consider how a rebellious child will often need external rules, severe deadlines and close supervision to hold him over until (hopefully) an internal moral change takes place. Rules, though a stop-gap measure, are hardly ideal.

Although the New Atheists belittle the Mosaic law for its ruthless strictness, it is an *accommodation* to a morally undeveloped ancient Near Eastern cultural mindset—with significant ethical improvements—as well as a response to the rebellious, covenant-breaking propensity of the Israelites.

4. The Mosaic law, Israel's history and varying ethical demands.

---

[40]Contra Avalos, "Paul Copan's Moral Relativism."

[41]Brevard S. Childs, *The Book of Exodus: A Critical, Theological Commentary* (Philadelphia: Westminster Press, 1974), p. 93.

[42]John H. Sailhamer, *The Pentateuch as Narrative: A Biblical-Theological Commentary*, Library of Biblical Interpretation (Grand Rapids: Zondervan, 1995), pp. 46-59; see also his *Introduction to Old Testament Theology: A Canonical Approach* (Grand Rapids: Zondervan, 1995), pp. 272-89.

Israel's variegated contexts or developmental stages suggest appropriately varied moral responses but also include permanent moral insights. We've noted the shift from an ancestral wandering clan to a theocratic nation, then to a monarchy or institutional state/kingdom, an afflicted remnant and finally a postexilic community/assembly of promise.[43] Each stage offers enduring moral insights—faithfulness and covenant-keeping, trusting in God, showing mercy. Our focus, though, is on the varying ethical demands on God's people. For example, in the first stage, Abraham, Isaac and Jacob are apolitical characters (except for Abram's rescuing Lot in response to an invasion [Gen 14]). After Israel's four-hundred-year wait, including bondage in Egypt, until the sin of the Amorites reaches full measure (Gen 15:16), they became a nation. This required land to inhabit. Yahweh fought on Israel's behalf while bringing just judgment upon an irredeemable Canaanite culture that had sunk hopelessly below any hope of moral return—with the rare exception of Rahab and her family; as Leviticus 18:28 declares, the land would "spew out" its inhabitants, and Israel itself was subject to the same judgment.

"Holy warfare" is perhaps the most emotionally charged point raised by the New Atheists. It is primarily located in the second stage and not throughout Israel's Old Testament history, although Israel, like neighboring nations, had persistent enemies to be fended off. So let me offer a few comments here.

First, Israel (whose history as God's Old Testament people, by the way, is unique, unrepeatable and not to be idealized or universalized for other nations) would *not* have been justified to attack the Canaanites without Yahweh's explicit command. Yahweh issued his command in light of a morally sufficient reason—the intractable wickedness of Canaanite culture.

Second, as I argue elsewhere,[44] we have strong archaeological evidence that the targeted Canaanite cities, such as Jericho and Ai, were

---

[43]Comments here are taken from chap. 3 in Goldingay, *Theological Diversity*.

[44]Paul Copan, "Yahweh Wars and the Canaanites," *Philosophia Christi* 11, no. 1 (2009): 73-90. I am indebted to the work of Richard S. Hess, especially his "War in the Hebrew Bible: An Overview," in *War in the Bible and Terrorism in the Twenty-First Century*, ed. Richard S. Hess and Elmer A. Martens (Winona Lake, Ind.: Eisenbrauns, 2008); Richard S. Hess, *Joshua: An Introduction and Commentary*, Tyndale Old Testament Commentary (Downers Grove, Ill.: InterVarsity, 1996).

not population centers with women and children but military forts or garrisons that protected noncombatant civilians in the hill country. Soldiers and political and military leaders—and occasionally female tavern-keepers (e.g., Rahab) could be found in these citadels. Indeed, the terms "city" (*'ir*) and "king" (*melek*) were typically used in Canaan during this period to refer, respectively, to "fortress/garrison" and "military leader."

In addition, Jericho probably had about one hundred or fewer soldiers in this outpost[45] (which is why the Israelites could encircle it seven times in one day and then do battle against it). So if Jericho was a fort, then "all" those killed therein were warriors—Rahab and her family being the exceptional noncombatants dwelling within this militarized camp.[46] The same applies throughout the book of Joshua. All of this turns out to be quite the opposite of what many have been taught in Sunday school classes!

Third, the Old Testament idea of "dedication to destruction" or the "ban" (*herem*) includes stereotypical language of "all" and "young and old" and "man and woman"—a language of totality even if women and children are not present. In fact, later on when Saul puts Israel's enduring enemy—the Amalekites—under the ban (1 Sam 15:3), the target could likewise be simply fortified Amalekite strongholds, not population centers. This is further suggested by the fact that the Amalekites were not at all annihilated: within the very same book (1 Sam 27:8; 30:1) we encounter an abundance of Amalekites. In these limited settings, *herem* is thoroughly carried out (involving even livestock [e.g., 1 Sam 15:9, 14])—though the term allows, and hopes for, exceptions (e.g., Rahab and her relatives).

Fourth, the "obliteration language" in Joshua (e.g., "He left no survivors" and "totally destroyed all who breathed" [Josh 10:40]) and in early Judges is clearly hyperbolic—another stock feature of ancient Near Eastern language. Consider how, despite such language, the latter part

---

[45]On the exaggeration of numbers in the ancient Near East and Old Testament, see Daniel M. Fouts, "A Defense of the Hyperbolic Interpretation of Numbers in the Old Testament," *Journal of the Evangelical Theological Society* 40, no. 3 (1997): 377-87. In military contexts in the Bible, *'eleph* (the Hebrew word for "thousand") can also mean "unit" or "squad."

[46]Richard S. Hess, "The Jericho and Ai of the Book of Joshua," in *Critical Issues in Early Israelite History,* ed. Richard S. Hess, Gerald A. Klingbeil and Paul J. Ray Jr. (Winona Lake, Ind.: Eisenbrauns, 2008), pp. 38-39.

of Joshua itself (along with Judges 1) assumes plenty of Canaanites still inhabit the land:

> For if you ever go back and cling to the rest of these nations, these which remain among you, and intermarry with them, so that you associate with them and they with you, know with certainty that the LORD your God will not continue to drive these nations out from before you. (Josh 23:12-13 NASB)

Joshua 9—12 utilizes the typical ancient Near Eastern literary conventions of warfare.[47]

The same assumption is evident in Deuteronomy 7:2-5: despite Yahweh's command to bring punishment to the Canaanites, they would not be obliterated—hence the warnings for Israel not to make political alliances or intermarry with them afterward. We see from this passage too that wiping out Canaanite religion was far more significant than wiping out the Canaanites themselves.[48]

Fifth, we should take seriously the numerous references of "driving out" the Canaanites (e.g., Ex 23:28; Lev 18:24; Num 33:52: Deut 6:19; 7:1; 9:4; 18:12; Josh 10:28, 30, 32, 35, 37, 39; 11:11, 14) or "dispossessing" them of their land (Num 21:32; Deut 12:2; 19:1). This clearing away the land for habitation does not require killing. Civilians—particularly women and children—would not wait to be killed, but would be the first to flee when their military strongholds were destroyed and thus no longer capable of protecting them (e.g., Jer 4:29).

Sixth, God's difficult command regarding the Canaanites as a limited, unique salvation-historical situation is in some ways comparable to God's difficult command to Abraham in Genesis 22. Yet we should no more look to the divinely mandated attack on Canaanites (a kind of corporate capital punishment) as a universal ideal for international military engagement than we should look to Abraham's sacrifice of Isaac as a timeless standard for "family values." Behind both of these hard commands, however, is the clear context of Yahweh's loving intentions and faithful promises. In the first place, God had given Abraham the miracle child Isaac, through whom God promised to make

---

[47]Wright, *Old Testament Ethics*, pp. 474-75; Iain Provan, V. Philips Long and Tremper Longman III, *A Biblical History of Israel* (Lousiville: Westminster John Knox, 2003), p. 149.
[48]Gordon Wenham, *Exploring the Old Testament: A Guide to the Pentateuch* (Downers Grove, Ill.: InterVarsity Press, 2003), p. 137.

Abraham the father of many. Previously, he saw God's provision when he reluctantly let Ishmael and Hagar go into the wilderness—with God reassuring Abraham that Ishmael would become a great nation. Likewise, Abraham knew that God would somehow fulfill his covenant promises through Isaac—even if it meant that God would raise him from the dead. Thus Abraham informed his servants, "We will worship, and then we will come back to you" (Gen 22:5 NRSV; cf. Heb 11:19). With the second harsh command regarding the Canaanites, Yahweh has already promised to bring blessing to all the families of the earth without exclusion (Gen 12:1-3; 22:17-18) and desires to include Israel's most hated enemies in this blessing (e.g., Is 19:25); so this should be set against the background of Yahweh's enemy-loving character (Mt 5:43-48; cf. Ex 34:6) and worldwide salvific purposes. In both cases, we have a good, promise-making God who has morally sufficient reasons for issuing these commands.

Seventh, the crux of the issue is this: if God exists, does he have *any* prerogatives over human life? The New Atheists seem to think that if God existed, he should have a status no higher than any human being and thus has no right to take life as he determines. Yet we should press home the monumental difference between God and ordinary human beings. If God is the author of life—the cosmic authority—he is not obligated to give us seventy to eighty years of life. The Lord gives and takes away (Job 1:21).[49] God can take Canaanite lives indirectly through Israel's armies—or directly, as with Sodom (Gen 19), according to his good purposes and morally sufficient reasons. Surely God's moral standing and wisdom (Job 38—41) are far above that of humans; indeed, for God to be God, he would have to pose an authority problem for human beings, but the New Atheists seem to ignore this.

5. The Law of Moses, the biblical canon and moral undertones. The Law of Moses, intended to be temporary rather than ultimate, still has its own deep moral warmth, but it finds fulfillment in the new cov-

---

[49]Avalos ("Paul Copan's Moral Relativism") writes: "If jihadist Muslims kill millions of Americans in order to wipe out our supposedly corrupt religion, then I suppose that would be morally acceptable by Dr. Copan's logic. It all depends on whether you accept the faith claim that Allah is the true God." My argument is that if God commanded it, then he had sufficient reason for doing so. This isn't to justify actions done by anyone in the name of God. See my discussion regarding "General Lin" in *When God Goes to Starbucks*, chap. 12; cf. chaps. 13-14.

enant fulfilled in Jesus Christ. The New Atheists tend to assume that the Mosaic law is comprehensively normative for the consistent Bible-believer. This huge presumption misses the flow of biblical revelation. We'll address this on a number of fronts.

First, Mosaic legislation isn't to be equated with the moral law. Laws are often a compromise between the ideal and the enforceable.[50] The Mosaic law is truly a moral improvement upon the surrounding ancient Near Eastern cultures—and is thus justifiably called "spiritual" and "good" (Rom 7:14, 16) and reflective of Yahweh's wisdom (Deut 6:5-8). Yet it is *self-confessedly* less than ideal. Contrary to the New Atheists' assumptions, the Mosaic law isn't the permanent, fixed theocratic standard for all nations.

Polygamy, for instance, is practiced—contrary to God's ideals in Genesis 2:24—perhaps in part because its prohibition would have been difficult to enforce, even if the biblical writers hoped for something better (cf. Deut 17:17; 1 Kings 11:3). Like divorce and other inferior moral conditions (cf. Mt 19:8), polygamy was tolerated rather than upheld as an ultimate moral standard.

Second, the Mosaic law reveals God's forbearance because of human hard-heartedness. Matthew 19:8 indicates that divorce was permitted—not commanded—because of hard hearts; it was not so "from the beginning." The same can be said of a strong patriarchalism, slavery, polygamy and warfare common in the ancient Near Eastern context; these are in violation of the creational ideals of Genesis 1—2. Rather than banishing all evil social structures, Sinaitic legislation frequently assumes the practical facts of fallen human culture while pointing Israel to God's greater designs for humanity.

God shows remarkable forbearance in the Old Testament. Romans 3:25 (NASB) indicates that God "passed over the sins previously committed." Elsewhere Paul declares:

> Therefore having overlooked the times of ignorance, God is now declaring to men that all people everywhere should repent, because He has fixed a day in which He will judge the world in righteousness through a Man whom He has appointed, having furnished proof to all men by raising Him from the dead. (Acts 17:30-31 NASB)

---

[50]Gordon J. Wenham, *Story as Torah: Reading Old Testament Narratives Ethically* (Grand Rapids: Baker Academic, 2000), p. 80.

In the Old Testament, God puts up with sinful human structures, but they remain less than ideal.

Third, the Mosaic law—an improved, more humanized legislation—attempts to restrain and control an inferior moral mindset without completely abolishing these negative structures. While negative aspects of slavery are retained, slaves achieve astonishing rights in the Old Testament, in contrast to the rest of the ancient Near East. Even so, Deuteronomy 15 expresses the hopeful goal of eventually eradicating slavery while both (a) diminishing the staying power of slavery in light of the exodus and (b) controlling the institution of slavery in light of the practical fact that misfortune in a subsistence culture could reduce anyone to poverty and indebtedness.[51] Yahweh often reminds Israel of its own history of slavery in hopes of engendering a loftier ideal: "You shall not oppress a stranger, since you yourselves know the feelings of a stranger, for you also were strangers in the land of Egypt" (Ex 23:9 NASB).

What is more, the three main texts regarding slave legislation (Ex 21; Lev 25; Deut 15) reveal a morally improved legislation as the text progresses. Christopher Wright sees Deuteronomy "modifying, extending, and to some extent reforming earlier laws, with additional explicit theological rationale and motivation." He goes so far as to say that while Exodus 21 emphasizes the humanness of slaves, even the ancient Israelite would recognize that Deuteronomy 15 was in tension with earlier legislation. So to obey Deuteronomy "necessarily meant no longer complying with Exodus." This point serves to illustrate the "living, historical and contextual nature of the growth of Scripture."[52] The same kind of progression is evident in legislation regarding primogeniture and the like.

Fourth, the Mosaic law contains seeds for moral growth, offering glimmers of light pointing to a higher moral path. Yes, God prohibits worship of other gods (the ultimate act of reality-denial), but his ultimate desire is that his people love him wholeheartedly. Love isn't reducible to the law's restraining influence, and enjoying God's presence isn't identical to idol avoidance.[53] The model of Yahweh's character and sav-

[51]McConville, *Grace in the End*, pp. 148-49.
[52]Christopher Wright, "Response to Gordon McConville," in *Canon and Biblical Interpretation*, ed. Craig Bartholomew et al. (Grand Rapids: Zondervan, 2006), p. 283. See Wright's fuller explanation in this chapter.
[53]Wenham, *Story as Torah*, p. 81. Interestingly, the last commandment of the Decalogue

ing action is embedded within and surrounding Israel's legislation—a "compassionate drift" in the law, which includes

> protection for the weak, especially those who lacked the natural protection of family and land (namely, widows, orphans, Levites, immigrants and resident aliens); justice for the poor; impartiality in the courts; generosity at harvest time and in general economic life; respect for persons and property, even of an enemy; sensitivity to the dignity even of the debtor; special care for strangers and immigrants; considerate treatment of the disabled; prompt payment of wages earned by hired labor; sensitivity over articles taken in pledge; consideration for people in early marriage, or in bereavement; even care for animals, domestic and wild, and for fruit trees.[54]

In their zealous preoccupation with the negative in Old Testament ethics, the New Atheists neglect these warm undertones in the law of Moses itself, exemplified in Yahweh's gracious, compassionate character and his saving action.

Fifth, the Mosaic law contains an inherent planned obsolescence, which is to be fulfilled in Christ. Despite the significant moral advances at Sinai, the law isn't the final word. A new covenant was promised that would progress beyond the old (e.g., Jer 31; Ezek 36—37). N. T. Wright notes that Torah "is given for a specific period of time, and is then set aside—not because it was a bad thing now happily abolished, but because it was a good thing whose purpose had now been accomplished."[55] According to the letter to the Hebrews, Jesus brings "substance" to the Old Testament's "shadows," fully embodying humanity's and Israel's story. Thus, if we stop at Old Testament texts without allowing Christ—the second Adam and the new, true Israel—to illuminate them, our reading and interpretation of the Old Testament will be greatly impoverished. Robin Parry reminds us that if we allow that the Christ-event is part of the plotline, then we are obligated to allow it to "cast its significance back onto our understanding of earlier texts."[56] If the New Testament brings out more fully the heart of God, then we must not let the "tail" (the Old Testament) wag

---

("You shall not covet") directs our ethical perspective in the direction of the heart's dispositions and intentions—*beyond* property and theft laws.

[54]Wright, *Old Testament Ethics*, p. 300.

[55]N. T. Wright, *Climax of the Covenant* (Minneapolis: Fortress, 1993), p. 181.

[56]Parry, *Old Testament Story and Christian Ethics*, p. 78.

the "dog" (the New Testament) as the New Atheists commonly do.

CONCLUDING REMARKS

As indicated throughout, I have attempted to condense much material into this brief essay. I've argued that Christians can readily acknowledge that the Mosaic law isn't the ideal, ultimate ethic. We can, with Daniel Dennett, "thank heaven" that those thinking that blasphemy or adultery deserves capital punishment are a "dwindling minority." However, let me here make a couple of statements regarding the New Atheists' trivialization of Yahweh and the inconsistency between their "objective" moral outrage and naturalism.

First, like Narnia's Aslan, gracious and compassionate Yahweh (Ex 34:6) isn't to be trifled with. He is good, but not "safe." The New Atheists resist the notion of Yahweh's rightful prerogatives over humans; they seem uncomfortable with the idea of judgment or cosmic authority. Yet God must reveal himself with holy firmness (at times, fierceness) to get the attention of human rebels—including Israel (Deut 9:6-7).

Dawkins's charge that God's breaking into a "monumental rage" when Israel "flirted with a rival god" is "sexual jealousy of the worst kind" seems to diminish the meaning of the marriage covenant—and, in particular, this unique bond between God and his people. Israel hadn't simply "flirted" with rival gods but cohabited with them, "playing the harlot" (cf. Ezek 16; 23); Israel did so on the "honeymoon" (Ex 32)! Hosea's notable portrayal of Israel as a prostitute—no mere flirt—is quite serious despite Dawkins's casual dismissal. The appropriate response to adultery is anger and hurt (cf. Is 5:4; 65:2-3; Ezek 6:9). When there is none, we rightly wonder how deeply and meaningfully committed to marriage one truly is.

Second, despite Dawkins's moral outrage, his metaphysic disallows it, admitting that a universe full of electrons contains "no evil and no good, nothing but blind pitiless indifference."[57] Indeed, science "has no methods for deciding what is ethical." Individuals and society decide.[58] Well, isn't this Dawkins's own individual preference—a merely contextual, relative matter rather than an objective one? As I've argued elsewhere,

---

[57]Richard Dawkins, *River Out of Eden: A Darwinian View of Life* (New York: Basic Books, 1995), pp. 132-33.
[58]Richard Dawkins, *A Devil's Chaplain* (New York: Houghton Mifflin, 2003), p. 34.

naturalism doesn't have the metaphysical resources to move from value-less matter to value (including rights-bearing human beings and objective morality). Theism is immensely better equipped metaphysically to provide such a context.[59]

Harris's attempt to "demolish the intellectual and moral pretensions of Christianity" is quite ironic for several reasons. First, despite historical deviations from Jesus' teaching (e.g., the Crusades, the Inquisition), biblical theism has historically served as a moral compass for Western civilization's advances.[60] Second, despite the New Atheists' appeals to science, they ignore the profound influence of the Jewish-Christian worldview on the West's scientific enterprise. In Paul Davies's words, "Science began as an outgrowth of theology, and all scientists, whether atheists or theists . . . accept an essentially theological worldview."[61] Third, the New Atheists somehow gloss over the destructive atheistic ideologies that have led to far greater loss of human life within just one century than "religion" (let alone "Christendom") with its wars, inquisitions and witch trials. Atheism has proven to be a far more destructive force than "religion." Finally, though Harris correctly defends knowledge of objective moral truths "without reference to scripture," he misses the greater point of how human value and dignity could emerge given naturalism's valueless, mindless, materialist origins. All humans are God's image-bearers, morally constituted to reflect God in certain ways; so atheists and theists alike can recognize an objective right and wrong and human dignity *without* special revelation (Rom 2:14-15). Naturalists, nevertheless, still lack the proper metaphysical context for affirming such moral dignity and value.

Though Old Testament ethics presents certain challenges, we've seen that the New Atheists often overstate and distort them. Their typical rhetoric and often-simplistic arguments may score points with popular

---

[59]Paul Copan, "God, Naturalism, and the Foundations of Morality" in *The Future of Atheism: Alister McGrath and Daniel Dennett in Dialogue*, ed. Robert Stewart (Minneapolis: Fortress Press, 2008).

[60]Alvin J. Schmidt, *How Christianity Changed the World* (Grand Rapids: Zondervan, 2004); Jonathan Hill, *What Has Christianity Ever Done For Us? How It Shaped the Modern World* (Downers Grove, Ill.: InterVarsity Press, 2005); Dinesh D'Souza, *What's So Great About Christianity?* (Washington, D.C.: Regnery Gateway, 2007); Rodney Stark, *The Victory of Reason* (New York: Random House, 2006).

[61]Paul Davies, *Are We Alone?* (New York: Basic, 1995), p. 96.

audiences, but their assertions present a lopsided picture of Old Testament ethics and Yahweh's character.

FOR FURTHER READING

Copan, Paul. *That's Just Your Interpretation*. Grand Rapids: Baker, 2001.

———. *How Do You Know You're Not Wrong?* Grand Rapids: Baker, 2005.

———. *When God Goes to Starbucks*. Grand Rapids: Baker, 2005.

———. "Yahweh Wars and the Canaanites," *Philosophia Christi* 11, no. 1 (2009): 73-90.

Goldingay, John. *Theological Diversity and the Authority of the Old Testament*. Grand Rapids: Eerdmans, 1995.

Hess, Richard S. "War in the Hebrew Bible: An Overview." In *War in the Bible and Terrorism in the Twenty-First Century*. Edited by Richard S. Hess and Elmer A. Martens. Winona Lake, Ind.: Eisenbrauns, 2008.

Millar, J. Gary. *Now Choose Life: Theology and Ethics in Deuteronomy*. Downers Grove, Ill.: InterVarsity Press, 2001.

Webb, William J. *Slaves, Women and Homosexuals: Exploring the Hermeneutics of Cultural Analysis*. Downers Grove, Ill.: InterVarsity Press, 2001.

Wenham, Gordon J. *Story as Torah: Reading Old Testament Narrative Ethically*. Grand Rapids: Baker Academic, 2004.

Wright, Christopher J. H. *Old Testament Ethics for the People of God*. Downers Grove, Ill.: InterVarsity Press, 2004.

10

How Could God Create Hell?

JERRY L. WALLS

Perhaps there is no word tossed about more casually in the English language that is virtually guaranteed to bring casual conversation to a dead stop than the word *hell*. This is particularly true if anyone dares to take it seriously or use it as anything more than a highly versatile slang phrase. You can use it as an adjective: "That was a hell of a (sometimes rendered 'helluva') game"; as a sort of exclamation: "Hell yes, I'm angry"; as an expression of puzzlement: "Hell if I know"; and so on. However, you are most likely to draw looks of suspicion, if not gasps of dismay, if you use it as a noun: "Well, yes, I do believe those who persist in rejecting God will wind up in hell."

The threat of hell has been disrupting polite conversation and eliciting passionate protests from atheists and other critics of Christianity for centuries. One such classic instance, as related by biographer Ernest Campbell Mossner, involves the famous Scottish philosopher David Hume, a real party animal who was noted for his cheerful disposition and good manners. During a social gathering one evening Hume was engaged in conversation with a minister, the Reverend John Warden, who apparently irritated Hume by mentioning a sermon by Jonathan Edwards titled "The Usefulness of Sin."[1] Hume put aside his customary gracious demeanor and went on the attack. If Edwards considers sin

---

[1]A much more famous sermon by Edwards is "Sinners in the Hands of an Angry God," which describes hell in rather vivid terms. It's a safe guess that mention of this sermon would also have set Hume off.

useful, Hume remarked, then he must agree with the notorious claim of the philosopher Leibniz, who argued that our world is the best of all possible worlds. Mossner then reports that Hume burst out: "But what the devil does the fellow make of hell and damnation?"[2]

This is indeed a good question that believers can hardly duck, dive, dip or dodge. It is often noted that the problem of evil is the main weapon in the atheist's arsenal. The question, simply put, is how the existence of evil and suffering can be compatible with the existence of a God of perfect love and power. Well, hell is the problem on steroids. As hard as it may be to make sense of evil in this life, the doctrine of hell seems to extend this suffering and misery into the next life that never ends.

This frightful possibility is also one that rational unbelievers cannot simply ignore. Here let us draw a distinction between issues that are existentially central and those which are existentially peripheral, an important distinction pointed out by my mentor at Notre Dame, Tom Morris.[3] As he observes, many academic, cultural and scientific controversies are such that we can safely and reasonably not care much about them; whatever is true in such cases does not impact our lives in any significant way. It is reasonable to be interested in such matters if one is naturally so inclined, but it may also be reasonable not to spend much time or effort worrying about them. One may rationally not care much about Helen of Troy and whether or not she really existed. One may understandably be indifferent about heliozoans or not even know what they are. One may sensibly yawn or shrug his shoulders about the legend of Helle and her ride on the ram with the golden fleece. But not to care about hell is another matter altogether. It represents par excellence an example of an existentially central issue which does affect our lives in profoundly significant ways. Not to care, and care deeply, about the truth of the matter where hell is concerned is nothing short of insane.

It is noteworthy that Richard Dawkins's discussion of hell in his book *The God Delusion* is largely focused on irrational fears engendered by the doctrine. He cites stories of persons who have been so traumatized by frightful depictions of hell woven by preachers and priests that they remained psychologically disturbed by those fears even after giving up

---

[2]Ernest Campbell Mossner, *The Life of David Hume*, 2nd ed. (Oxford: Clarendon, 1980), p. 570.
[3]Thomas V. Morris, *Making Sense of It All: Pascal and the Meaning of Life* (Grand Rapids: Eerdmans, 1992), pp. 21-22.

their faith in God. In saying that it is insane not to care about hell, I have no interest in defending sensational accounts of the doctrine or in using it to frighten anyone into embracing a faith that has no appeal for them. Given what is at stake in the doctrine, however, no rational person can be indifferent to whether it is true or not.

But Dawkins's comments suggest that concern about hell can be dismissed by rational persons because it is clearly the creation of mean-spirited people who have devised the doctrine as a means of manipulation and intimidation. And let's not forget self-righteous: those who believe in the existence of hell are always self-righteous hypocrites who take delight in the damnation of others. Dawkins writes:

> Whatever they believe hell is actually like, all these hell-fire enthusiasts seem to share the gloating *Schadenfreude* and complacency of those who know they are among the saved, well conveyed by that foremost among theologians, St Thomas Aquinas, in *Summa Theologica*: "That the saints may enjoy their beatitude and the grace of God more abundantly they are permitted to see the punishment of the damned in hell." Nice man.[4]

Dawkins has a footnote to this passage quoting the brimstone-flinging Ann Coulter: "I defy any of my co-religionists to tell me they do not laugh at the idea of Dawkins burning in hell." No doubt there is a comic element in the idea of Dawkins in hell if for no other reason than because of the bemused look that would be on his face as he exclaimed, "Well I'll be damned, it's real after all." But at a deeper level I must disagree with Coulter, for I am confident that most of my co-religionists share my hope that Dawkins will eventually end up in heaven, where, no doubt, he would have an even more amusing, albeit sheepish, grin on his face, exclaiming "I'll be damned, it's real after all!" with heavy irony.

At any rate, Dawkins's take on hell is a variation on a theme that has been a popular one at least since Nietzsche, whose account of what he called "the genealogy of morals" has been highly influential in postmodern thought. As he saw it, Christian moral ideals such as kindness, forgiveness and mercy were actually a clever ploy on the part of weak people to gain an advantage over the strong. Everyone, whether self-consciously or not, is acting out of the "will to power." Those who talk about compassion for the poor and service to the downtrodden are engaged in a

---

[4]Richard Dawkins, *The God Delusion* (Boston: Houghton Mifflin, 2006), pp. 320-21.

devious form of manipulation and control over the elite of this world. In the same vein, Nietzsche thought the Christian doctrines of heaven and hell were a way for weak, dishonest people to get vengeance on their powerful enemies. Such doctrines allow the losers of the world to console themselves with the thought that in the end the tables will be turned and they will triumph while their enemies toast.

I have no doubt that at least some of the people who believe in hell have been motivated by such unsavory thoughts and desires. Belief in hell that is fueled by hatred or vindictiveness can rightly be dismissed as irrational and reprehensible. For that matter, there is something deeply incoherent about hatefully believing in hell, because hatred is one of the things that makes one a good candidate for ending up there. However, no one should make the mistake of concluding that the doctrine of hell is false because some, if not many, persons who have believed in it have done so for irrational or emotional reasons.[5] To so conclude would make one guilty of a basic logical error known as the genetic fallacy.

This famous fallacy slides from noting the dubious origin of a belief to the falsity of the belief itself. But alas, to do so can lead to some monumental mistakes. For instance, consider your neighborhood resident who has the irrational belief that everyone is out to get him. Well, can you be sure just because his belief has dubious origins that no one is out to get him? Obviously not, as we can see from the famous observation: "Just because you are paranoid does not mean they are not out to get you!" Likewise, just because you are a hypochondriac does not mean you never get sick. And just because some people believe in hell for dubious reasons and motivations does not mean the doctrine is false.

WHEN WAS HELL LISTED ON THE REAL ESTATE MARKET?

If the doctrine of hell is true, who created it? If there really is a hell besides the hateful fantasy spun out of the vindictive emotions of spiteful people, where did it come from? Who or what accounts for its existence? The answer, I suggest, is that those primarily responsible for the existence of hell are mean-spirited, self-righteous people. However, I mean this in an entirely different sense than Nietzsche and Dawkins meant it.

The basic Christian doctrine of creation is summed up nicely in the

---

[5]For a more thorough discussion of this point, see my book *Hell: The Logic of Damnation* (Notre Dame: University of Notre Dame Press, 1992), chap. 1.

first line of the Nicene Creed: "We believe in one God the Father Almighty, Maker of heaven and earth, and of all things visible and invisible." The important claim here is that God created everything that exists apart from himself. Moreover, everything he created was good. Now this claim, which is essential to Christianity, can easily heighten the perplexity about hell. For if God created everything that exists, then he must have created hell, but hell is obviously not a good thing.

The perplexity only increases when we step back and reflect on the nature of God himself, the One who created all things visible and invisible. Let me come at this matter from a bit of an ironic angle, by citing Nietzsche, famous for his soliloquies on the death of God as well as his diatribes against Christianity and Christian morality. One of the things that struck me recently in reading one of his most famous books were his numerous references to dancing and his desire to dance. In one rather poignant passage titled "The Tomb Song" that seems to describe his loss of adolescent faith and dreams, he wrote the following:

> And once I wanted to dance as I had never danced before: over all the heavens I wanted to dance. Then you persuaded my dearest singer. And he struck up a horrible dismal tune. . . . My highest hope remained unspoken and unredeemed. And all of the visions and consolations of my youth died![6]

In view of his dancing aspirations, it is perhaps not surprising that earlier in the same book, he even admits an attraction to the idea of a dancing god. "I would believe only in a god who could dance. And when I saw my devil I found him serious, thorough, profound, and solemn: it was the spirit of gravity—through him all things fall."[7]

Nietzsche is my favorite atheist, so I do not mind agreeing with him at many points and this is one of them. Now let me pair this quote from Nietzsche with a couple of my favorite descriptions of God from Christian writers. First, consider this passage from John Wesley, the eighteenth-century theologian and evangelist who founded the Methodist Church. Wesley notes that God created us for happiness and we can hardly be blamed for chasing after it since he designed us for that very purpose, though we typically find ourselves looking for it in all the

---

[6]Friedrich Nietzsche, *Thus Spoke Zarathustra*, trans. Walter Kaufmann (New York: Penguin, 1954), p. 112.
[7]Ibid., p. 41.

wrong places. In response to this, Wesley pointed us toward the true source of what we crave: "In this alone can you find the happiness you seek; in the union of your spirit with the Father of spirits; in the knowledge and love of Him who is *the fountain of happiness*, sufficient for all the souls he has made."[8]

Next, let us consider some thoughts from C. S. Lewis as he explains the doctrine of the Trinity. As he points out, this doctrine is the ultimate explanation for the seemingly simple truth that God is love. Since God contains more than one person, love has existed among the three persons of the Trinity for all eternity. So God did not need to create us in order to express love. Nevertheless, he created us out of love, and his choice to create us is an overflow of who he is in his eternal nature. What this means is that God is not a static thing, but rather a "dynamic, pulsating activity, a life, almost a kind of drama. Almost, if you will not think me irreverent, a kind of dance."[9] Lewis goes on to point out, like Wesley, that God is the only possible source of true happiness for us.

> If you want to get warm, you must stand near the fire: if you want to be wet you must get into the water. If you want joy, power, peace, eternal life, you must get close to, or even into, the thing that has them. They are not a sort of prize which God could, if He chose, just hand out to anyone. They are a great fountain of energy and beauty spurting up at the very centre of reality. If you are close to it, the spray will wet you: if you are not, you will remain dry.[10]

Notice the images and pictures of God in these passages. God is a fountain of happiness, a pulsating activity, a drama, a dance, a fountain of energy and beauty at the heart of reality. No wonder Wesley, Lewis and countless other Christian thinkers and writers have made the point that our only true satisfaction will be found in God. It is because we are made in his image that nothing else will do the trick. He is perfect love, and joy, and truth, and beauty, and goodness. That is what we were made for, and that is what will bring us the true happiness and satisfaction we naturally and persistently crave. As Lewis remarked, there is nothing arbitrary about the fact that there is no other possible way to

---

[8]John Wesley, *The Works of John Wesley*, 3rd ed. (1872; reprint Grand Rapids: Baker, 1979), 6:434 (my italics).

[9]C. S. Lewis, *Mere Christianity* (San Francisco: HarperSanFrancisco, 2001), p. 175.

[10]Ibid., p. 176.

achieve happiness. God is the ultimate source of it, and if we seek it elsewhere we will inevitably come up short and be disappointed.

And yet, it is understandable, in a way, that we are inclined to seek it elsewhere. Everything God created is good and—if rightly used—can bring us joy. Moreover, everything he created is in some sense a reflection of him. But notice, they are only a reflection of God; they are not God. Our mistake is to seize onto these things as if they are the final reality, rather than to realize that they are only finite gifts of one who is himself the ultimate gift of infinite worth.

Now we are in a position to answer the question of where hell came from and in what sense God is responsible for it. The question as raised by skeptics is often put like this: if God is a God of love, how could he send anyone to hell? Well, I want to suggest that it is precisely because God is a God of love that people may wind up in hell.

Let us come back to the doctrine of the Trinity, the distinctive Christian claim that the one God exists in three persons: Father, Son and Holy Spirit. The three persons of the Trinity have existed from all eternity in a mutual relationship of love, joy and delight. Now this God created us in his image precisely for the purpose of a relationship with himself. As Wesley and Lewis saw it, God wants us to enter the fountain of energy and beauty at the center of reality; he wants us to get wet! Or to use another image, he wants us to join the dance of joy that energizes the three persons of the Trinity. He wants us to take our place in the drama of life, vitality and pulsating energy that represents our truest and deepest satisfaction.

But here is how our creation in the image of a God of love has enormous implications for the question of hell. Love, by its very nature, is not the sort of thing that can be compelled, programmed or manipulated. Rather, it must be given freely as well as received. For us to enter into and maintain the sort of relationship that God desires, we must freely love, trust and obey him. Consider, in this light, the following words of Jesus: "If anyone loves me, he will obey my teaching. My Father will love him, and we will come to him and make our home with him. He who does not love me will not obey my teaching" (Jn 14:23-24). Now this is an exhilarating but staggering thought. God wants to enter our lives in such a way that we will be "at home" with him. By loving obedience to the teaching of Jesus, we can open our lives to the very source of life, the fountain of happiness, the eternal dance of love and joy. But the heartrending reality is that we may not choose to obey and thereby close ourselves off from this life-giving relationship.

This is the key to understanding how hell is created. God created all the raw material for it in a sense when he chose to create free beings in his image. As noted before, God created everything that exists apart from himself. So hell must be composed in some sense of things God created. When God created beings with free will, he created *the possibility of hell*. That is to say, implicit in the relational freedom God gave us is the possibility that we will choose not to love, trust and obey him. Rather than accepting the invitation to plunge into the fountain and relish its refreshing pleasure, it is possible that some might choose to hold back and remain dry. Rather than embrace the opportunity to dance, some might choose to reject the offer and attempt to construct their own substitute for joy. If these choices are made and persisted in, then the possibility of hell becomes reality.

So in short, hell is created when free beings use (more accurately, abuse) the freedom God has given them not to embrace him but to reject him. In so doing, they reject the only possible source of deep and lasting happiness, and thereby consign themselves to frustration, misery and suffering.

Let us pursue this point by reflecting further on the image of God as a dance. And let us think about this in terms of the fact that God requires us to love and obey him in order to have a relationship with him. As Wesley put the point, holiness and happiness are inseparably joined. "When he has taken full possession of our heart; when he reigns there without a rival, the Lord of every motion there; when we dwell in Christ, and Christ in us we are one with Christ, and Christ with us; then we are completely happy."[11]

A few years ago I took some basic ballroom dancing lessons when one of my students, who had been a dance instructor, offered lessons at my school. I had never danced before but had watched on the sidelines with some degree of envy as others enjoyed themselves. So I decided to give it a shot to see if I might enjoy it too. Well, to be honest, it did not come naturally to me, but with the help of the instructor and some very patient and gracious dance partners, I finally started to learn the rhythm

---

[11]Wesley, *Works*, 6:430.

and steps. I am still not very good at it, but I have made reasonable progress, and now I can do a decent fox trot, swing and, my favorite, rhumba. (I still have trouble with the waltz, a dance that is particularly beautiful and graceful for those who have more skill than I.)

You really begin to enjoy dancing only when you have learned the steps well enough that you can get into the flow of the music and begin to feel at home in doing so. You have to submit to the pattern and structure of the dance in order to enjoy the freedom of dancing with some degree of naturalness and pleasure. So then learning the dance steps to the point that we internalize them is like becoming holy. Learning to love and trust and obey God is what we need to do to be at home with God in the divine dance of the Trinity. It is precisely in submission to his will that we discover our true freedom and experience the delight and pleasure and satisfaction for which we were created.

Grasping this also helps us get a better picture of hell. In light of our discussion we could say that hell is the long-term result of refusing to learn the dance steps. It is the experience of choosing to remain on the sidelines rather than submitting to the order necessary to participate in the joy. It is the outcome of convincing yourself that you really don't want to dance and that you are better off without it. So who is mainly responsible for creating hell? Those who will not dance.

It is most important to underscore that hell is inhabited by those who simply refuse the invitation to participate in the dance. Hell has sometimes been pictured as a sort of masochistic torture chamber whose denizens are held against their will, who would do anything to escape hell, but alas they cannot. In contrast to this notion, C. S. Lewis has remarked that "the damned are, in one sense, successful, rebels to the end; that the doors of hell are locked on the *inside*."[12]

Given the biblical account of God's overwhelming love for his estranged children, I think Lewis's picture is far more accurate than the fiery torture chamber image of hell that has often been depicted. This is not to deny that hell is miserable, but the point is that the misery is self-inflicted. Indeed, the Bible makes clear that God has gone to extreme lengths to extend his love to us and persuade us to accept it. The death of Christ on the cross is God's ultimate statement that he wants us to come home to him and learn to dance.

---

[12]C. S. Lewis, *The Problem of Pain* (New York: Macmillan, 1962), p. 127.

We noted earlier Nietzsche's confession that he wanted to dance, and his admission that he would like a God who danced. Well, that God wants to dance with Nietzsche, and he will do everything he can to get Nietzsche—and Dawkins—in the dance. God has made it clear that he will go to any length to save us—short of overriding our freedom, which would be a violation of the very love he offers to us. He wants us freely to accept his love and freely to love him in return. It is the persistent choice to resist this offer of love that builds up the walls of hell, locks its doors shut and encloses its inhabitants in their self-created suffering.

THE CURIOSITY OF CUB FANS: WHY CHOOSE HELL?

Here we face a most perplexing question, or rather, a set of questions. Why would anyone make this sort of choice? Why would anyone persist in choosing isolation and estrangement from God at the cost of his or her own happiness? Why would anyone choose hell over heaven?

It is perhaps understandable why people choose evil in the short run. They may do so out of weakness or out of a misguided notion that so choosing will liberate them from narrow constraints, bringing them ful-fillment and happiness. But if evil breaks its promises and inevitably ends up causing disappointment and misery to those who choose it, how can we make sense of anyone persisting in such choices to the point of damnation?

When I wrote my doctoral dissertation defending the doctrine of hell, these were the questions I struggled with the most, and they are still the ones I find most difficult in trying to make sense of the doctrine of eternal hell. The thinker whose work has perhaps challenged me the most in this regard is the philosopher Tom Talbott, who has argued that there simply is no intelligible motive for choosing hell. If the choice of evil does indeed lead to greater and greater misery for those who so choose, it is simply incoherent, he claims, to think any person could persist in such a choice.[13]

C. S. Lewis took up this challenge more than a half-century ago in

---

[13]For those who would like to follow up these issues in more detail, see my critique of Talbott in my book *Hell: The Logic of Damnation*, pp. 113-38. More recently, see Talbott's essay and my response in *Universalism: The Current Debate*, ed. Robin A. Parry and Christopher H. Partridge (Grand Rapids: Eerdmans, 2003), and my essay "A Hell of a Choice: Reply to Talbott," *Religious Studies* 40 (2004): 203-16. The same volume has a reply by Talbott and my rejoinder.

The Great Divorce. He develops this provocative premise: a group of people from hell take a bus ride to heaven and are given the option of staying there if they wish. Indeed, they are encouraged in every conceivable way to stay. The inhabitants of heaven implore them to remain with powerfully persuasive and winsome speeches and other forms of enticement. Now the immediate reaction one may have who has not read the book is to think that of course they would stay. How could anyone prefer returning to hell rather than staying in heaven? But this is the stunning thing about the book: most of the characters opt for returning to hell. And what is chilling about the book is that Lewis manages to narrate their choices in a way that is psychologically and morally plausible.

At one point, the narrator of the story asks the question of just what motivates the choice to return to hell.

> "Milton was right," said my teacher. "The choice of every lost soul can be expressed in the words 'Better to reign in Hell than serve in Heaven.' There is always something they insist on keeping even at the price of misery. There is always something they prefer to joy—that is to reality. You see it easily enough in a spoiled child that would sooner miss its play and its supper than say it was sorry and be friends."[14]

Unfortunately, it is not just spoiled children who make these sorts of misguided choices. Throughout the book Lewis depicts numerous adult versions of the same fundamental choice. For instance, early in the book he describes a character who arrives in heaven and is surprised to find that one of the people there is a man who had worked for him in this life and who he looked down upon as an inferior. To make matters worse, the man had been a murderer. Now the man has been forgiven and is urging his former boss to repent of his own sins so he, too, can be in heaven. The boss finds this insulting and intolerable. He had come to heaven to get his rights, not to be urged to repent by a bloody murderer.

> "So that's the trick, is it?" shouted the Ghost, outwardly bitter, and yet I thought there was a kind of triumph in its voice. It had been entreated: it could make a refusal: and this seemed to it a kind of advantage. "I thought there'd be some damned nonsense. . . . Tell them I'm not coming, see? I'd rather be damned than go along with you. . . ." It was almost happy now that it could, in a sense, threaten.[15]

---

[14]C. S. Lewis, *The Great Divorce* (San Francisco: HarperSanFrancisco, 2001), p. 71.
[15]Ibid., pp. 30-31.

Here we see a sort of twisted logic in the ultimately irrational choice of evil that leads to hell. There is a kind of perverse pleasure in holding to resentment and bitterness. There is no real happiness here, but there is a shadowy substitute that may almost pass for happiness for those in the grip of evil. There is no real righteousness, but there is the deceptive sense of satisfaction that comes from self-righteousness. So hell is a sort of mirror image of heaven. It is not the real thing, but it offers its own distorted imitations of true joy, pleasure, righteousness and satisfaction.

At the end of the day, as perplexing as it is to make sense of hell rationally and intellectually, perhaps it gains credibility when we look into our own hearts and realize how often we have been tempted by the shadowy substitutes for real joy, or have even found ourselves under their spell. True torment—in this life and the next—results less from sulfurous flames and more from the self-will and misguided desires that lead us to refuse the eternal dance. Perhaps Nietzsche unwittingly summed up the essence of hell when he penned these wrenching words: "And all of the visions and consolations of my youth died!"[16]

FOR FURTHER READING

Crockett, William, ed. *Four Views of Hell*. Grand Rapids: Zondervan, 1992.

Kvanvig, Jonathan. *The Problem of Hell*. New York: Oxford University Press, 1993.

Lewis, C. S. *The Great Divorce*. San Francisco: HarperSanFrancisco, 2001.

Seymour, Charles. *A Theodicy of Hell*. Dordrecht: Kluwer, 2000.

Walls, Jerry L. *Hell: The Logic of Damnation*. Notre Dame: University of Notre Press, 1992.

---

[16]Thanks to David Baggett, Claire Brown, Philip Tallon and Elizabeth Turner for helpful comments on an earlier draft of this essay.

Part **4**

WHY IT MATTERS

11

Recognizing Divine Revelation

CHARLES TALIAFERRO

There is a famous photograph of the aftermath of a napalm-bomb attack during the Vietnam War. Nine-year-old Kim Phuc is running, naked, her clothes having been burned. Soon after the photograph was taken, she lost consciousness. She spent fourteen months in a hospital and had seventeen operations.

> Although I suffered from pain, itching and headaches all the time, the long hospital stay made me dream of becoming a doctor. But my studies were cut short by the local government. They wanted me as a symbol of the state. I could not go to school anymore. The anger inside me was like a hatred as high as a mountain. I hated my life. I hated all people who were normal because I was not normal. I really wanted to die many times. I spent my daytime in the library to read a lot of religious books to find a purpose for my life. One of the books that I read was the Holy Bible. In Christmas 1982, I accepted Jesus Christ as my personal savior.[1]

Kim Phuc professes to have found Jesus Christ through the Bible.

It is one thing to describe and reflect on God in the Bible. Virtually anyone, regardless of whether one thinks there actually is or is not a God, can explore God or the person Jesus Christ found in the text. "Christ the Redeemer" or "God" may be treated as a character one finds in a narrative that may or may not be true. It is another matter, however,

---

[1]Kim Phuc, "The Long Road to Forgiveness," *All Things Considered,* June 30, 2008 <www
.npr.org/templates/story/story.php?storyId=91964687>.

to encounter God *through* the Bible. On this reading, searching Scripture may actually constitute a search for God.

Is it possible that the Bible is a means through which we can encounter God? Or, to rephrase slightly, could it be that God provides, through the Bible, a means by which there can be a genuine discovery of God? In this chapter, I offer an overview of the very idea of divine revelation and then take up the question of why anyone might believe that a divine revelation has occurred or is occurring and available today.

My principal goal is to address what I shall call *the framework of inquiry*. Given certain frameworks, the case for divine revelation does not stand a chance. I shall be challenging these frameworks, however, and recommending a more open-ended method for assessing the possibility of divine revelation. I believe that a balanced, open methodology can recognize the profundity and authenticity of experiences like Kim Phuc's.

REVELATION AS DISCLOSURE

What is revelation? Traditionally, Christians have distinguished between *general* and *specific* revelation. The first concerns the ways in which the world itself may manifest or disclose the reality and nature of God. Like many of the contributors to this book, I have argued that philosophical reflection on the world has given us reasons for a belief in God. Special revelation, however, concerns a more focused, historical disclosure of God.[2]

For traditional Christians, the Bible itself is a divine revelation, though some Christians prefer seeing the Bible as either *containing* divine revelation (use of the Bible's content enables God to be disclosed to persons) or as *a record of God's revelation* (the Bible records the life of Christ which discloses God incarnate). On either of these interpretations, divine revelation involves what is believed to be God's special, specific activity in disclosing the divine nature and will. Such disclosures are believed to have occurred through miraculous events (the resurrection); auditions, or spoken or written statements in the form of commands; divinely inspired history; and through parables, poetry, songs, proverbs, dialogues, as well as visions. While some biblical narratives suggest that

---

[2]Charles Taliaferro, *Contemporary Philosophy of Religion* (Malden, Mass.: Blackwell, 1998), pp. 427-42; and Charles Taliaferro, *Evidence and Faith: Philosophy and Religion Since the Seventeenth Century* (New York: Cambridge University Press, 2005).

revelation took place by way of a strict recording of divine speech, other parts of the Bible suggest that God worked to achieve a revelation through inspiring a person's own insights and creative imagination (Isaiah and Jeremiah).

To fill out an account of just how an inspired divine disclosure may develop, consider this overview by Evelyn Underhill of the experiences of Madame Guyon (1647-1717), St. Teresa of Ávila (1515-1582) and William Blake (1757-1827):

> Madame Guyon states in her autobiography, that when she was composing her works she would experience a sudden and irresistible inclination to take up her pen; though feeling wholly incapable of literary composition, and not even knowing the subject on which she would be impelled to write. If she resisted this impulse it was at the cost of the most intense discomfort. She would then begin to write with extraordinary swiftness; words, elaborate arguments, and appropriate quotations coming to her without reflection, and so quickly that one of her longest books was written in one and a half days. "In writing I saw that I was writing of things which I had never seen: and during the time of this manifestation, I was given light to perceive that I had in me treasures of knowledge and understanding which I did not know that I possessed."
>
> Similar statements are made of St. Teresa, who declared that in writing her books she was powerless to set down anything but that which her Master put into her mind. So Blake said of "Milton" and "Jerusalem," "I have written the poems from immediate dictation, twelve or sometimes twenty or thirty lines at a time, without premeditation and even against my will. The time it has taken in writing was thus rendered non-existent, and an immense poem exists which seems to be the labour of a long life, all produced without labour or study."[3]

Christians who believe that the Bible as a whole is the inspired medium or mediation of God's acts and nature tend to see the meaning of parts of the Bible in relation to the Bible as a whole, and to subsequent Christian reflection. Consider, for example, a text in Isaiah where it appears that there is a prophecy (or prediction) of Jesus: "The virgin will be with child and will give birth to a son, and will call him Immanuel" (Is 7:14). Was Jesus likely to have been in the mind of the author(s) of this text? It is highly doubtful, as it is also doubtful that they could

---

[3]Evelyn E. Underhill, *Mysticism: The Nature and Development of Spiritual Consciousness* (Oxford: Oneworld, 2001), p. 66.

possibly have had a concept of the Trinity. Nonetheless the meaning and significance of this passage need not be seen as confined to the original intention of the author. Rather, Christians may look back at this after Christ's birth, life, death and (believed) resurrection and come to see that Jesus was foreshadowed in earlier texts that hint at a future act of God in saving his people.

Given the Christian conviction that God is omnipresent and active in disclosing his nature and will over time, it is natural that Christians sometimes describe revelation itself in dynamic terms. There is a scriptural reference to the word of God being alive (Heb 4:12: "For the word of God is living and active"). Arguably, a text or an event constitutes a revelation only if there is a bona fide disclosure. If the living God is not disclosed to a person studying the Bible, there is a sense in which the text is not (as it were) living or functioning as revealing or disclosing God's life. From a Christian's point of view, this may be a case in which God's living word and disclosure are obscured; in its place we merely have an ancient text or a book that was at one time the most influential reference book in the Western and Near Eastern worlds. My aim here is to propose that *if* the Bible does authentically disclose God's nature and will, this may be seen as a *living* disclosure insofar as it reveals in the present the life of God in relation to human history. Thus, if one reads and assents to a scriptural testimony about God (for example, 1 Jn 4:8: "God is love"), one thereby encounters a disclosure of God as God *is*, and not just as God was once thought of or experienced once upon a time.

WHY WOULD ANYONE BELIEVE IN DIVINE REVELATION?

If there is some reason to believe there is a good God, there is some reason to believe this God would provide some means for awareness of and a relationship with God. In traditional Christianity God is seen as a powerful, loving being who calls us to a life of justice and mercy, and who especially calls persons to confession, repentance and, ultimately, a complete transformation through the redemptive life of Christ. On this view, the Bible can play a vital role in the shaping and sustaining of an individual's and a community's identity.

Some Christians—especially Reformed or Protestant traditions—see the Bible as the uncompromising exclusive means of a life of faith in God (this teaching is sometimes represented in the phrase *sola scriptura* or "Scripture only"), whereas others see the Bible as a primary source of divine revelation and definitive of faith while also appealing to tradition and reason as amplifying and serving as a source of divine revelation (Anglicans have promoted a threefold foundation for faith: Scripture, reason and tradition). But if we grant that there may be some good involved in fostering a loving relationship with God through divine revelation, we are still some distance away from having grounds that such a revelation is real.

Traditionally Christians have sought to build a case for the authenticity of the Bible as a divine disclosure on the grounds of miracles, religious experience, its internal coherence and beauty, and its coherence with what may be known of God independently through, for example, philosophical arguments. As for miracles, Christian apologists have highlighted fulfilled prophecy and eyewitness testimony about the resurrected Christ. Religious experience comes in many forms, one of which is the perceived or experiential awareness that persons seem to have of God through Scripture. As for coherence and beauty, an analogy may be useful. Imagine you come across what appears to be a manual for a machine that is highly complex and coherent, and provides a detailed, elegant account of discoveries made by using the machine that also seems coherent. Imagine, however, that there is no sign of the machine itself (the thought experiment may be likened to discovering a manual and account of a telescope or microscope before you have heard of or seen either). Of course, internal coherence, detail and beauty may define many novels that are fiction, but I suggest that a manual with sufficient coherence may be, along with a body of observations that appear to have been made possible by the machine, some evidence that there was some kind of machine at one time. Similarly, it may be argued that the beauty and coherence of the Bible can be seen as some reason to think that something like its narrative is true. This reasoning would need careful articulation (we would need to suppose that the Bible does not conflict with what is known to be false, and so on), but it could be one reason among others to entertain the Bible as divine revelation. The Bible has also been defended by philosophers who argue that it is compatible with, and confirms much of, what is known about God through independent argument.

FOUR REASONS FOR DENYING DIVINE REVELATION

In a single chapter, it is impossible to offer a full positive case for divine revelation. I shall concentrate instead on presenting and then replying to four influential objections to the idea of divine revelation, thus paving the way toward taking divine revelation seriously. Consider the following objections: the problem of fairness, the objection that the God of the Bible is vicious, the inadequacy of religious experience and an objection to miracles.

The problem of fairness. Isn't special, divine revelation unfair? Monotheistic religions seem to support the idea that God is just, but wouldn't it be unjust for God to privilege some people with a divine disclosure and not others? Related to this is a worry that making a claim to possessing a divine revelation could be a reflection of vanity or misplaced pride. Why think God should privilege *your* people or religion rather than others?

Vanity and jealousy of God. A problem with seeing the Bible as a divine revelation may lie not just in the vanity of believers in the revelation but in the apparent vices of its chief character. Richard Dawkins advances the following colorful portrait of the God of the Bible:

> The God of the Old Testament is arguably the most unpleasant character in all fiction; jealous and proud of it; a petty, unjust, unforgiving control-freak; a vindictive, bloodthirsty ethnic cleanser; a misogynistic, homophobic racist, infanticidal, genocidal, filicidal, pestilential, megalomaniacal, sadomasochistic, capriciously malevolent bully. . . . The oldest of the three Abrahamic religions, and the clear ancestor of the other two, is Judaism: originally a tribal cult of a single fiercely unpleasant God, morbidly obsessed with sexual restrictions, with the smell of charred flesh, with his own superiority over rival gods and with the exclusiveness of his chosen desert tribe.[4]

This charge, of course, seeks to undermine any temptation to see the Bible or its God as beautiful!

The inadequacy of religious experience. I offer only one version of this objection here, coming from Daniel Dennett, a foremost contributor to philosophy of mind. He charges that religious experience cannot possibly count as evidence for religious beliefs. Dennett is deeply suspicious

---

[4]Richard Dawkins, *The God Delusion* (Boston: Houghton Mifflin, 2006), p. 31.

of relying on the testimony of others and introspection about what people seem to experience when they feel as though they are in the presence of God or the sacred. He claims that the only reliable data that we can muster about religious experience concern the external behavior that is involved in religious avowals. So, we may study what people say and how they act when they profess to encounter the sacred, but we can make no headway with respect to their inner states. We are all, as he puts it, "outsiders" and may even lack comprehension about the nature of one's own experiences and beliefs concerning religion.

> When it comes to interpreting religious avowals of others, *everybody is an outsider.* Why? Because religious avowals concern matters that are beyond observation, beyond meaningful test, so the only thing *anybody* can go on is religious behavior, and, more specifically, the behavior of *professing.* A child growing up in a culture is like an anthropologist, after all, surrounded by informants whose professings stand in need of interpretation. The fact that your informants are your father and mother, and speak in your mother tongue, does not give you anything more than a slight circumstantial advantage over the adult anthropologist who has to rely on a string of bilingual interpreters to query the informants. (And think about your own case: weren't you ever baffled or confused about just what you were supposed to believe? You know perfectly well that *you* don't have privileged access to the tenets of the faith that you were raised in. I am just asking you to generalize the point, to recognize that others are in no better position.)[5]

If Dennett is correct, an appeal to the experiential testimony about divine disclosure cannot get off the ground.

The no miracles objection. The most famous case against the plausibility of miracles goes back to David Hume (1711-1776), who argued that it will always be more reasonable to conclude that reports of miracles stem from fear, a love of wonder, an overactive imagination and so on than to believe a miracle actually occurred. For Hume, a miracle is a violation of the laws of nature; all the evidence of our senses that there are certain laws (e.g., laws that entail that upon physical death there is no resurrection) counts as evidence that there was no violation of the law (e.g., reports of a resurrection are not true).

---

[5]Daniel C. Dennett, *Breaking the Spell: Religion as a Natural Phenomenon* (New York: Viking, 2006), p. 240.

It has been further argued by Bede Rundle, Matthew Bagger, Jan Narveson and others that explanations involving God are simply unacceptable. Theistic explanations do not, for example, have the adequacy and precision of scientific explanations. Jan Narveson offers the following critique of theism.

> It ought to be regarded as a major embarrassment to natural theology that the very idea of something like a universe's being "created" by some minded being is sufficiently mind-boggling that any attempt to provide a detailed account of how it might be done is bound to look silly, or mythical, or a vaguely anthropomorphized version of some familiar physical process. . . . It is plainly no surprise that details about just *how* all this was supposed to have happened are totally lacking when they are not, as I say, silly or simply poetic. For the fundamental idea is that some infinitely powerful mind simply willed it to be thus, and, as they say, Lo! it was so! If we aren't ready to accept that as an explanatory description— as we should not be, since it plainly doesn't *explain* anything, as distinct from merely asserting that it was in fact done—then where do we go from there? On all accounts, we at this point meet up with mystery. "How are we supposed to know the ways of the infinite and almighty God?" . . . Why does water boil when heated? The scientific story supplies an analysis of matter in its liquid state, the effects of atmospheric pressure and heat, and so on until we see, in impressive detail, just how the thing works. An explanation's right to be called "scientific" is, indeed, in considerable part earned precisely by its ability to provide such detail.[6]

If Narveson is correct, then theistic accounts of miracles or any events in history or even creation itself are philosophically and scientifically pointless.

THE FRAMEWORK OF INQUIRY

Before replying to the four objections to divine revelation, let us consider a general point regarding philosophical inquiry. Sometimes the method we employ to describe or explain a given phenomena will unfairly lead to a substantial conclusion. I offer two examples.

Can you observe yourself? This may seem an odd question, but several philosophers have maintained that self-observation is either impossible or clearly not the case. They believe that the self is not an individual

---

[6]Jan Narveson, "God by Design?" in *God and Design: The Teleological Argument and Modern Science,* ed. N. A. Manson (London: Routledge, 2003), pp. 93-94.

thing or subject that one can observe. David Hume offered the following case for the conclusion that a person either does not or cannot observe himself.

> When I enter most intimately into what I call myself, I always stumble on some particular perception or other, of heat or cold, light or shade, love or hatred, pain or pleasure. I never catch myself at any time without perception, and never can observe any thing but the perception.[7]

Hume's thesis has some plausibility. It would be odd to think one can observe oneself the way one observes a color or hears a noise or detects pain. Before accepting his conclusion, however, it is important to question Hume's framework. Hume assumes that if you can observe yourself, you will be like an object of experience in your visual field or in some sense in front of you. But this is not the only framework. Consider an alternative thesis: you experience yourself in virtually all your experiences and can make due observation of yourself. When you feel pain, don't you feel *yourself* in pain? When you feel heat, aren't you *yourself* feeling hot? When you see color, it is you who are experiencing (for example) the blue and green. When you love something, don't you experience yourself as loving (or have self-awareness of yourself as a lover)? Hume's case against self-observation has traction as long as we do not allow for the possibility of a broader framework in which to recognize the self.

My point here is not that Hume is *obviously* wrong or that merely shifting frameworks decisively refutes his stance. My point, rather, is that if you broaden your method to consider both Hume's method as well as take seriously philosophers who believe we observe the self as a substantial subject that has sensations and so on, then we are better able to reach a fair conclusion.

A second case where it seems that frameworks can interrupt open inquiry concerns free will. Some philosophers deny that we have the freedom to act in ways that are not fully determined because they only recognize two possibilities when it comes to human behavior: either the behavior is determined or it is random. Given those alternatives, the idea that a person could act responsibly in a way that is not determined looks

---

[7]David Hume, *A Treatise of Human Nature* (London: Harvard University Press, 1888), p. 251.

quite hopeless. After all, can a person be responsible if her "free" acts are actually random (or without cause)? The case for freedom opens up only when you consider the possibility that our apparent experience of freedom involves a third possibility: persons have the power to consider more than one act and to make a choice between them when they could do otherwise. There is not space to fill in all the details, but the main point to note is that open-ended, fair-minded inquiry should, at least in principle, be open to a third form of explanation.

These observations about the importance of frameworks are intended to pave the way for considering the four objections to divine revelation.

FOUR REPLIES AND SOME POSITIVE REASONS FOR RECOGNIZING DIVINE REVELATION

The problem of fairness. The objection from fairness assumes that a just, all-good God would not distribute goods that gave only some persons unearned or undeserved advantages. Taken to an extreme, this sort of objection might rule out God creating creatures with unequal powers that conferred unmerited advantages of any kind. Would a fair creation have to be homogenous or only modestly differentiated? I do not think so, given the good of fecundity or plentitude (*bonum variationis*). Insisting on some strictly equal distribution of goods makes sense if the framework is an elected official distributing a surplus, but the framework of creation does not seem to require equality or homogeneity. But apart from questioning whether a good creator can allow for different degrees of power and value in the created order, it should be noted that Judaism and Christianity hold that the special divine revelation as embodied or conveyed through the Bible is intended for *all* people. The goal is equal access to divine revelation for all.

The idea that God would have a "chosen people" has traditionally been understood as a means of blessing all people. In Genesis 28:14 (NASB) the divine revelation of God to Jacob is couched in terms of a universal blessing: "Your descendants will . . . spread out to the west and to the east and to the north and to the south; and in you and in your descendents shall all the families of the earth be blessed." Followers of Christ are enjoined or commissioned to welcome all into a fellowship made possible by the divine disclosure in Christ. In the course of conveying this divine revelation more people come to have their own encounter with the *living* Word of God.

It should also be appreciated that divine revelation can be humbling and burdensome. Part of the content of the biblical revelation is a story of human evil, violence, murder, rape and so on. The Bible as a whole does not offer a flattering portrait of human life at its best. Hence, the charge that biblical devotion may be a reflection of human vanity is not compelling.

The idea that divine revelation is to be extended humbly and lovingly by persons reflects the biblical understanding of God as personal or as a person. J. R. Lucas draws out the implications of thinking about God in personal terms:

> If God is a person, it follows that our relations with God are personal relations. . . . God is not a Thing. Nor is he an Idea. If we were Platonists, we might believe that there was some technique whereby we could emancipate ourselves from the shackles of our earthly existence and put ourselves on a level with the Forms. But God, being a living spirit, has a different sort of existence from the dead timelessness of the Forms. Knowledge of him is not like knowledge of mathematical truths, which any man can set himself to come to know, but like knowledge of persons, and is essentially an interchange between two parties, requiring not only our wish to know, but his willingness to be known.[8]

Because biblical revelation is essentially the revelation of a divine person, there is some fittingness to the notion that divine revelation itself is to be personally communicated (Mt 28:19, 20). The Bible does, indeed, locate divine revelation as specific and focused in its inception and reception, and revelation is received at one place and time in human history in order to be communicated personally throughout the world. Because of this call to make divine revelation universally accessible, the objection from unfairness seems to be met.

The vanity and jealousy of God. Dawkins's portrait of God requires a lengthy reply, but here I shall have to focus on his charge that the God of the Bible is vain and jealous. If we think only of earthly rulers or human beings, the desire to be worshiped is the height of vanity. And for an earthly ruler to be jealous of any other ruler and to desire for our complete fealty seems also to be a matter of megalomania. But if we take seriously the biblical and subsequent theological identifica-

---

[8]J. R. Lucas, *Freedom and Grace* (London: SPCK, 1976), p. 26.

tion of God with goodness, matters change.

If God is essentially good (God can do no evil) and the goods of the cosmos reflect God's goodness (for example, there would not be the good of friendship between persons unless God created and sustains them in being), then to worship God is to take delight in and respond in reverence and awe to goodness itself. Worship is not, then, paying compliments to a massive ego but reverencing the goodness that makes created goods possible.

God *is* depicted as jealous in the Bible, but is jealousy always a vice? Imagine, again, that God is good, and a relationship with God is itself good. What would be amiss if, say, a creature's desire for self-destruction aroused God to call this person back to a good life of harmony with God and if this calling was out of *jealousy*? Assuming God to be the good creator of all, this would not be akin to a human being making inappropriate claims to a relationship with another human being.

But even if we used human jealousy as an analogy or image of God's character, would this be a matter of vice? Image a healthy, good relationship between parents and a child until the child goes to school and becomes infatuated with an alcoholic, drug-pushing, pornography-watching, narcissistic philosophy professor whom the child calls "Daddy." Wouldn't the parents properly feel jealous (as well as perhaps angry) in response to this scenario? The biblical portrait of a jealous God can be part of the biblical injunction to live fully and forsake violence: "Choose life in order that you may live" (Deut 30:19 NASB).

Dawkins's failure to recognize the centrality of goodness in the Christian concept of God is explicit in his book *The God Delusion*. Dawkins defines what he calls "the God Hypothesis":

> There exists a superhuman, supernatural intelligence who deliberately designed and created the universe and everything in it, including us. . . . Goodness is not part of the definition of the God Hypothesis, merely a desirable add on.[9]

But in Christian tradition, *goodness* is the key reference point, the essential mark of divinity and no mere "add on" or afterthought. This is also central to Judaism. The Bible offers a progressive or evolving portrait of God, beginning with a divine revelation to a nomadic "desert

---

[9]Dawkins, *God Delusion,* pp. 31, 106.

tribe" and then reaching out to the breathtaking dimensions of the great Hebrew prophets with their universal teachings of peace and justice (Isaiah, Jeremiah). The key to answering Dawkins lies, in part, in taking seriously the theistic framework in which goodness is the central nature of God.

Dennett's religious experience. Is the case for treating the Bible as a divine disclosure stymied because we simply are complete outsiders to the experience of others and because religious experience is (by its very nature) "beyond observation"? In this reply I shall use what philosophers call an ad hominem argument. I have chosen to focus on Dennett both because of the popularity of his work and because he represents an important case of a situation where the framework he uses to reject religious experiences is so severe that he himself is not able to maintain it consistently.

First, I simply note that Dennett denies what many of those who have religious experiences assert, namely that they have an observational or experimental awareness of the divine. I have defended the evidential force of such experiences elsewhere, as have William Alston, Keith Yandell, Caroline Davis and others.[10] But here I note that Dennett's skepticism about accessing other people's states of mind is in conflict with what he reports as accessing the thoughts and experiences of his child.

In the same book in which he professes only to study "the behavior of professing" and to forgo trying to decipher "the inner mind," Dennett offers the following account for how he managed to grasp and alter "the inner mind" of his daughter.

> One's parents—or whoever are hard to distinguish from one's parents— have something approaching a dedicated hotline to acceptance, not as potent as hypnotic suggestion, but sometimes close to it. Many years ago, my five-year-old daughter, attempting to imitate the gymnast Nadia Comaneci's performance on the horizontal bar, tipped over the piano stool and painfully crushed two of her fingertips. How was I going to calm down this terrified child so I could safely drive her to the emergency room? Inspiration struck: I held my own hand near her throbbing little hand and sternly ordered: "Look, Andrea! I'm going to teach you a secret! You can push the pain into *my* hand with your hand. Go ahead, *push!*

---

[10]See also my *Contemporary Philosophy of Religion* (Malden: Blackwell, 1998); and *Evidence and Faith: Philosophy and Religion Since the Seventeenth Century* (New York: Cambridge University Press, 2005).

Push!" She tried—and it worked! She'd "pushed the pain" into Daddy's hand. Her relief (and fascination) were instantaneous. The effect lasted only for minutes, but with a few further administrations of impromptu hypnotic analgesia along the way, I got her to the emergency room, where they could give her the further treatment she needed. (Try it with your own child, if the occasion arises. You may be similarly lucky.) I was exploiting her instincts—though the rationale didn't occur to me until years later, when I was reflecting on it. (This raises an interesting empirical question: would my attempt at instant hypnosis have worked as effectively on some other five-year-old, who hadn't imprinted on me as an authority figure? And if imprinting is implicated, how young must a child be to imprint so effectively on a parent? Our daughter was three months old when we adopted her.)[11]

Dennett is seeking to bolster the claim that religious beliefs can achieve authority though parental and other authorities using quasi-hypnotic techniques. In this story, Dennett does not treat his daughter (nor does she treat him) as an outsider; Dennett seems perfectly willing to reference subjective mental experiences that go well beyond his daughter's verbal profession of pain and her physical behavior. I would go so far as to claim that the above case seems like a straightforward incident of when the daughter felt the love of her solicitous, caring father.

Dennett's framework for critiquing religious testimony would not only sweep away the testimony of Kim Phuc, it would make nonsense of his shared emotional loving bond with his daughter. If Dennett can access the inner mind of his daughter, anthropologists can assess and evaluate the inner minds of religious believers. More modestly, I propose this anecdote reveals that in many cases we can assess a person's inner states (the daughter's apparent observation of her father's love, for examples), and so we should at least be open to the profession of the religious believer to experience the presence of a sacred, divine reality.[12]

No miracles? If one assumes at the outset that theism is false, no reported miracles need to be taken seriously. But it is becoming harder to dismiss theism out of hand. Daniel Dennett does in a handful of pages of *Breaking the Spell*, but he is evidently unaware of the revival of theism in

---

[11]Dennett, *Breaking the Spell*, p. 130.
[12]I return to this point below when considering the importance of taking into account the value of evidence.

philosophy since the 1970s.[13] If one allows for the possibility of theism, however, Hume's and Narveson's verdicts are not at all self-evident.

Narveson's own outlook raises a question similar to the one raised about Dennett. In his framework he may rule out not only divine agency but also human agency. He suggests that we should not accept explanations in which an agent willed that something take place and "Lo!, it was so." He appears to want some kind of complex mediation as in an account of water boiling in terms of atomic particles and heat. Two points are worth making in reply: If human activity is genuinely to be accounted for in terms of reasons and desires (I turned on a light switch so that I could see you), then my reasons cannot be reduced to or undermined by an impersonal scientific account as to why I turned on the switch. Arguably, persons must have a basic power to act on reasons. Thus power is enabled, supported and limited by our brains, our anatomy and environment, but its power is not something that can be eliminated from a plausible account of human agency. Second, most accounts of physical causation allow that on a foundational material level, some causal powers are basic and not further explainable. Why does a quarter have a certain spin? Eventually (to avoid an infinite regress) one has to posit basic powers. If there are basic powers possessed at the subatomic level, why can't persons themselves have basic powers? I suggest that explanations by human agents are intelligible in part because we take purposive, reasoned explanations as basic and not substituted by impersonal forces. If so, there is no reason in principle to dispatch with explanations that appeal to divine agency.

As for a positive case for the experience of God through the Bible, this is a matter of assessing not just theories and probabilities but values.

LOOKING FOR VALUES

So far I have largely sought to clear the ground for recognizing divine revelation, rather than argue in detail, for example, that it is reasonable to believe in the resurrection of Christ and therefore to plausibly believe that this life needs to be seen as involving *more* than natural causes and events. I refer you to Richard Swinburne's fine work *The Resurrection of God Incarnate* for detailed argument. I want to conclude this chapter with the proposal that when you do look further into such detailed argu-

---

[13]See my *Evidence and Faith*.

ments, you consider not just frameworks but the overall *values that are at stake*. I will back this proposal up with a tragic illustration.

The greatest opponent of miracle reports, David Hume, was a racist or, more technically, a white supremacist. This does not itself undermine his case against miracles in the slightest. But there is an interesting, similar pattern in Hume's case against miracles and his case against reports of black intelligence. Here is a notorious passage that captures Hume's prejudice against blacks:

> I am apt to suggest the Negroes and in general all of the other species of men (for there are four or five different kinds) to be naturally inferior to the whites. There never was a civilized nation of any other complexion than white, nor even any individual eminent either in action or speculation. No ingenious manufactures amongst them, no arts, no sciences. On the other hand, the most rude and barbarous of the whites, such as the ancient Germans, the present Tartars, have all still something eminent about them, in their valor, form of government, or some other particular. Such a uniform and constant difference could not happen, in so many countries and ages, if nature had not made an original distinction betwixt these breeds of men. Not to mention our colonies, there are Negro slaves dispersed all over Europe, of which none ever discovered any symptoms of ingenuity, tho' low people without education will start up amongst us, and distinguish themselves in every profession. In Jamaica indeed they talk of one Negro as a man of parts and learning; but 'tis likely he is admired for very slender accomplishments like a parrot, who speaks a few words plainly.[14]

Hume may begin this passage with "I am apt to suspect"; however, this show of tentativeness quickly gives way. By his estimation, there has been a uniform and constant association of whites and superior intelligence. He acknowledges reports of exceptions (the man from Jamaica) but dismisses this talk in light of his view of the regular, uniform, exceptionless character of nature. He is so convinced of this that he offers an explanation of ostensible anomalies. It is more probable (likely) that blacks merely simulate intelligence, the way a bird may merely simulate language, without being intelligent; presumably both may be accounted for within the bounds of what Hume conceives the laws of nature to be.

Hume's strategy was to define the nature of black persons so as to

---

[14]David Hume, *Of National Characters* (London: Longmans, 1886), p. 225.

make any reported exceptions to nature implausible. He does the same thing with reported miracles. He defines nature as an arena in which, if there is a reported miracle, it amounts to a report of an event that *violates* nature.

Hume was aware in his day both that there were widespread reports of miracles historically and that there were reports of intelligence among nonwhites. The man from Jamaica was Francis Williams, who held a degree from Cambridge University, headed a school and was known for his Latin poetry. There were some ten thousand blacks in London during Hume's tenure there. A black American poet, Phillis Wheatly (1753-1784), went to London where she publicly wrote and received poetry. Why wasn't Hume open to taking Wheatly and other remarkable black artists, scholars and so on seriously? I believe he was not open to such counterevidence because he defined nature in such a way as to make reports of black intelligence profoundly implausible. The tragic results of this racial foreclosure are that Hume lost both an appreciation for the abundant, evident goods that stem from productive interracial activity, and he provided reasons that were employed by slave owners to practice their race-based slavery. By not being open to black equality, he encouraged white supremacy.

The lesson to draw from Hume's predicament is not that Hume was wrong about blacks and thus wrong about God and divine revelation. All a follower of Hume needs to do is to separate the cases and claim Hume was wrong about blacks and right about God. And it could be that, if Dawkins, Christopher Hitchens and other New Atheists are right about religion being poisonous (to use Hitchens's phrase), we may have a moral reason to encourage a highly skeptical evaluation of the credibility of religion. But if, like Kim Phuc, we find in religion (or at least in a biblically based religion) more of an antidote than a poison, we have reason to make sure our frameworks do not rule out what may be of profound value. Given the possibility that divine religion provides us with a means for an authentic, transforming encounter with God, then a framework broader than Hume's, Dennett's, Dawkins's and Narveson's is worthy of pursuit. This section may be summarized succinctly: provided one has the same reason to be open to theism, one should not define nature and explanations so as to make recognizing divine presence as difficult as Hume made recognizing blacks' intelligence.

The overall case for recognizing and experiencing the Bible as God's living word will depend on your overall view of nature, history and values. As you consider the merit (or supposed demerits) of the Bible, one thing is crucial not to omit: it is one thing to look *at* the Bible, but if you only look at it, your investigation will be as limited as if you only looked at a telescope. I also recommend trying to look *through* the Bible to see what or who might be revealed through it.[15]

FOR FURTHER READING

Abraham, William. *Canon and Criterion in Christian Theology.* Oxford: Clarendon, 1998.

Dawkins, Richard. *The God Delusion.* Boston: Houghton Mifflin, 2006.

Dennett, Daniel C. *Breaking the Spell: Religion as a Natural Phenomenon.* New York: Viking, 2006.

Hume, David. *Of National Characters.* London: Longmans, 1886.

———. *A Treatise of Human Nature.* London: Harvard University Press, 1888.

Lucas, J. R. *Freedom and Grace.* London: SPCK, 1976.

Manson, N. A., ed. *God and Design: The Teleological Argument and Modern Science.* London: Routledge, 2003.

Swinburne, Richard. *Revelation: From Metaphor to Analogy,* 2nd ed. Oxford: Oxford University Press, 2007.

Taliaferro, Charles. *Contemporary Philosophy of Religion.* Malden: Blackwell, 1998.

———. *Evidence and Faith: Philosophy and Religion Since the Seventeenth Century.* New York: Cambridge University Press, 2005.

Underhill, Evelyn. *Mysticism: The Nature and Development of Spiritual Consciousness.* Oxford: Oneworld, 2001.

Wolterstorff, Nicholas. *Reason Within the Bounds of Religion.* Grand Rapids: Eerdmans, 1976.

———. *Divine Discourse.* New York: Cambridge University Press, 1995.

---

[15]I thank Elizabeth Clark, Aaron Stauffer and Elsa Marty for helpful comments on this essay.

12

The Messiah You Never Expected

SCOT McKNIGHT

When most first-century Jews observed Jesus, the first thing that came to mind was not the word *Messiah*. His contemporaries had all kinds of terms for him: some thought he was a lawbreaker, demon-possessed, a glutton and drunkard, a blasphemer, a false prophet, a claimant for "King of the Jews"; others thought he was nothing more than an illegitimate child, a *mamzer* in the Hebrew of his day.[1] It wasn't just the Jewish leaders or even ordinary Jewish folk who had trouble with Jesus. Even his family at one point thought he was "out of his mind" (Mk 3:21).

But Jesus' followers saw something else. They thought he was the Son of God and Messiah and the Son of Man and Lord and Teacher and Prophet like Moses. As we read the New Testament, titles for Jesus multiply to where it becomes quite obvious what happened: what these Jews first believed about the Jewish God, YHWH by name, was what they came to believe also about Jesus. In their mind, Jesus was God, the God of Israel in flesh. John 1:1 says it explicitly.

But we are not interested in this chapter in how Jesus' followers saw him. We have another question, one that gets behind why so many of his contemporaries did not use the word *Messiah* for him. If he was the Messiah, he wasn't what most of them were expecting. What I'm suggesting

---

[1]You can chase down these accusations against Jesus if you read Luke 14:1-6, Mark 7:1-20, Mark 3:20-27, Matthew 11:16-19, Mark 14:53-65, Matthew 27:62-64, Mark 15:1-20 and John 8:39-47.

is not that there were lots of views of the Messiah in Judaism; there were. What I'm saying is that, in spite of the welter of views about Messiah, when some compared what they thought the Messiah would be to what Jesus was doing, it just didn't add up to "Therefore, Jesus is our Messiah." Jesus confused them because he didn't live the script they had written for the Messiah. His confusing of his contemporaries leads me to a question: what did they see?

I'd like to sketch some items the contemporaries of Jesus most likely saw when they listened to and watched Jesus. What we will discover if we have the patience to think about Jesus in the terms of those who saw him from the outside—as if for the very first time—is that Jesus pressed upon his observers one major question: "Who do you think I am?" They were led to that question, I suggest, by ten things they observed.

1. JESUS WAS FREE

Jews believed the book of Leviticus was from God; that meant eating kosher foods. By the time of Jesus they had extended food laws to include eating only with those who ate kosher, which meant they didn't eat with Gentiles or sinful people. As in our day, not only was the Bible seen as inspired, but traditional interpretation (called *halakah*) of the Torah (the "Law of Moses") was just as authoritative. If someone came along and tossed some shrimp on the barbie or pulled out a ham sandwich at lunch, that person would be seen as a flagrant violator of the Torah.

Those who watched Jesus eating with others, however, observed something: Jesus didn't seem to care for the standard *halakah* on some things; he ate with those who were considered "sinners." Some of his contemporaries saw what he did and listened to what he said, and they said this: "Here is a glutton and a drunkard, a friend of tax collectors and sinners" (Mt 11:19). These aren't words describing how much Jesus ate or drank but technical words from the Torah of Moses. They come straight from Deuteronomy 21:18-21:

> If someone has a stubborn and rebellious son who does not obey his father and mother and will not listen to them when they discipline him, his father and mother shall take hold of him and bring him to the elders at the gate of his town. They shall say to the elders, "This son of ours is stubborn and rebellious. He will not obey us. He is a *profligate and a drunkard*." Then all the men of his town are to stone him to death. You must

purge the evil from among you. All Israel will hear of it and be afraid. (TNIV, emphasis added)

The words of the observers of Jesus, based in Torah according to official interpretation, were that Jesus was a "rebellious son" and he should be stoned. These words were a legal category designed for prosecution. What the observers saw, then, was that Jesus not only knew these words of Moses and how his contemporaries interpreted them, but he didn't seem to care what they thought they meant. He was *free* from that interpretation. And so he did what he thought was right: he ate with those considered sinners.

What they would have seen was not what they expected of the Messiah; the Messiah would be the quintessential son of the Torah and a master interpreter—which, ironically, he was, but they didn't see that his interpretation was different from theirs. I think observers of Jesus saw him as wild. G. K. Chesterton, in his book called *Orthodoxy*, pins great words on what the observers of Jesus saw: "The more I considered Christianity, the more I found that while it had established a rule and order, the chief aim of that order was to give room for good things to run wild."[2] Jesus, too, was running wild.

2. JESUS WAS CONFIDENT

Observers of Jesus in the first century would have noticed something else immediately: his chutzpah. Every observant Jew began and ended the day reciting the *Shema*, roughly the words we now find in Deuteronomy 6:4-9, which reminded them to love God with every globule of their being. Not only that, they said this whenever they left their house and entered back into that house. And they recited the *Shema* when they were on the path with their children to remind them of the central creed of Judaism: to love God by obeying God's commands.[3]

Jesus was free from that sacred duty as well. But there's more. Not only was he free but he exempted his followers. It's found now in Luke 9:59-60, where we find Jesus summoning three different individuals to

---

[2]G. K. Chesterton, *Orthodoxy* (New York: Doubleday, 1990), p. 95.

[3]The only exception for reciting *Shema* was in the event of a father's death. We learn this from a later rabbinic text called the *Mishnah* (Berakot 3.1). I'm not sure this *halakah* was in effect in the first century, but it can serve to illustrate just how sacred a duty was to bury one's father.

follow him. To the second man, Jesus said: "Follow me."

> But he replied, "Lord, first let me go and bury my father."
> Jesus said to him, "Let the dead bury their own dead, but you go and proclaim the kingdom of God." (TNIV)

Jesus thought *following him* was more important than burying one's father. To be sure, the Jewish burial process involved immediately placing one's father's corpse in a niche in a stone wall and waiting for the body to decompose. That took about a year. Then the eldest son checked to make sure the body had decomposed sufficiently, removed the bones and placed them in a bone box (ossuary) to be permanently buried. Even if this prolonged process is the proper historical setting for Jesus' words, however, the words come off as full of chutzpah. The sacred duty to bury your father, Jesus was saying, is not as important as following *me*. "I am more important than sacred tradition," Jesus was saying.

Elsewhere (Mt 12:1-8) Jesus scuffles with his contemporaries over the sabbath. We need to remind ourselves of how Matthew 11 ended: Jesus said *he* could give his disciples *rest*. That word *rest* is golden; it is what sabbath is all about, and that means the opening point of Matthew 12, that Jesus is lord even of the sabbath, is a way of saying that *he* was the sabbath, *he* was the rest. The famous Jewish scholar Jacob Neusner reads this passage and concludes that "what we face is an irreconcilable conflict. Either 'Remember the Sabbath Day to keep it holy' or 'The son of man is the Lord of the Sabbath'—but not both."[4] Neusner sees here a claim on the part of Jesus to be the sabbath himself—to be the one in whom the rest is found. That's what I mean by *chutzpah*.

The natural response of the ordinary Jew to these words of Jesus was this: "Who in the world do you think you are?"

3. JESUS WAS A LIGHTNING ROD

For a variety of reasons Jesus was a lightning rod. After watching the same actions and hearing Jesus say the same things, two groups came to two different conclusions: Peter and Mary Magdalene believed Jesus was the answer to age-old questions and the climax of the story of Israel; many of the Pharisees thought Jesus was a menace to piety and sacred tradition. When the Pharisee saw a converted prostitute anointing Jesus'

---

[4]Jacob Neusner, *A Rabbi Talks with Jesus* (New York: Doubleday/Image, 1994), p. 70.

feet with expensive oil, his response was "If this man were a prophet, he would know who is touching him and what kind of woman she is—that she is a sinner" (Lk 7:39 TNIV). But the woman saw things differently: she thought Jesus was the one who acknowledged her, showed her compassion and gave her a new start in life. As Luke tells the story, Jesus saw in *her* (not him) the true model of adoration.

> Then he [Jesus] turned toward the woman and said to Simon, "Do you see this woman? I came into your house. You did not give me any water for my feet, but she wet my feet with her tears and wiped them with her hair. You did not give me a kiss, but this woman, from the time I entered, has not stopped kissing my feet. You did not put oil on my head, but she has poured perfume on my feet. Therefore, I tell you, her many sins have been forgiven—as her great love has shown. But whoever has been forgiven little loves little." Then Jesus said to her, "Your sins are forgiven."

Not surprisingly, the question of those who saw what happened was "Who is this who even forgives sins?" (Lk 7:44-49 TNIV).

The Roman authorities didn't like Jesus either. Once the Pharisees came to Jesus and said, "Leave this place and go somewhere else. Herod wants to kill you." Jesus' response:

> Go tell that fox, "I will keep on driving out demons and healing people today and tomorrow, and on the third day I will reach my goal." In any case, I must press on today and tomorrow and the next day—for surely no prophet can die outside Jerusalem! (Lk 13:31-33 TNIV)

We can trust the Pharisees on this one to have known the inside story: Rome saw Jesus as a threat.

Like the Pharisees and Romans, the Sadducees made Jesus a lightning rod of opposition. Many of us learned the parable of the Good Samaritan as kids, and sometimes we were taught the parable in a way that avoids the subversive nature of the story. It was, after all, a priest and Levite—probably Sadducees—who were on their way from Jerusalem, and that means they form the foil for the Samaritan—hardly a priest!—who showed compassion (Lk 10:25-37). John the Baptist, the son of a priest and relative of Jesus, was beheaded by Herod Antipas. In the Sadducees' opinion, Jesus was a follower of John and was threatening their positions with the Romans. During Jesus' last week, when he went toe to toe with the Sadducees and their associates (Mk 11:27-33; 12:13-17,

18-27), there was a history of bad blood at work. Jesus wasn't backing down, and neither were they. The perfect storm to put him away had been congealing for more than a year.

Any casual observer with open eyes and ears could not have missed that behind the scenes a plot was in motion. The question this plot raises is: Why did they think Jesus had to be killed? What sort of person is such a threat to so many that they need to put him away to deal with him?

4. JESUS WAS AN ACTIVIST

If we compare Jesus to Socrates or Plato or the apostle Paul or to Augustine we observe that all of them, in their own way, were intellectuals. By reading about them and by reading what they wrote or taught, we know they can sustain an argument for pages. What reader hasn't wondered what Paul was up to in Romans 7 or Augustine in *The City of God*?

No one wants to say Jesus wasn't intelligent, but his style was not that of an intellectual. Instead, Jesus' style was that of an activist who gathered people around and plotted and organized and orchestrated an all-out agenda to get his people to respond to the message of the kingdom of God. You can see this sort of thing at work in Luke 10:1-12 as Jesus organizes and commissions seventy evangelists. Jesus moved from village to village doing this one day after the next (Lk 9:51-56).

True, Jesus gave sermons, and some of them have been remembered and set down for our own learning. We think here of the Sermon on the Mount (Mt 5—7) or what Luke calls the Sermon on the Plain (Lk 6:17-49). But Jesus did not write any books, at least that we know about, and his style was homey stories and clever lines and insightful remarks. One reason this is the way we remember Jesus is because he was so active that he seemed not to have the time or the inclination to turn his ideas into dissertations. When we think of Jesus, we are not to think of a professor type but of a local pastor, activist and community worker all rolled into one personality. We are to think of who Jesus was and how he would have struck those who observed him in his day.

5. JESUS WAS PREACHY

Anyone who took an interest in Jesus at all would have observed that he told people what he thought and sometimes had to tell people off. The kind of rhetoric we find in the Bible might surprise us today, and I know a recent study surprised me when I tried to put together James's concern with the tongue (Jas 3:1-12) and the sharp criticisms he offers (Jas 4:1-12; 4:13—5:6). But that kind of rhetoric was common in the ancient world, and Jesus fit right in. We've mentioned the Sermon on the Mount, but Matthew records four others: the missionary discourse (Mt 10), the parable discourse (Mt 13), the church discourse (Mt 18) and a discourse that warns of Jerusalem's imminent destruction (Mt 23—25). John's Gospel is laced together with lengthy sermons by Jesus (cf. Jn 6). Perhaps Matthew 23 alone stands as some of the strongest, preachy rhetoric of Jesus, and those who were watching would have come away thinking Jesus was courageous and could be rhetorically potent if he needed to be. But more often his preachiness moved in other directions.

Everyone noticed Jesus' parables, short stories that invite the listener in and, if the listener stays long enough, either turn his world upside down or—like the wardrobe that gives children entrance into C. S. Lewis's Narnia or the painting that welcomes Lewis's Eustace aboard the Dawn Treader—draw him into a new world with a new vision that leads to a new life.

Jesus' style was to tell stories. Aristotle's style was that of a chemist working in a mortuary! Aristotle dissected everything; Jesus "stori-fied" everything. Sometimes the listener discovered late in the game that the story was on him.

Let's set Jesus' preaching and parables in context: Jesus is on a mission to restore Israel, and he is being opposed. His weapon is to preach about his vision of the kingdom of God, and he tells stories to make clear to others what is really going on. When he senses the wind of opposition, instead of opening his sails to fly away, he lowers his nose and heads right into it. For Jesus, there is no looking back. He sets his sight on Jerusalem, enters the sacred temple, tips over tables and then, when asked about his behavior, gives his audience a memorable, breathtaking story:

> A man planted a vineyard. He put a wall around it, dug a pit for the winepress and built a watchtower. Then he rented the vineyard to some farmers and moved to another place. At harvest time he sent a servant to the tenants to collect from them some of the fruit of the vineyard. But they seized him, beat him and sent him away empty-handed. Then he sent another servant to them; they struck this man on the head and treated

him shamefully. He sent still another, and that one they killed. He sent many others; some of them they beat, others they killed.

He had one left to send, a son, whom he loved. He sent him last of all, saying, "They will respect my son."

But the tenants said to one another, "This is the heir. Come, let's kill him, and the inheritance will be ours." So they took him and killed him, and threw him out of the vineyard.

What then will the owner of the vineyard do? He will come and kill those tenants and give the vineyard to others. Haven't you read this passage of Scripture:

"The stone the builders rejected
    has become the cornerstone;
the Lord has done this,
    and it is marvelous in our eyes"?

The story ends, and then "the chief priests, the teachers of the law and the elders looked for a way to arrest him because they knew he had spoken the parable against them. But they were afraid of the crowd; so they left him and went away" (Mk 12:1-12 TNIV).

Jesus' story is a good one, depending of course on who you are. Jesus forces his hearers to run the gauntlet—whose side are they on? Are they with the "son" or are they with the vine-growers? Of course, they think, they are with the "son" who was obviously treated unjustly. But then everything shifts into nothing less than a showdown: Jesus points out that he is the "son" and that the vine-growers are the leaders of Jerusalem—chief priests and Pharisees. Those who took the time to listen to him recognized in Jesus' story not some moral tale but a devastating critique of their attitude toward his mission to bring the kingdom of God. Unlike the Zealots, Jesus' "sword" was the word, usually in story form.

The observers of Jesus in this kind of situation—and this was as commonplace for Jesus as questions about policy are for presidential candidates—could not have failed to ask: Why is there so much concern with Jesus? Why does what he has to say matter so much? Who is he? They had plenty of opportunity to watch and hear because Jesus was an activist preacher who did this all day long for three years.

6. JESUS HAS A RADAR FOR HYPOCRISY

We can begin with the observation that Jesus despised the ostentatious practice of religious acts. As an activist he saw lots of it; as a preacher he was compelled to reveal it.

Perhaps the gentle wit of an English novelist can help us out. When Lord Middleton invited two young women, cousins at that, home without informing his dear wife, Jane Austen (in *Sense and Sensibility*) informs us of the following:

> As it was impossible, however, now to prevent their coming, Lady Middleton resigned herself to the idea of it with all the philosophy of a well-bred woman, contenting herself with merely giving her husband a gentle reprimand on the subject five or six times every day.[5]

It might be observed that Jesus had the same apparent approach to "helping" hypocrites see their failings, though he avoided the subtlety of Austen's indirection. Over and over this happens, and it can't but strike anyone who reads the Gospels how sensitive Jesus was to the matter. In Mark 7 Jesus points out that fastidiousness over washed hands needs to be met with an even more intense desire to be pure in heart. In Jesus' last week, he remonstrates at length with the Pharisees and scribes over their hypocrisies.

What Jesus observed in certain leaders of his day has its counterparts among many in ours, including leaders in the church. Even if we are to make sure the same is not true of us, that does not mean that we don't at times think that Jesus "got 'em but good." And we smile with approval, because the words he used carried their own punch. It would not be far from the mark to suggest that Flannery O'Connor's brilliant exposés of religious pretense, dressed up as they are in the grotesque images she chooses to employ, owe their origins to the ancient prophets of Israel, like Micah or Isaiah, and to Jesus' own excoriations in Matthew 23. Perhaps her words best comment on Jesus': "I doubtless hate," she wrote to Maryat Lee in June of 1957, "pious language worse than you because I believe the realities it hides."[6] The realities O'Connor believed in were those created by Jesus, and he hated pious language for the same reason. He knew the truth, and wanted people to live in the truth. In fact, he was the truth (Jn 14:6), and that made hypocrisy detestable. His sitting in judgment on others made people wonder who he thought he was.

---

[5]Jane Austen, *Sense and Sensibility* (New York: Dover, 1996), p. 79.
[6]Flannery O'Connor, *Collected Works* (New York: Library of America, 1988), p. 1035.

7. JESUS WAS CHARISMATIC

I use the word *charismatic* because I think ordinary observers would have said it about Jesus. When he entered the village, folks gathered to him; when he came to dinner, folks wanted to sit near him; when he sauntered out to the village well for a drink, others got thirsty. Mark's quiet words map the life of Jesus:

> Jesus withdrew with his disciples to the lake, and a large crowd from Galilee followed. When they heard all he was doing, many people came to him from Judea, Jerusalem, Idumea, and the regions across the Jordan and around Tyre and Sidon. Because of the crowd he told his disciples to have a small boat ready for him, to keep the people from crowding him. For he had healed many, so that those with diseases were pushing forward to touch him. (Mk 3:7-10 TNIV)

Sometime sit down with one Gospel, read it and mark down every time someone asks Jesus a question. What is surprising is how rarely Jesus initiates his actions or his teaching. Far more often someone asks Jesus a question because they want to know what he thinks. Everyone recognized this, even the opponents of Jesus. Notice the potent irony in two scenes from John 12, one in which the leaders of Judaism reject Jesus while ordinary Greeks embrace him, an irony that perfectly illustrates Jesus as charismatic:

> Now the crowd that was with him when he called Lazarus from the tomb and raised him from the dead continued to spread the word. Many people, because they had heard that he had performed this sign, went out to meet him. So the Pharisees said to one another, "See, this is getting us nowhere. Look how the whole world has gone after him!"
>
> Now there were some Greeks among those who went up to worship at the Festival. They came to Philip, who was from Bethsaida in Galilee, with a request. "Sir," they said, "we would like to see Jesus." Philip went to tell Andrew; Andrew and Philip in turn told Jesus. (Jn 12:17-22 TNIV)

There's another sense of charismatic; I will turn to that now. But being charismatic in the above sense led people to ask what it was about Jesus that made him so attractive.

8. JESUS WAS SPIRITUAL

Ordinary observers of Jesus, those who were neither committed to him nor against him, would have been struck by the spirituality of Jesus. At Jesus' baptism he had a vision of some sort (Mk 1:9-11). He was transfigured in the very presence of his followers (Mk 9:2-13). He somehow saw Satan fall like lightning (Lk 10:18). Jesus was known for prayer, the kind of prayer that intimately related to God as *Abba* (Aramaic for "Father"), and he taught his disciples a prayer (Lk 11:2-4). He healed people and exorcised demons (Mt 4:23-25) and he multiplied bread (Mk 6:30-44). We could multiply the examples, but the point has been made: only deeply spiritual, charismatic people do things like this.

A point needs to be made here. Some argue from these kinds of claims that Jesus was God, and I think he was. But we miss something when we make this move all the time. We should see something else: Jesus did these things not because he was God but because, in his humanity, the power of God the Father was given to him. This dependence on God is the constant witness of John's Gospel, and Jesus did these things because he was in tune with and empowered by the Spirit of God (Lk 3:22; 4:1, 18; Mt 12:28).[7]

At the time of Jesus there were others who were called "holy men" or *Hasidim*. Each is different, but they fall into a pattern. No doubt many would have seen Jesus as Jewish *hasid*. Notice this text from the later Jewish rabbinic text, the *Mishnah*:

C. They said to Honi, the circle drawer, "Pray for rain."

D. He said to them, "Go and take in the clay ovens used for Passover, so that they not soften [in the rain which is coming]."

E. He prayed, but it did not rain.

F. What did he do?

G. He drew a circle and stood in the middle of it and said before Him, "Lord of the world! Your children have turned to me, for before you I am like a member of the family. I swear by your great name—I'm simply not moving from here until you take pity on your children!"

H. It began to rain drop by drop.

I. He said, "This is not what I wanted, but rain for filling up cisterns, pits, and caverns."

---

[7]A book should be mentioned here: Gerald Hawthorne, *The Presence and the Power* (Waco, Tex.: Word, 1991).

J. It began to rain violently.

K. He said, "This is not what I wanted, but rain of good will, blessing, and graciousness."

L. Now it rained the right way, until Israelites had to flee from Jerusalem up to the Temple Mount because of the rain.[8]

Each Jewish *hasid* is distinct, not the least of whom would have been Jesus, but each also fits into a pattern of someone who is charismatic in the sense of having direct access to God, and everyone knew this about Jesus. And yet they observed lots of differences between Jesus and the others. He, after all, was the only one who ended up crucified. Why?

9. JESUS HAD COMPASSION

Jesus was known for the company he kept and the tables at which he ate. Every evening became a banquet, every night a symposium, every home a dining hall. And to the table came all sorts of the marginalized. Take note of these sorts whom you find on every page of Jesus' life: fishermen, Zealots, tax collectors, prostitutes, lepers, demonized and women aplenty. He created the first socially correct Sesame Street dinner table, and he did so because he believed his Father loved all people. He anticipated Mr. Rogers and his neighborhood, because Jesus thought everyone was "special" and that his table could be the start of both a new "neighborliness" and a new "neighborhood." He did this because he believed all humans—whether "pure" or not, whether "observant" or not and whether morally sound or not—were made in God's image. And, like Augustine after him, he knew that people weren't fully persons until they turned to God.

What, we can ask, do you think the Samaritan woman said about Jesus when she got home (Jn 4)? Or the lepers who were healed when each of them got back home (Lk 17:11-19)? Or the poor man about whom Jesus told the story of Dives and Lazarus (Lk16:19-31)? Or the woman caught in the act of whatever by whomever but who was suddenly freed for a new life (Jn 7:53—8:11)? The lines these people remember from Jesus were things like this: "Be healed" or "Be forgiven" or "Be restored." They remembered Jesus as someone who looked them in the eye, saw who and what they were, disregarded it because he knew who had

---

[8]Translation: Jacob Neusner, *The Mishnah* (New Haven: Yale, 1988).

made them, and invited them home. Jesus was for big tables in a big house, with places reserved for all sorts. What kind of person, they would have asked, does stuff like this?

10. JESUS WAS AT HOME, NOT AT HOME

The last characteristic is a double image: Jesus was both *at home in Judaism* and at the same time *not completely comfortable with the Judaism of his day*. In 1973 Geza Vermes, a Jew who became a priest and then converted back to Judaism, brought to the scholarly world's attention that Jesus is only understood if he is understood in Jewish terms.

Jesus is at home in Judaism; he speaks like it, he thinks like it, and he worships like it. His piety is Judaism's. He taught its themes, he told its stories, and he used its connections. Until you and I understand Judaism, we really can't get a good hold on Jesus. Until we understand "Torah" and "purity" and "temple" and "land" and the like, we can't grasp what Jesus was saying and what he was doing. In other words, Jesus' mission was a "Jewish" mission—a mission to Jews and for Jews and about Jews and in the terms of the Jews. His vision was rooted in Israel's Scriptures, his God is the God of Israel's Scriptures, his prophetic stance over against Israel is drawn from Israel's prophets, and his family—Joseph, Mary and his extended family (John the Baptist and his parents, Zechariah and Elisabeth)—thoroughly Jewish and concerned with things Jewish. It is more than likely that Jesus worshiped at the temple on High Holidays; he would have taken part in sacrificing lambs for Passover; he would have helped to build the "tents" for *Sukkoth;* and he would have participated in synagogue services and the like in Nazareth. He was a Jew among Jews, and nothing he did or said (really ever) was anything but Jewish.

However, what he did and what he said created tensions—not because what he did or said was not Jewish but because it bucked the establishment and called for a new day. Which leads to the final characteristic about Jesus. Jesus was simply not comfortable with the Judaism of his day.

Jesus told this little parable, really little more than a wisdom riddle (with a little adjustment by me): "No one but a dumb cluck puts new wine in an old wineskin" (Mk 2:22). That tells the whole story about Jesus: he came not to break the Torah but to fulfill it; he came not to tear

apart the feasts of Israel but to set them on a new level—that is what the
Lord's Supper is to *Pesach* (the Hebrew term for "Passover"); he came
not to abolish redemption but to restore it. So Jesus is himself the new
wine in an old wineskin—he is (according to himself and his followers)
Jewish wine but cranked up so that the old wineskin of Judaism just
can't contain his ferment. If you fill that wineskin with the juice that is
Jesus, the skin will burst and the whole place will be a mess. And no one
likes messes.

This all came to a head during the Feast of Unleavened Bread and
Passover. Jesus entered the city of Jerusalem, pierced his way into the
temple courts and started tipping over tables as an acted parable of what
was about to happen to the temple itself if the leaders refused to listen to
him. By the end of the week he had been tried and summarily executed
on a cross just outside the city.

The Gospels tell us Jesus predicted not only that he would die but that
his death would bring saving benefits to his followers. In one text, Jesus
says that "even the Son of Man did not come to be served, but to serve,
and to give his life as a ransom for many" (Mk 10:45 TNIV). And, along the
same line of understanding, in the Last Supper, Jesus suddenly broke with
the Passover custom and said, "This is my body" and "This is my blood of
the covenant, which is poured out for many. . . . Truly I tell you, I will not
drink again of the fruit of the vine until that day when I drink it new in the
kingdom of God" (Mk 14:22, 24-25 TNIV). Jesus believed his death was
beneficial; it was a death that absorbed the wrath of God against the sins
of his people and the world, turned violence on its head, and brought
kingdom redemption to his followers. From this point on, association
with Jesus is association with the Crucified One.

Even if Jesus thought his death was saving, he still died. His death
almost undid his followers—but only until Sunday morning, when the
report quickly spread among the followers that Jesus had somehow come
back to life. He had been raised. They announced this because the tomb
was empty, for which there are only two possible explanations: either
the body was removed by the followers of Jesus and they were all liars,
and Christianity is foisted up by a pack of rebel liars; or, the body was
raised by God, and the Christian preaching of hope through resurrection is the gospel. There are no other reasonable alternatives: either the
disciples are liars or they are truth-tellers.

What Brutus said about Mark Antony, or at least what Shakespeare depicts him as saying, may be what the Roman Pontius Pilate thought of that small band of Jesus' followers:

> For he can do no more than Caesar's arm
> When Caesar's head is off.[9]

But what, one may ask, if the Ruler comes back to life? What then, Brutus? Does the arm come back to life too? Does the arm that has come back to life learn to see Messiah in a new set of categories? The witness of history is that it did. The Messiah who was expected was transformed by the Messiah who came.

The idea for approaching Jesus from the outside comes from reading G. K. Chesterton's *The Everlasting Man*. In part two of this sometimes quite wonderful but always punchy book, he sought to describe Jesus by an imaginary man from the moon who discovers the Gospels but had never heard of Jesus prior to reading them. Chesterton tells the truth about the Gospels with this: "If we *could* read the Gospel reports as things as new as newspaper reports, they would puzzle us and perhaps terrify us much *more* than the same things as developed by historical Christianity. . . . [T]he moral is that the Christ of the Gospel might actually seem more strange and terrible than the Christ of the Church."[10]

How about you? Who do you think he was?[11]

FURTHER READING

Copan, Paul, and Craig A. Evans, eds. *Who Was Jesus?* Louisville: Westminster John Knox, 2001.

France, R. T. *The Man They Crucified*. London: Inter-Varsity Press, 1975.

McKnight, Scot. *The Story of the Christ*. Grand Rapids: Baker, 2006.

Neusner, Jacob. *A Rabbi Talks with Jesus*. New York: Doubleday, 1994.

Wright, N. T. *The Challenge of Jesus: Rediscovering Who Jesus Was and Is*. Downers Grove, Ill.: InterVarsity Press, 1999.

---

[9]William Shakespeare *Julius Caesar* 2.1.182-83.

[10]G. K. Chesterton, *The Everlasting Man* (San Francisco: Ignatius, 1993), pp. 192-93.

[11]This chapter is rooted in three of my publications: *The Story of the Christ* (Grand Rapids: Baker, 2006), pp. 45-62; "Calling Jesus *Mamzer*," *Journal for the Study of the Historical Jesus* 1 (2003): 73-103; *Who Do My Opponents Say That I Am? An Investigation of the Accusations Against the Historical Jesus*, ed. S. McKnight and J. B. Modica, Library of New Testament Studies 327 (London: T & T Clark, 2008).

13

Tracing Jesus' Resurrection to Its Earliest Eyewitness Accounts

Gary R. Habermas

Early Christians claimed that Jesus rose from the dead and appeared to many. How close were these accounts to the events in question? Scholars point out that the earliest New Testament writings began to appear about twenty years after Jesus' death. My purpose here will be to argue that two epistles unanimously recognized as Paul's, 1 Corinthians and Galatians, provide the basis for showing that the original resurrection proclamation was exceptionally early and linked to the initial eyewitnesses themselves. This indicates that the resurrection appearances are securely grounded in the historical tradition.

A BRIEF WORD ABOUT THE MINIMAL HISTORICAL FACTS

Most evangelical scholars begin their treatment of Jesus' resurrection by arguing for the general historical reliability of the four Gospels. While I think these texts provide much helpful information that contributes to the construction of such a case,[1] that will not be my approach here. Rather than attempting to employ these sources as a whole, in this essay I will utilize only those historical data that critical scholars think can be established according to more skeptical standards. Though I cannot provide

---

[1] Most notably on the Gospels, see Richard Bauckham, *Jesus and the Eyewitnesses: The Gospels as Eyewitness Testimony* (Grand Rapids: Eerdmans, 2006). Cf. James D. G. Dunn, *Jesus Remembered*, vol. 1 of *Christianity in the Making* (Grand Rapids: Eerdmans, 2003).

the basis for these historical facts here, I have done so elsewhere.[2]

This method is often misunderstood. Some object that the Bible cannot be used as a source. However, *I am using only data that critical scholars allow*, and this acknowledgment by them comes for a reason: there is a strong basis which grounds this material.

In any study that employs the principles of historiography, whether ancient or modern, arguably the two major requirements are to secure testimony that is both eyewitness and as close as possible to the events in question. It is especially crucial to have enough information to address any major alternative scenarios. To have both eyewitness and early testimony is fairly uncommon in the ancient world, but where they are available, especially together, they usually play a crucial role. This was recognized in ancient times as well.[3]

THE CRUCIFIXION OF JESUS—GROUND ZERO

The point of departure for our timeline is Jesus' death by crucifixion, generally dated at either A.D. 30 or 33. The precise time will not be debated here; Raymond Brown thinks that it is almost impossible to choose between them, but neither date poses a problem.[4] John Dominic Crossan asserts that "Jesus' death by execution under Pontius Pilate is as sure as anything historical can ever be."[5] The remainder of the events on which we will concentrate our efforts occur over the next twenty-five years.

TWO TO THREE DECADES AFTER THE CROSS: THE "AUTHENTIC" PAULINE EPISTLES

The majority of scholars today regard Paul's epistles as the starting point

---

[2]For examples, Gary R. Habermas, *The Risen Jesus and Future Hope* (Lanham, Md.: Rowman and Littlefield, 2003); *The Historical Jesus: Ancient Evidence for the Life of Christ* (Joplin, Mo.: College Press, 1996).

[3]Second-century historian Lucian of Samosata addressed the removal of subjective factors from the historian's work (6:7-15, 72-73, 39-43), as well as the proper function of eyewitness testimony, unlike the ancient writer who claimed to have been a witness, although Lucian decided that the facts opposed his claim (6:43-47)! See Lucian's *How to Write History,* vol. 6 of *Lucian in Eight Volumes,* trans. K. Kilburn, Loeb Classical Library (Cambridge, Mass.: Harvard University Press, 1959).

[4]Raymond E. Brown, *The Death of the Messiah,* 2 vols. (Garden City, N.Y.: Doubleday, 1994), esp. p. 1376; cf. pp. 1350-78. The former date is more commonly chosen by scholars, though nothing depends on our being specific.

[5]John Dominic Crossan, *Who Killed Jesus? Exposing the Roots of Anti-Semitism in the Gospel Story of the Death of Jesus* (San Francisco: HarperCollins, 1995), p. 5.

when discussing early Christianity. Of the thirteen books that bear this apostle's name, even critics accept at least six as authentic: Romans, 1-2 Corinthians, Galatians, Philippians and 1 Thessalonians. Even skeptical scholars agree that these books are written by Paul and date in the decade between A.D. 50 and 60.[6]

Critical scholars prefer these "authentic" Pauline epistles because we can be certain of the author and dates of these writings. While Paul mentions fewer details of Jesus' earlier life in these works, he provides important specifics regarding the gospel message of Jesus Christ's death and resurrection appearances, and from a much earlier time than the Gospels.

The key text in this regard is certainly 1 Corinthians 15:3-8. In the previous two verses, Paul refers to his earlier preaching to the Corinthians. This epistle was written in approximately A.D. 54-55, whereas Paul's original preaching in the city would have been dated at least a couple of years earlier, perhaps as early as 50, as Koester acknowledges.[7] So Paul wrote concerning Jesus' death and resurrection appearances in this crucial text just twenty-five years after the crucifixion of Jesus, while having preached the same message to the Corinthian church several years earlier, or about twenty years after the events.

This last date is only half the time span from Jesus to the Gospel of Mark, and less than one-third the distance between Jesus and the Gospel of John. But Paul's account also provides other crucial reasons to prefer it above the Gospels. In a straightforward remark that is exceptionally well-recognized by critical scholars, Paul explains that he received the material in 1 Corinthians 15:3-7 from another source: "For what I received I passed on to you as of first importance" (1 Cor 15:3). This comment offers an entirely different perspective on the reliability of Paul's information. Could this possibly provide an insight into the nature of the earliest apostolic teaching between the years of A.D. 30 and 50, prior to the writing of the first New Testament book? Even the book of Acts is regularly dated between A.D. 65 and 85, or from thirty-five

---

[6]For examples, Bart D. Ehrman, *The New Testament: A Historical Introduction to the Early Christian Writings,* 2nd ed. (New York: Oxford University, 2000), pp. 43-44; Helmut Koester, *Introduction to the New Testament,* vol. 2, *History and Literature of Early Christianity* (Philadelphia: Fortress, 1982), pp. 103-4.

[7]Koester, *History and Literature,* pp. 103-4.

to fifty-five years after the crucifixion.[8] Both this date and the writings of the Gospels come from a very respectable time frame for ancient reports. But what if we had material from even prior to the early Pauline epistles?

Besides 1 Corinthians 15:3, several other New Testament texts also mention the passing on of early tradition.[9] This follows the well-known Jewish practice of insuring doctrinal and pastoral continuity by reproducing faithful teaching. Even without the presence of explicit statements that a tradition is being passed on, critical scholars are widely in agreement with regard to a number of these ancient texts. The presence of such a tradition is often indicated by the sentence structure, diction, textual parallelism, stylized wording and so on. Sometimes these texts are apparent because of the syntax breaks between the citation and the larger text. On still other occasions, texts contain brief theological snippets that are best explained as existing in this form for purposes of memorization. Another example is what is generally agreed to be a Christological hymn in Philippians 2:6-11.

One benefit of these early traditions (also called "creeds" or "confessions") is that they reproduce teachings that are earlier than the book or writing in which they appear. Therefore, if this material is known to be reliable, especially if it appears to be apostolic in nature, then it most likely exhibits trustworthy comments that are also early, sometimes exceptionally so.[10]

In order to see if the material in 1 Corinthians 15:3-7 is even earlier and more authoritative, we must determine the most likely scenario for Paul's reception of this tradition. The apostle claims in a forthright manner that he passed this information on just as he received it. Do we have any information regarding when Paul may have received this account? Who most likely gave it to him? Since it concerns the death and resurrection appearances of Jesus, the very center of early Christianity, it would be crucially important if we were to have some indication of Paul's source.

---

[8]John Drane, *Introducing the New Testament* (San Francisco: Harper & Row, 1986), pp. 236-38.
[9]See 1 Corinthians 11:2, 23; 2 Thessalonians 3:6; 1 Timothy 1:15; 3:1; 4:9; 2 Timothy 2:2, 11; Titus 1:9.
[10]For the classic treatment of this subject, see Oscar Cullmann, *The Earliest Christian Confessions*, trans. J. K. S. Reid (London: Lutterworth, 1949); cf. Joachim Jeremias, *The Eucharistic Words of Jesus* (London: SCM Press, 1966).

A HALF DECADE AFTER THE CROSS: PAUL'S FIRST TRIP
TO JERUSALEM

Strangely enough, the next stage in the process was discovered not by
biblical conservatives, but by critical scholars. Further, there is near
unanimity among those who address these issues. Paul asserts more
than once that he received traditions from others and passed them on to
his hearers. Does he provide any indications of where and when he obtained these data?

From everything we know, Paul was a careful scholar. He had been
trained well in the Old Testament tradition, referring to himself as an
individual who was exceptionally zealous for the law, as a Pharisee and
"a Hebrew of Hebrews" (Phil 3:4-6). He had advanced beyond others of
his own age and distinguished himself by supporting without question
the tradition of Judaism. As such, he violently persecuted early Christians (Gal 1:13-14). Then he testified that he met the risen Jesus,
accounting for the total transformation of his life (1 Cor 9:1; 15:8-10;
Gal 1:15-16).

Paul attests that immediately after his conversion, he did not consult
with anyone. Since he had seen the risen Jesus, and had been instructed
by him to preach to the Gentiles, he did not think it was necessary to
confirm this with others. Jesus' authority was greater than that of anyone
else. However, three years later he did visit Jerusalem and spent fifteen
days with Peter and James the brother of Jesus (Gal 1:15-18).

What happened during this incredible meeting involving these three
great Christian leaders? It must have been eventful, to say the least. In
the now famous words of Cambridge University New Testament scholar
C. H. Dodd, "We may presume that they did not spend all the time talking about the weather."[11]

So what did they discuss? It might be said that the first rule of literary
criticism is to interpret a text in its context. When we apply that rule
here, the context both immediately before and after Paul's statement
concerns the nature of the gospel message. Therefore, critical scholars
conclude that clearly this subject formed the center of this historic meeting. Besides, what else would Paul and the other two apostles more likely
discuss other than the very center of their faith? For these two reasons,

---

[11]C. H. Dodd, *The Apostolic Preaching and Its Developments* (Grand Rapids: Baker, 1980),
p. 16.

it is widely concluded that the gospel content constituted the focus of their conversation.

Further, the majority of critical scholars who answer the question think that Paul received the early tradition recorded in 1 Corinthians 15:3-7 during this visit to Jerusalem, and that he received it from Peter and James, who, incidentally, are the only other individuals besides Paul whose names appear in the list of Jesus' resurrection appearances. Based on the usual date for Paul's conversion of between one and three years after Jesus' crucifixion, Paul's reception of this material in Jerusalem would be dated three years later, or from approximately A.D. 34 to 36. On many occasions, I have documented this critical scholarly conclusion as to when and from whom Paul received this material.[12] Richard Bauckham has also recently noted the scholarly consensus on this point.[13]

Besides the subject matter itself and the three individual names in the list of appearances, another hint regarding this process is found in Galatians 1:18. When speaking of his time with Peter and James, Paul used the Greek term *historēsai* (taken from the term *histōr*), which is often defined as gaining knowledge by personal inquiry or investigation.[14] So Paul apparently meant for the reader to understand that he was using this quality time with the other two apostles in order to probe their understanding of the gospel message. But even without him telling us this, it makes the most sense of his taking a trip to Jerusalem to speak with the major apostles there. Moreover, the topic was very important to Paul, for he paused afterward to tell his reader: "I assure you before God that what I am writing you is no lie" (Gal 1:20).

It is absolutely crucial that we keep in mind here the vital difference between the formal tradition that Paul passed along to others, which as far as we know was written down for the first time in 1 Corinthians 15:3-7, and the particular *content* that this tradition summarizes. Virtually nothing depends on Paul having received this exact tradition during

---

[12]For examples, see Habermas, *Historical Jesus*, esp. pp. 152-57; Gary R. Habermas, "The Resurrection Appearances of Jesus," in *In Defense of Miracles: A Comprehensive Case for God's Action in History,* ed. Douglas Geivett and Gary R. Habermas (Downers Grove, Ill.: InterVarsity Press, 1997), esp. pp. 263-70.

[13]Bauckham, *Jesus and the Eyewitnesses,* pp. 265-66.

[14]See William Farmer, "Peter and Paul, and the Tradition Concerning 'The Lord's Supper' in 1 Corinthians 11:23-25," *Criswell Theological Review* 2 (1987): 122-30.

precisely this meeting in Jerusalem, even though that is when critical scholars tend to place it. By far the more important matter concerns Paul's knowledge of the gospel content as preached by Peter and James the brother of Jesus, which comprises the creed. Thus, all we really need to know here is that Paul investigated the gospel particulars with them, and this seems well-assured.

In fact, critical scholars are so sure about this last conclusion that Dodd concluded, "The date, therefore, at which Paul received the fundamentals of the Gospel cannot well be later than some seven years after the death of Jesus Christ. It may be earlier." Therefore, "Paul's preaching represents a special stream of Christian tradition which was derived from the main stream at a point very near to its source." And lest some say that Paul confused this message, Dodd concludes, "Anyone who should maintain that the primitive Christian Gospel was fundamentally different from that which we have found in Paul must bear the burden of proof."[15]

But we do not have to take Dodd's word for this; dozens of contemporary critical scholars, including skeptics, espouse the general scenario outlined here.[16] Therefore, the majority of critical scholars who address the issue think that Paul received his traditional material on the death and resurrection of Jesus from Peter and James the brother of Jesus while he was in Jerusalem, approximately a half dozen years after the crucifixion of Jesus. Further, even if one questions the precise time and place of Paul's actual reception of this creedal material, it is exceptionally difficult to avoid the conclusion that these three apostles at least ascertained the nature of the gospel content at that time.

LESS THAN TWO DECADES AFTER THE CROSS: PAUL'S LATER TRIP TO JERUSALEM

Here we must digress a bit in our timeline, before we keep moving backward toward Jesus' death. But this occasion was better left until after the previous discussion. Immediately after describing his initial trip to Jerusalem, Paul relates that he visited the city again, fourteen years later (Gal 2:1). During what year did this second meeting occur? Paul dates it from his previous discussion in Galatians 1, causing scholars to wonder whether Paul meant the time of his conversion, or from his first trip to

---

[15]Dodd, *Apostolic Preaching*, p. 16.
[16]For these lists, see Habermas, *Risen Jesus and Future Hope*, esp. nn. 75-102.

Jerusalem. Also, scholarly opinion varies as to whether the meeting in Galatians 2:1-10 is the same as the account in Acts 15:1-31. Regardless, the difference is slight. Koester prefers a date of A.D. 48.[17]

Once again, Paul's topic is clearly that of the gospel. In one of the most incredible comments in the New Testament, Paul attested that he specifically journeyed to Jerusalem to visit the leading apostles in order to set before them the gospel message that he had been preaching "for fear that I was running or had run my race in vain" (Gal 2:1-2). What an incredible admission! Here we have the "apostle to the Gentiles" acknowledging that he submitted himself to the apostolic authorities in Jerusalem in order to ascertain if the gospel message he was preaching was on target. Had he been mistaken, there could have been dire circumstances for the Gentile members of the early church; hence Paul's hesitation.

Besides Peter and James the brother of Jesus, the apostle John was also present (Gal 2:9). Along with Paul, it is difficult to miss the stellar composition of this group. One could hardly imagine a single authority in the early church who was more influential than these four. We are told that Paul's companions Barnabas and Titus were also present (Gal 2:1). It is to this group that Paul presented his gospel message, for their inspection. The verdict was that the other three apostolic leaders "added nothing to my message" (Gal 2:6). Further, they extended fellowship to Paul and Barnabas, recognizing their mission to the Gentiles (Gal 2:9). The other apostles did exhort them to also take care of the poor, which Paul states he was eager to do anyway (Gal 2:10).[18]

Paul could not have hoped for a better verdict! We assume that he, Peter and James were all on the same page during Paul's first visit to Jerusalem. But here he specifically asked for a judgment regarding the central message that he preached to the Gentiles and found that there was no conflict between his gospel teaching and that of the other apostles. Especially when we consider that these were the most influential leaders in the early church, the value of such a positive verdict could hardly be overemphasized. They were all united regarding the most sacred proclamation in early Christianity.

---

[17]Koester, *History and Literature*, p. 103.
[18]See Paul's efforts to take up offerings on behalf of poor believers (1 Cor 16:1-4; 2 Cor 8:1-15).

Again we are reminded of Dodd's statement that Paul and the other early apostles all agreed when it came to the gospel message.[19] Paul made it clear that early gospel preaching was concerned with the person of Christ, his death, burial, resurrection and appearances (1 Cor 15:3-4). Paul is clear about this in other places as well, where he also quotes other very early creedal traditions (such as Rom 1:3-4; 10:9). Similarly, the book of Acts also defines the early apostolic preaching of the gospel as referring to the deity, death and resurrection of Jesus.[20] Many critical scholars also consider a number of these texts in Acts to be other early traditions that predate the book itself. Dodd was one of the leading specialists here, and he found the same gospel specifics in these Acts texts as in the writings of Paul.[21]

After Paul cites the early creedal text in 1 Corinthians 15:3-7, he mentions the other apostles and affirms that they were preaching the same message of Jesus' resurrection appearances that he was (1 Cor 15:11; cf. 15:12-15). So his readers could get the same information from either him or them—they were in agreement. This is the reverse of Galatians 2:1-10. There, the three chief apostles affirmed Paul's gospel message. In Corinthians, Paul asserts that they were all teaching the same central message of the resurrected Christ that he preached.[22]

For ancient texts, perhaps never do we see this sort of cross-checking by the major authorities, all at such an early date. Howard Clark Kee amazingly asserts that this material is so strong that "it can be critically examined and compared with other testimony from eyewitnesses of Jesus, just as one would evaluate evidence in a modern court or academic setting."[23] We conclude that Paul, Peter, John and James the brother of Jesus were the right people, at the right place, at the right time, all proclaiming the same resurrection message!

---

[19]Dodd, *Apostolic Preaching*, p. 16.

[20]For a number of these passages, see Acts 1:21-22; 2:22-36; 3:13-16; 4:8-10; 5:29-32; 10:39-43; 13:28-31; 17:1-3, 30-31.

[21]Dodd, *Apostolic Preaching*, pp. 17-31, esp. pp. 19, 24, 26, 31.

[22]For this agreement between Paul and the other apostles on the nature of the gospel message, see Martin Hengel, *The Atonement* (Philadelphia: Fortress, 1981), pp. 38, 69; John Meier, *A Marginal Jew: Rethinking the Historical Jesus* (New York: Doubleday, 1987), p. 118; Hans Dieter Betz, *Galatians: A Commentary on Paul's Letter to the Churches in Galatia* (Philadelphia: Fortress Press, 1979), p. 76; Ben Meyer, "Resurrection as Humanly Intelligible Destiny," *Ex Auditu* 9 (1993): 15; Bauckham, *Jesus and the Eyewitnesses*, p. 266.

[23]Howard Clark Kee, *What Can We Know About Jesus?* (Cambridge: Cambridge University Press, 1990), pp. 1-2.

IMMEDIATELY AFTER THE CROSS: BACK TO THE DATE OF THE ACTUAL EVENTS

After our brief backtracking in order to place Paul's later trip to Jerusalem in its proper perspective, we are now ready to move to the final scene on our timeline. Here we want to ask about those who had knowledge of these historical events prior to Paul's own reception of the data, including the creedal formulation. After all, Paul's obtaining the knowledge of these events before his own appearance of the risen Jesus was not an end in itself. We must backtrack to the original occurrences themselves.

Working backward before Paul, then, these accounts had already been cast into succinct oral summaries for use in teaching, especially because the majority of hearers were apparently illiterate. Prior to that are the original accounts of these occurrences by those who actually participated in them. As noted, we know that the entire process took place very quickly, based on the precise data we have regarding the actual events, the teaching about them and the formulation into a succinct creedal statement. Then it was recorded just a relatively short time later. Critical scholars readily concede that the early Christians believed that certain events had taken place with regard to the risen Jesus.

Therefore, prior to Paul's trip to Jerusalem and his discussion with Peter and James regarding the gospel data (which was perhaps also the time when he received the original creedal tradition in 1 Cor 15), Paul was obviously not the first one to have heard their report about the appearances. At least the other two apostles, presumably along with others, had to know the information before Paul did. Now we are getting close to the beginning, since both Peter and James are listed among those who saw the risen Jesus, as is especially clear in 1 Corinthians 15:4, 7. The only more foundational data are the actual events themselves.

How should we date each of these strands? We have seen that Paul's first trip to Jerusalem is usually placed at A.D. 34 to 36, and Paul's conversion at three years before that, or about A.D. 31 to 33. Since Paul believed that he saw an appearance of the recently dead and now risen Jesus, the crucifixion would have occurred earlier still, but not very long beforehand. If any of the early confessions embedded in the Acts sermons[24] also represent reliable reconstructions of the earliest teaching, as granted by most critical scholars, then we have additional reasons for

---

[24]Such as those listed in note 20 above.

holding that the resurrection was preached from the very beginning, immediately after Jesus' death.

Do critical scholars agree on the date of this pre-Pauline creed? Even radical scholars like Gerd Lüdemann think that "the elements in the tradition are to be dated to the first two years after the crucifixion . . . not later than three years after the death of Jesus."[25] Similarly, Michael Goulder contends that Paul's testimony about the resurrection appearances "goes back at least to what Paul was taught when he was converted, a couple of years after the crucifixion."[26]

An increasing number of exceptionally influential scholars have very recently concluded that at least the teaching of the resurrection, and perhaps even the specific formulation of the pre-Pauline creedal tradition in 1 Corinthians 15:3-7, dates to A.D. 30! In other words, there never was a time when the message of Jesus' resurrection was not an integral part of the earliest apostolic proclamation.[27] No less a scholar than James D. G. Dunn even states regarding this crucial text: "This tradition, we can be entirely confident, was *formulated as tradition within months of Jesus' death.*"[28]

Therefore, Paul received creedal material in Jerusalem just five years or so after Jesus' crucifixion that was actually formulated earlier, perhaps dating even all the way back to very shortly after the death of Jesus. But regardless of where we date this creedal tradition itself, the underlying *content* of the gospel message regarding the death and resurrection of Jesus Christ goes back to the very beginning. In other words, it was the central message of the early apostolic church from its inception.

A COMMON OBJECTION

At present, perhaps the most frequently heard charge, especially from the ranks of the New Atheist devotees, is that Christianity copied its message from other earlier ancient religions. For instance, Christopher

[25]Gerd Lüdemann, *The Resurrection of Jesus*, trans. John Bowden (Minneapolis: Fortress, 1994), p. 38.

[26]Michael Goulder, "The Baseless Fabric of a Vision," in *Resurrection Reconsidered*, ed. Gavin D'Costa (Oxford: Oneworld, 1996), p. 48.

[27]Larry W. Hurtado, *How on Earth Did Jesus Become a God? Historical Questions About Earliest Devotion to Jesus* (Grand Rapids: Eerdmans, 2005), esp. p. 4; N. T. Wright, *The Resurrection of the Son of God* (Minneapolis: Fortress, 2003), p. 319; cf. Bauckham, *Jesus and the Eyewitnesses*, pp. 264-68, 307-8.

[28]Dunn, *Jesus Remembered*, p. 825 (emphasis in the original).

Hitchens wonders about some of the supernatural events that reportedly surrounded Jesus' birth, when similar things were said to have happened to other religious personages like Buddha and Krishna.[29] These similarities are also mentioned or hinted at regularly with regard to the resurrection of Jesus.[30]

The real oddity about this charge is the very real disconnect between *popular* skeptical critiques and treatments by equally skeptical *specialists* in the relevant fields. Seemingly a large percentage of the former adopt these complaints about parallel religions as if they are simply accepted by everyone except Christians, who apparently have their heads stuck in the sand. However, while the scholarly skeptics may occasionally note this or that minor similarity, they very rarely charge that early Christianity derived its resurrection teachings from prior religions. Why this huge disconnect between skeptical popularists and their scholarly counterparts? Could it be that the historical data simply do not support such commonly repeated charges?

Even if we do not stray very far from the material in this essay alone, this popular thesis is substantially challenged at every juncture. First, the fashionable charge that stories of crucified and risen saviors were rampant in the ancient world prior to Christianity has been dismissed by critical scholars, especially during the last few decades. For starters, the pagan stories were generally of persons who never lived and involved religious messages that actually contradicted major Christian teachings, and these ancient accounts had very little influence in ancient Palestine. Much more significantly, the central historical points of contact are simply missing: The reports of Buddha and Krishna come hundreds of years afterward. No other major religious founders in ancient times were ever crucified. Further, it cannot be demonstrated that there is even a single pagan resurrection account prior to Jesus, whether mythological or historical.[31] This is certainly significant in any attempt to press these so-called parallels.

---

[29]Christopher Hitchens, *God Is Not Great: How Religion Poisons Everything* (New York: Hachette, 2007), pp. 22-23.

[30]Richard Dawkins, *The God Delusion* (Boston: Houghton Mifflin, 2006), pp. 119-20.

[31]For a classical treatment on the dating of the pagan stories, see Günther Wagner, *Das religionsgeschichtliche Problem von Römer 6, 1-11* (Zürich: Zwingli Verlag, 1962), especially Wagner's excellent summary in part 3, sects. A-B. Even Helmut Koester includes similar comments, particularly in *Introduction to the New Testament*, vol. 1 (Philadelphia: Fortress, 1982), pp. 190, 193.

Second, and in utter contrast, we have outlined the scholarly unanimity regarding especially 1 Corinthians 15:3-7, along with early sermon summaries in Acts, that date the incredibly early proclamation of the resurrection message to about A.D. 30. It shows that this message was linked directly to the life and ministry of Jesus Christ, with no sign of legendary origin.

Third and even more crucially, with respect to Jesus' resurrection skeptical scholars are persuaded almost unanimously that the appearance reports came *from the eyewitnesses themselves*, based on their own original experiences, not ancient myths and legends. In other words, the resurrection belief was derived from real experiences rather than amorphous rumors from elsewhere.

Further, this scenario was confirmed during Paul's visits to Jerusalem to discuss the nature of the gospel message with the key apostles (Gal 1:18-20; 2:1-10). Paul knew what the other apostles were teaching regarding the resurrection appearances of Jesus and commended their message (1 Cor 15:11-15). This tight framework indicates that the original proclamation was based from start to finish on actual historical occurrences.

Many additional problems beset the legendary thesis as well. These experiences transformed the disciples so that they were willing to die specifically for their gospel teaching. This indicates that they utterly believed the truth of this resurrection message. Paul's own appearance and conversion from church persecutor are left unexplained by ancient myths, as is Jesus' brother James' conversion from skepticism to belief in the risen Christ (although we have not discussed this here). Lastly, the empty tomb is heavily evidenced[32] but is unexplained by this alternative thesis.

Although additional critiques could be mentioned,[33] this indicates why the vast majority of scholars reject legends as the origin of the early resurrection proclamations, which arose from actual, eyewitness experiences. As Wolfhart Pannenberg asserts: "Under such circumstances it is an idle venture to make parallels in the history of religions responsible for the *emergence* of the primitive Christian message about Jesus' resurrection."[34]

---

[32]For several major reasons, see Habermas, *Risen Jesus and Future Hope*, pp. 23-24.

[33]For a detailed discussion and critique, see Gary R. Habermas, *The Resurrection of Jesus: A Rational Inquiry* (Ann Arbor, Mich.: University Microfilms, 1976), pp. 146-71.

[34]Wolfhart Pannenberg, *Jesus: God and Man*, trans. Lewis Wilkins and Duane Priebe (Phila-

CONCLUSION: COMPLETING THE ARGUMENT

Contemporary critical scholars agree that, besides Paul's own appearance, he obtained his early message of the gospel from others before him. He probably received at least the content of the tradition in 1 Corinthians 15:3-7 from Peter and James when he visited Jerusalem in the very first years after Jesus died on the cross. For these apostles, in turn, the resurrection appearances were of course earlier still.

It is this argument, more than any other, that has convinced the bulk of critical scholars today that Jesus' resurrection was proclaimed in the earliest church. Likewise, scholars think that the cause of this early message was the experiences of Jesus' earliest disciples, who were utterly convinced that they had seen appearances of their risen Lord.[35] This message did not occur at some later date, and was definitely not concocted or copied from the teachings of others. As Bauckham emphasizes clearly, "There can be no doubt that . . . Paul is citing the *eyewitness testimony* of those who were recipients of resurrection appearances."[36]

This explains the incredible value of Paul's report in 1 Corinthians 15:3-7. It definitely addresses the two most crucial historiographical issues by linking the reports of the *original eyewitnesses* which were demonstrably taken from the *very earliest period*. This argument has stunned a generation of critical scholars, causing them to realize that Jesus' resurrection appearances, unlike later parallels which may have borrowed from Christianity, are firmly grounded in the historical tradition.

FOR FURTHER READING

Bauckham, Richard. *Jesus and the Eyewitnesses: The Gospels as Eyewitness Testimony.* Grand Rapids: Eerdmans, 2006.

Craig, William Lane. *The Son Rises: Historical Evidence for the Resurrection of Jesus.* Chicago: Moody Press, 1981.

Cullmann, Oscar. *The Earliest Christian Confessions,* trans. J. K. S. Reid. London: Lutterworth, 1949.

Dodd, C. H. *The Apostolic Preaching and Its Developments.* Grand Rapids: Baker, 1980.

---

delphia: Westminster Press, 1977), p. 91 (emphasis in the original).

[35]For details, see Gary R. Habermas, "Experiences of the Risen Jesus: The Foundational Historical Issue in the Early Proclamation of the Resurrection," *Dialog: A Journal of Theology* 45 (2006): 288-97.

[36]Bauckham, *Jesus and the Eyewitnesses,* p. 308 (emphasis in the original).

Habermas, Gary R. *The Historical Jesus: Ancient Evidence for the Life of Christ.* Joplin, Mo.: College Press, 1996.

———. *The Risen Jesus and Future Hope.* Lanham, Md.: Rowman & Littlefield, 2003.

Wright, N. T. *The Resurrection of the Son of God.* Minneapolis: Fortress, 2003.

14

Why Faith in Jesus Matters

MARK MITTELBERG

Everybody has faith.

It's true! Every person you know—including the one in the mirror —trusts something she believes in but which she can't prove or know in an absolute sense.

The serious Buddhist lives as if the eightfold path of Buddhism will lead to spiritual enlightenment. He can't prove that the tenets of his faith are sound, but he carries on in the hope that these are the right ideas that will lead to the best possible outcome.

The dedicated Hindu banks on the belief that reincarnation is real, and that through constant effort and faithful devotion, over many lifetimes, her bad karma can be worked off. She hopes this process leads to the point where she will finally be purified and find liberation from this illusory world of "maya." She can't prove it will happen, but she seeks to live as if it is true.

Devout Muslims try to live by the five pillars of Islam, believing that Allah is God, Muhammad is his prophet and the Qur'an is God's holy book. They can't know for certain that these things are true—there isn't a way to personally verify them—but they live by faith that they are right.

Committed Christians, myself included, live in the trust that God exists and Jesus is who he claimed to be—the unique Son of God. We believe that his death on the cross was allowed by God to atone for our sins, Jesus paying the spiritual death penalty in our place. We're convinced we have good reasons and evidence to conclude that these things are correct, and we stake our future on that trust. But it's *trust* just the same; we don't have absolute proof.

What about the casual Buddhist, Hindu, Muslim or Christian who merely pays lip service to his particular faith system but largely ignores it in daily life? There are millions of these people too—and they're living by faith that faith issues aren't very important to live by. Even the person who casually says, "Oh, I never worry about things like that!" lives by faith that people need not concern themselves about these matters.

This might surprise you, but even atheists live by faith—including the so-called New Atheists. They operate in the belief that there is no Creator, no higher moral law to which they are accountable, no divine judgment and no afterlife. They can't prove any of these things. They don't *know* for a fact that there is no God, spiritual standard, day of reckoning or existence after death. In fact, most people in the world believe that denying these things goes against the evidence as well as human experience and therefore requires *more* faith.

I'll say it again: *everybody* has faith—*in something*. So why am I arguing that we should put our faith in Jesus, and why am I so convinced that this is really important?

Great questions. Let's start with the first one: *Why trust in Jesus?*

WHY TRUST IN JESUS?

To begin, faith of any kind is only as good as what it is focused on. Trusting in a bridge over a canyon is beneficial only if the bridge being crossed is, in fact, trustworthy. Belief in a medication is helpful only if that medication is appropriate for the ailment and therefore beliefworthy. (Some medications help, some don't do anything, and some can cause serious harm.) And faith in a philosophy or religious point of view is worthwhile only if that viewpoint is actually true and helpful, and thus "faithworthy." So what makes Jesus more faithworthy than the other options?

Jesus had credentials like no other leader, teacher, philosopher or prophet, and these credentials give us solid reasons to trust in him. Let me put it in the terms of this book: *God is great, God is good—and so is Jesus.*

I don't know if you've noticed the parallels, but in spite of his human nature, Jesus and his early followers gave strong evidence that he also exhibited the characteristics of God. Let's look at a few examples, beginning with the area of *greatness*.[1]

Part of God's greatness is his infinite power—what theologians call *omnipotence*. Yet we see through the historical record that in the New Testament Jesus had the ability to take control of nature, calming fierce storms with simply a word. He was able to do the miraculous, from changing water into wine to walking on water itself. He healed the sick, gave sight to the blind and sometimes even raised the dead to life. His ultimate show of power was when he came back from the grave himself on the third day after his brutal death by crucifixion.

Another aspect of God's greatness is his infinite knowledge, or *omniscience*. But we see in Jesus, too, the ability to know people's thoughts before they said a word—sometimes before they were even in his presence. He knew Judas would betray him, and when and where he would do it, and he predicted Peter's unlikely denial of him before it happened. He also prophesied that he would suffer and that the "temple" of his body would be destroyed, but that he would raise it up again three days later. Further, he foresaw the demolition of the Jewish temple, the city of Jerusalem and the nation of Israel. All of this was fulfilled by the Roman Emperor Titus about four decades after Jesus said it would happen.

God is also described as *eternal* and beyond time—a claim Jesus made for himself when he told his religious opponents in John 8:58, "Before Abraham was, I am." They understood the immensity of this declaration—he was claiming to have preexisted the patriarch Abraham, who had lived some two thousand years before their time. More than that, they recognized that he was applying the biblical name for God—"I Am" from Exodus 3:14—to himself. In fact, they were so incensed about his claim of divinity that they accused him of blasphemy and picked up stones to kill him.

Notice, however, that Jesus never tried to correct or change their perceptions. He didn't say: "Hold on, fellows, you've misunderstood what I

---

[1]I'll quote from the Bible to illustrate my points. I think the evidence is overwhelming that the Bible is historically reliable, giving us accurate information on the events as they actually happened. Beyond that, I believe the Bible has credentials that show it to be a supernaturally inspired book. For a summary of my thoughts on this see *Choosing Your Faith . . . in a World of Spiritual Options* (Wheaton, Ill.: Tyndale House, 2008). And for a fuller introduction to this information, read Lee Strobel's classic *The Case for Christ* (Grand Rapids: Zondervan, 1998).

was trying to communicate!" Rather, he reinforced his claims to deity when he said in John 10:30, "I and the Father are one"—and again they called it blasphemy and tried to stone him!

The writers of the New Testament, who walked and talked with Jesus (or who associated closely with those who did) and who knew for certain what he said and did, reinforced these claims. We see this throughout the Gospels, as well as in the letters to the churches. For example, the belief in Jesus' eternal nature was underscored when the writer of Hebrews penned these classic words: "Jesus Christ is the same yesterday and today and forever" (Heb 13:8). And the apostle Paul taught Jesus' deity clearly in many of his writings, including Colossians 1:15-16, where he declared Jesus "the image of the invisible God, the firstborn over all creation. For by him all things were created: things in heaven and on earth, visible and invisible, whether thrones or powers or rulers or authorities; all things were created by him and for him."

In fact, God's power is demonstrated best in his act of *creating* the heavens and the earth (Gen 1:1), and yet Jesus' disciple John, in harmony with what Paul said in Colossians, states clearly in his Gospel that Jesus "was with God in the beginning. Through him all things were made; without him nothing was made that has been made" (Jn 1:2-3). In other words, Jesus is eternal, and prior to his incarnation as a man he participated with the Father as a cocreator of the universe. (It's from passages like this that we begin to understand the biblical doctrine of the Trinity—that there is one God who exists eternally in three persons: Father, Son and Holy Spirit.) The writer of Hebrews echoed these thoughts when he declared that God "has spoken to us by his Son, whom he appointed heir of all things, and through whom he made the universe" (Heb 1:2).

Granted, we don't see these characteristics of omnipotence, omniscience, eternality or divine creativity expressed in their fullest measure in Jesus. According to Philippians 2, that's because Jesus, in the act of taking on human nature, temporarily let go of the equal position he had with the Father (Phil 2:6-7), and humbled himself by taking the form of a servant (Phil 2:7-8). In so doing he was not stripped of his divine attributes, but he willingly curtailed his expression of them, at least for a season. Thus we see him operating without fully accessing the knowledge and power that were inherently his, in order to complete his earthly mission. But even in this self-limited situation, we still see clear glimpses of his divine attributes peeking through—qualities and abilities not seen in any other religious leader before or since then.

More than just sharing the Father's greatness, Jesus also exhibited divine *goodness* as well. So many religious leaders over the ages have talked in ways that made themselves look good, but then utterly failed to live up to their own rhetoric. The closer we look, the less impressive they appear. The moral microscope is not kind; even exceptional people manifest weakness and failure under close scrutiny.

That's why it's so amazing that nobody ever found fault with Jesus—for anything. That included his closest companions, who would have easily picked out any character flaws, moral or ethical inconsistencies, or old-fashioned human error and frailty. But nothing was reported in terms of moral defects or weakness—not even from Jesus' own mother, who certainly would have known!

This is important not because a leader needs to be perfect in order to be followed but because Jesus repeatedly claimed to be the Son of God, meaning he uniquely shared the Father's divine nature. If that claim was true, it would certainly require that he be sinless and without flaw.

Throughout the Gospels we see Jesus' enemies trying to catch him doing something—*anything*—wrong. But even they were left quibbling over peripheral details, like whether Jesus kept certain obscure rules to the letter of the law. In the end, these opponents had to hire false witnesses to invent stories in order to try to accuse Jesus. Knowing as they did that none of it was true, you can imagine their frustration when at one point Jesus threw the reality of his sinless life back at them: "Can any of you prove me guilty of sin?" (Jn 8:46).

When it was all said and done, the only accusation that they could level against Jesus was the one mentioned earlier: blasphemy. And he would have been guilty as charged—had he not so clearly demonstrated through his moral goodness, supernatural power, divine insights and clear teachings that we was, in fact, the Son of God.

Jesus was also consistently loving, patient and kind to the people he encountered. He could be direct and challenging, but he always mixed in grace too. He was like the heavenly Father in every way, and he presented himself as one who could be followed with confidence. There never has been, nor will there ever be, another person like Jesus. He looks good from any distance. In fact, the closer you observe him, the more impressive he becomes.

We all have faith in something, so why not put your faith in the one who won't disappoint, the one who demonstrated that he could be trusted? As we put it earlier, he is faithworthy.

We've responded to the first question, Why trust in Jesus? Now let's turn to the second question, *Why is faith in Jesus important?*

WHY IS FAITH IN JESUS IMPORTANT?

Going back to the broader themes of this book, let me state part of the answer like this: *God is great, God is good—but we're neither.* It seems that to the degree Jesus is similar to God, we are dissimilar.

Consider again God's greatness. He is, as we have seen, incredibly powerful. We are by comparison puny. Think of those who are great by our standards: those with power, or those who have fame or money. Doesn't wisdom (along with time) show us that these things are fleeting? Kings and rulers once considered great often fall to the very ones they had led. Politicians seen as rising stars can soon become the scorn of their own party—even of their entire nation. And those who abuse power are usually the ones whose defeat is the most dramatic. There's even a popular phrase to describe this: the higher they climb, the harder they fall.

Fame? Pop stars who were the hottest tickets ten or twenty years ago are often forgotten or, worse yet, demeaned and ridiculed. Many leaders in entertainment, media, television and film look back and realize they were merely enjoying fifteen minutes of fame. Even those who get years of fame come to realize how empty it is; suicide seems to be at least as prevalent among celebrities as it is among ordinary folks. Notoriety doesn't fix personal problems; it magnifies them. Thus fame often ends in infamy.

And wealth? It does not bring lasting joy, power or influence. It can bring a measure of happiness and satisfaction, but often the person ends up empty and alone. And even with the benefits it can offer, money can't indefinitely forestall the inevitable onset of aging, weakness and death. As the saying goes, the one who dies with the most toys . . . still dies.

God also has unlimited knowledge and wisdom—but we have more questions than answers. For all of our learning we're still trying to crack the code of how God put it all together in the first place. Fifteenth-century German astronomer Johannes Kepler is credited with saying that science is simply "thinking God's thoughts after him"—and it's apparent that even now we have a lot of catching up to do. The renowned astronomer Robert Jastrow famously wrote: "For the scientist who has lived by his faith in the power of reason, the story ends like a bad dream. He has scaled the mountains of ignorance; he is about to conquer the highest peak; as he pulls himself over the final rock, he is greeted by a band of theologians who have been sitting there for centuries."[2]

In the New Testament, Paul summed up the situation powerfully: "Where is the wise man? Where is the scholar? Where is the philosopher of this age? Has not God made foolish the wisdom of the world? . . . For the foolishness of God is wiser than man's wisdom, and the weakness of God is stronger than man's strength" (1 Cor 1:20, 25).

And there's also no point in trying to compare our longevity with God's eternality. God's words in the Old Testament book of Isaiah make the contrast clear:

> All men are like grass,
>   and all their glory is like the flowers of the field.
> The grass withers and the flowers fall,
>   because the breath of the LORD blows on them.
>   Surely the people are grass.
> The grass withers and the flowers fall,
>   but the word of our God stands forever. (Is 40:6-8)

By whatever standard we measure human greatness, it falls far short of God's incredible and infinite greatness. And need we even discuss our goodness compared to God's? The history of our race is not pretty. Our track record is littered with examples of our constantly disregarding God's commandments as well as our own consciences.

That was true in the distant past, but now things are getting better, right? With education, knowledge and modernization, we're learning and moving further toward more excellent moral behavior, aren't we? The short answer is no; education has not provided the progress we hoped for. In many ways, it has been the opposite. C. S. Lewis observed, "Education without values, as useful as it is, seems rather to make man a more clever devil." Theodore Roosevelt noted that "a man who has never gone to school may steal from a freight car; but if he has a univer-

---

[2]Robert Jastrow, *God and the Astronomers*, 2nd ed. (New York: W. W. Norton, 1992), p. 107.

sity education he may steal the whole railroad." Dinesh D'Souza, author of *What's So Great About Christianity*, explains some of what we've seen in our purportedly enlightened modern era when he reports that "in the past hundred years or so, the most powerful atheist regimes—Communist Russia, Communist China, and Nazi Germany—have wiped out people in astronomical numbers. . . . [They] have in a single century murdered more than one hundred million people."[3]

That hardly sounds like enlightenment or progress. But the problem is not just in the past, on the other side of the ocean or with some foreign regime. Local news today reveals murders, kidnappings, shootings, rapes and robberies. These things are becoming so common that most of us have a hard time paying attention to the frequent reports.

But let's be really honest. These evils aren't just "out there" in our communities. They're in our workplaces, neighborhoods, families, and ultimately in our own minds and souls. The Hebrew prophet declared: "The heart is deceitful above all things, and desperately wicked" (Jer 17:9 KJV). Jesus explained that the everyday sin of anger is really like murder; the commonplace sin of lust is actually like adultery. When we understand morality in that way, we begin to understand how pervasive the problem really is—in each of us. Even on our best days our thoughts are tainted and our motives mixed. British author G. K. Chesterton once replied to the question "What's wrong with the world?" by simply and honestly saying: *"I am."*

Contrast all of this to God's goodness—what the Scriptures refer to as his *holiness*—and it's clear that we fail to come anywhere close to his standards. In fact, the Bible says plainly: "All have sinned and fall short of the glory of God" (Rom 3:23). This is the bad news of the Christian message. As that passage explains a few verses earlier:

> There is no one righteous, not even one;
>> there is no one who understands,
>> no one who seeks God.
> All have turned away,
>> they have together become worthless;
> there is no one who does good,
>> not even one. (Rom3:10-12, quoting Ps 14:1-3; 53:1-3;
>> Eccles 7:20)

---

[3]Dinesh D'Souza, *What's So Great About Christianity* (Washington D.C.: Regnery, 2007), p. 214.

The Bible adds even more sobering information a couple of pages later, where we're warned that "the wages of sin is death" (Rom 6:23). That's the reality that ultimately makes faith in Jesus so important. It's the realization that God is good, and we're not. We fall far short of his moral standard and even rebel against it. We deserve punishment for our sins and failings, and the payment is spiritual death. This "death" means separation from God in a place of regret for all of eternity. And here's the real killer: there's nothing we can do about it. We owe a debt before God but have nothing in our moral bank account with which to pay it.

Thankfully there is also good news. He doesn't want to leave us in our helpless, hopeless condition. We can explain it like this: *God in his goodness still cares about us, and in his greatness God made a way for us— through Jesus.*

The most famous verse in the Bible, John 3:16, tells us "God so loved the world that he gave his one and only Son, that whoever believes in him shall not perish but have eternal life." God came to earth as one of us, in Jesus, not only to teach us what is right but also to die in our place. He was our substitute who came to pay for all that we had done wrong. "The wages of sin is death," Romans 6:23 states, but it goes on to say that "the *gift of God* is eternal life in Christ Jesus our Lord" (emphasis added).

Why is faith in Jesus so important? *Because we so desperately need what he offers!* In fact, Jesus himself, early in his ministry, sums up his mission in two statements: "The Son of Man came to seek and to save what was lost" (Lk 19:10)—namely, *us!* And "The Son of Man did not come to be served, but to serve, and to give his life as a ransom for many" (Mt 20:28). That "ransom" was the payment he would make on the cross, when he died to cover our moral debt and pave the way for us to receive his forgiveness, his leadership and a relationship with God as his adopted son or daughter.

Jesus also warned us that there was no other payment, and no other religious leader, book or organization that could ultimately lead us back to God. "I am the way and the truth and the life," he explained clearly. "No one comes to the Father except through me" (Jn 14:6). This can be a very unpopular message, but Jesus—*the one with divine credentials*— backed it up with his life—as well as his resurrection!

Yet it's not enough to just know all of this. You can nod your head in agreement that God is great and God is good—and so is Jesus. You can even admit that you're very unlike him, and that you fall short of his standards. This is an important first step, but biblically defined, faith entails more than a mere nodding of the head or the acknowledging of certain truths. It includes those things—we must start by understanding and agreeing with the right ideas—but then we must respond to them.

Think of it in terms of flying. It's not enough to just believe in aviation, to spend time in airports, to affirm the skills of airline pilots. No, that will not get you to Pittsburgh. You need to act on those beliefs by actually climbing on board an airplane. That's real faith, and it can get you where you want to go.

Likewise, John 1:12 says, "Yet to all who received him, to those who believed in his name, he gave the right to become children of God." Yes, we need to *believe the truth* about Jesus, but we also need to personally *receive him*. Genuine faith in Jesus entails both elements.

This book may have convinced you that God exists. Or maybe you already believed in him, but it has helped you to better understand his greatness and goodness. And perhaps this chapter has given you a stronger appreciation of the shared nature of Jesus and the Father. If so, that's wonderful. But it's not enough. It would be a tragedy if the only impact of this book was to help you become a more astute theist or a better educated theologian. Some of the most miserable people in the world are religious men and women who fill their heads with information but don't let it affect what they do or who they become. Contrasted to that, Jesus said he came so that we "may have *life*, and have it to the *full*" (Jn 10:10, emphasis added).

Saul was one of the most religiously zealous people to ever walk the planet, but his heart was full of poison as he sought to destroy God's work among the early Christians. Saul became famous for his persecution of the church, including his support of the murder of one of its first leaders, Stephen (Acts 6—8). It wasn't until Saul finally met the risen Jesus, and understood and embraced the grace of God that was paid for by Jesus' death on the cross, that Saul found real *life*. Today we know him as the apostle Paul, the man who took the message of God's grace to the ends of the earth.

As Saul, or Paul, later looked back over his life he summed it up by saying this:

> Everything else is worthless when compared with the infinite value of knowing Christ Jesus my Lord. For his sake I have discarded everything else, counting it all as garbage, so that I could gain Christ and become one with him. I no longer count on my own righteousness through obeying the law; rather, I become righteous through faith in Christ. For God's way of making us right with himself depends on faith. (Phil 3:8-9 NLT).

That's why faith in Jesus matters so much! In a sense, Paul's story is also my own story—and it can be your story, too, if you'll climb on board with Christ by responding to him in faith. I hope and pray that you will. The God who is great and the God who is good is ready and waiting for you to come home to him.

FOR FURTHER READING

Bowman, Robert, and J. Ed Komoszewski. *Putting Jesus in His Place: The Case for the Deity of Christ.* Grand Rapids: Kregel, 2007.

Evans, Craig A. *Fabricating Jesus: How Modern Scholars Distort the Gospels.* Downers Grove, Ill.: InterVarsity Press, 2006.

McDowell, Josh, and Sean McDowell. *More Than a Carpenter,* rev. ed. Wheaton, Ill.: Tyndale House, 2009.

Mittelberg, Mark. *Choosing Your Faith . . . in a World of Spiritual Options.* Wheaton, Ill.: Tyndale House, 2008.

———. *Faith Path: Helping Friends Find Their Way to Christ,* DVD and Workbook. Colorado Springs: David C. Cook, 2009.

———, ed. *Choosing Your Faith New Testament.* Wheaton, Ill.: Tyndale House, 2008.

Strobel, Lee. *The Case for Christ: A Journalist's Personal Investigation of the Evidence for Jesus.* Grand Rapids: Zondervan, 1998.

———. *The Case for Faith: A Journalist Investigates the Toughest Objections to Christianity.* Grand Rapids: Zondervan, 2000.

Postscript

My Pilgrimage from Atheism to Theism
A Discussion Between Antony Flew and Gary Habermas

Antony Flew and Gary Habermas met in February 1985 in Dallas, Texas. The occasion was a series of debates between atheists and theists, featuring many influential philosophers, scientists and other scholars.[1] A short time later, in May 1985, Flew and Habermas debated at Liberty University before a large audience. The topic that night was the resurrection of Jesus.[2] Although Flew was arguably the world's foremost philosophical atheist, he had intriguingly also earned the distinction of being one of the chief philosophical commentators on the topic of miracles.[3] Habermas specialized on the subject of Jesus' resurrection.[4] Thus, the

---

[1]"Christianity Challenges the University: An International Conference of Theists and Atheists," Dallas, Texas, February 7–10, 1985, organized by Roy Abraham Varghese.

[2]See Gary R. Habermas and Antony G. N. Flew, *Did Jesus Rise from the Dead? The Resurrection Debate,* ed. Terry L. Miethe (San Francisco: Harper & Row, 1987; Eugene, Ore.: Wipf and Stock, 2003).

[3]Some examples by Antony Flew include "Miracles and Methodology," in *Hume's Philosophy of Belief: A Study of His First Inquiry* (London: Routledge and Kegan Paul, 1961); "The Credentials of Revelation: Miracle and History," in *God and Philosophy* (New York: Dell, 1966); "Miracles," in *Encyclopedia of Philosophy,* ed. Paul Edwards (New York: Macmillan, 1967); "The Impossibility of the Miraculous," in *Hume's Philosophy of Religion* (Winston-Salem, N.C.: Wake Forest University Press, 1985); introduction to *Of Miracles* by David Hume (La Salle, Ill.: Open Court, 1985); "Neo-Humean Arguments About the Miraculous," in *In Defence of Miracles: A Comprehensive Case for God's Action in History,* ed. R. Douglas Geivett and Gary R. Habermas (Downers Grove, Ill.: InterVarsity Press, 1997).

[4]Some examples by Gary Habermas include *The Risen Jesus and Future Hope* (Lanham, Md.: Rowman and Littlefield, 2003); *The Historical Jesus: Ancient Evidence for the Life of Christ* (Joplin, Mo.: College Press, 1996); *The Resurrection of Jesus: An Apologetic* (Grand Rapids:

ensuing dialogue on the historical evidence for the central Christian claim was a natural outgrowth of their research.

Over the next twenty years Flew and Habermas developed a friendship, writing dozens of letters, talking often and dialoguing twice more on the resurrection. In April 2000 they participated in a live debate on the Inspiration Television Network, moderated by John Ankerberg.[5] In January 2003 they again dialogued on the resurrection at California Polytechnic State University–San Luis Obispo.[6]

During a couple telephone discussions shortly after their last dialogue, Flew explained to Habermas that he was considering becoming a theist. While Flew did not change his position at that time, certain philosophical and scientific considerations were causing him to do some serious rethinking. He characterized his position as that of atheism standing in tension with several huge question marks.

A year later, in January 2004, Flew informed Habermas that he had indeed become a theist. While still rejecting the concept of special revelation, whether Christian, Jewish or Islamic, nonetheless he had concluded that theism was true. In Flew's words, he simply "had to go where the evidence leads."[7]

The following interview took place in early 2004 and was subsequently modified by both participants throughout the year. This nontechnical discussion sought to engage Flew over the course of several topics that reflect his move from atheism to theism.[8] The chief purpose was not to pursue the details of any particular issue, so we bypassed many avenues that would have presented a plethora of other intriguing questions and responses. These were often tantalizingly ignored, left to ripen for another discussion. Neither did we try to persuade each other of alternate positions. Our singular purpose was simply to explore and

---

Baker, 1980; Lanham, Md.: University Press of America, 1984); "Knowing That Jesus' Resurrection Occurred: A Response to Stephen Davis," *Faith and Philosophy* 2 (1985): 295-302; "Resurrection Claims in Non-Christian Religions," *Religious Studies* 25 (1989): 167-77; "The Late Twentieth-Century Resurgence of Naturalistic Responses to Jesus' Resurrection," *Trinity Journal* 22 (2001): 179-96. For a more popular treatment, see Habermas and Michael R. Licona, *The Case for the Resurrection of Jesus* (Grand Rapids: Kregel, 2004).
[5]Gary R. Habermas and Antony G. N. Flew, *Resurrected? An Atheist and Theist Debate,* ed. John Ankerberg (Lanham, Md.: Rowman and Littlefield, 2005).
[6]The dialogue took place as a part of the Veritas Forum and is accessible at <www.veritasforum.com/talks/httm>.
[7]Telephone conversation, September 9, 2004.
[8]Both participants also agreed to the title of the interview.

report Flew's new position, allowing him to explain various aspects of his pilgrimage. We thought that this in itself was a worthy goal. Along the way, an additional benefit emerged, as Flew reminisced about various moments from his childhood, graduate studies and career.

• • •

HABERMAS: You recently told me that you have come to believe in the existence of God. Would you comment on that?

FLEW: Well, I don't believe in the God of any revelatory system, although I am open to that. But it seems to me that the case for an Aristotelian God who has the characteristics of power and also intelligence is now much stronger than it ever was before. And it was from Aristotle that Aquinas drew the materials for producing his five ways of, hopefully, proving the existence of his God. Aquinas took them, reasonably enough, to prove—if they proved anything—the existence of the God of the Christian revelation. But Aristotle himself never produced a definition of the word *God,* which is a curious fact.

But this concept still led to the basic outline of the five ways. It seems to me that from the existence of Aristotle's God, you can't infer anything about human behavior. So what Aristotle had to say about justice (justice, of course, as conceived by the Founding Fathers of the American Republic as opposed to the "social" justice of John Rawls)[9] was very much a human idea, and he thought that this idea of justice was what ought to govern the behavior of individual human beings in their relations with others.

HABERMAS: Once you mentioned to me that your view might be called deism. Do you think that would be a fair designation?

FLEW: Yes, absolutely right. What deists such as Thomas Jefferson, who drafted the American Declaration of Independence, believed was that while reason, mainly in the form of arguments to design, assures us that there is a God, there is no room either for any supernatural revelation of that God or for any transactions between that God and individual human beings.

HABERMAS: Then would you comment on your "openness" to the no-

[9]John Rawls, *A Theory of Justice* (Cambridge, Mass.: Harvard University Press, 1971).

tion of theistic revelation?

FLEW: Yes. I am open to it, but not enthusiastic about potential revelation from God. On the positive side, for example, I am very much impressed with physicist Gerald Schroeder's comments on Genesis 1.[10] That this biblical account might be scientifically accurate raises the possibility that it is revelation.

HABERMAS: You very kindly noted that our debates and discussions had influenced your move in the direction of theism.[11] You mentioned that this initial influence contributed in part to your comment that naturalistic efforts have never succeeded in producing "a plausible conjecture as to how any of these complex molecules might have evolved from simple entities."[12] Then in your recently rewritten introduction to the forthcoming edition of your classic volume *God and Philosophy,* you say that the original version of that book is now obsolete. You mention a number of trends in theistic argumentation that you find convincing, like big bang cosmology, fine-tuning and intelligent design arguments. Which arguments for God's existence did you find most persuasive?

FLEW: I think that the most impressive arguments for God's existence are those that are supported by recent scientific discoveries. I've never been much impressed by the kalam cosmological argument, and I don't think it has gotten any stronger recently. However, I think the argument to intelligent design is enormously stronger than it was when I first met it.

HABERMAS: So you like arguments such as those that proceed from big bang cosmology and fine-tuning arguments?

FLEW: Yes.

HABERMAS: You also recently told me that you do not find the moral argument to be very persuasive. Is that right?

FLEW: That's correct. It seems to me that for a strong moral argument, you've got to have God as the justification of morality. To do this makes

---

[10]Gerald L. Schroeder, *The Science of God: The Convergence of Scientific and Biblical Wisdom* (New York: Broadway Books, 1998).

[11]Letter from Antony Flew, November 9, 2000.

[12]Antony Flew, "God and the Big Bang" (lecture, 2000), pp. 5-6; this is a lecture commemorating the 140th anniversary of the British Association meeting regarding Charles Darwin's *The Origin of the Species.*

doing the morally good a purely prudential matter rather than, as the moral philosophers of my youth used to call it, a good in itself. (Compare the classic discussion in Plato's *Euthyphro*.)

HABERMAS: So, take C. S. Lewis's argument for morality as presented in *Mere Christianity*.[13] You didn't find that to be very impressive?

FLEW: No, I didn't. Perhaps I should mention that, when I was in college, I attended fairly regularly the weekly meetings of C. S. Lewis's Socratic Club. In all my time at Oxford these meetings were chaired by Lewis. I think he was by far the most powerful of Christian apologists for the sixty or more years following his founding of that club. As late as the 1970s, I used to find that, in the United States, in at least half of the campus bookstores of the universities and liberal art colleges which I visited, there was at least one long shelf devoted to his very various published works.

HABERMAS: Although you disagreed with him, did you find him to be a very reasonable sort of fellow?

FLEW: Oh yes, very much so, an eminently reasonable man.

HABERMAS: And what do you think about the ontological argument for the existence of God?

FLEW: All my later thinking and writing about philosophy was greatly influenced by my year of postgraduate study under the supervision of Gilbert Ryle, the then professor of metaphysical philosophy in the University of Oxford, as well as the editor of *Mind*. It was the very year in which his enormously influential work on *The Concept of Mind* was first published.[14] I was told that, in the years between the wars, whenever another version of the ontological argument raised its head, Gilbert forthwith set himself to refute it.

My own initial lack of enthusiasm for the ontological argument developed into strong repulsion when I realized from reading Leibniz's *Theodicy*[15] that it was the identification of the concept of Being with the concept of Goodness (which ultimately derives from Plato's identification in

---

[13]C. S. Lewis, *Mere Christianity* (New York: Macmillan, 1980), esp. bk. 1.

[14]Gilbert Ryle, *The Concept of Mind* (London: Hutchinson, 1948).

[15]G. W. Leibniz, *Theodicy*, ed. A. Farrer, trans. E. M. Huggard (1710; London: Routledge and Kegan Paul, 1965).

the *Republic* of the Form or Idea of the Good with the Form or Idea of the Real) which enabled Leibniz in his *Theodicy* validly to conclude that a universe in which most human beings are predestined to an eternity of torture is the "best of all possible worlds."

HABERMAS: So of the major theistic arguments, such as the cosmological, teleological, moral and ontological, the only really impressive ones that you take to be decisive are the scientific forms of teleology?

FLEW: Absolutely. It seems to me that Richard Dawkins constantly overlooks the fact that Darwin himself, in the fourteenth chapter of *The Origin of Species,* pointed out that his whole argument began with a being which already possessed reproductive powers. This is the creature the evolution of which a truly comprehensive theory of evolution must give some account. Darwin himself was well aware that he had not produced such an account. It now seems to me that the findings of more than fifty years of DNA research have provided materials for a new and enormously powerful argument to design.

HABERMAS: As I recall, you also refer to this in the new introduction to your *God and Philosophy.*

FLEW: Yes, I do; or, since the book has not yet been published, I will!

HABERMAS: Since you affirm Aristotle's concept of God, do you think we can also affirm Aristotle's implications that the First Cause hence knows all things?

FLEW: I suppose we should say this. I'm not at all sure what one should think concerning some of these very fundamental issues. There does seem to be a reason for a First Cause, but I'm not at all sure how much we have to explain here. What idea of God is necessary to provide an explanation of the existence of the universe and all which is in it?

HABERMAS: If God is the First Cause, what about omniscience, or omnipotence?

FLEW: Well, the First Cause, if there was a First Cause, has very clearly produced everything that is going on. I suppose that does imply creation "in the beginning."

HABERMAS: In the same introduction, you also make a comparison between Aristotle's God and Spinoza's God. Are you implying, with some interpreters of Spinoza, that God is pantheistic?

FLEW: I'm noting there that *God and Philosophy* has become out of date and should now be seen as a historical document rather than as a direct contribution to current discussions. I'm sympathetic to Spinoza because he makes some statements which seem to me correctly to describe the human situation. But for me the most important thing about Spinoza is not what he says but what he does not say. He does not say that God has any preferences about or any intentions concerning human behavior or about the eternal destinies of human beings.

HABERMAS: What role might your love for the writings of David Hume play in a discussion about the existence of God? Do you have any new insights on Hume, given your new belief in God?

FLEW: No, not really.

HABERMAS: Do you think Hume ever answers the question of God?

FLEW: I think of him as, shall we say, an unbeliever. But it's interesting to note that he himself was perfectly willing to accept one of the conditions of his appointment, if he had been appointed to a chair of philosophy at the University of Edinburgh. That condition was, roughly speaking, to provide some sort of support and encouragement for people performing prayers and executing other acts of worship. I believe that Hume thought that the institution of religious belief could be, and in his day and place was, socially beneficial.[16]

I, too, having been brought up as a Methodist, have always been aware of this possible and in many times and places actual benefit of objective religious instruction. It is now several decades since I first tried to draw attention to the danger of relying on a modest amount of compulsory religious instruction in schools to meet the need for moral education, especially in a period of relentlessly declining religious belief. But all such warnings by individuals were, of course, ignored. So we now have in the UK a situation in which any mandatory requirements to instruct pupils in state funded schools in the teachings of the established

---

[16]Donald W. Livingston, *Philosophical Melancholy and Delirium: Hume's Pathology of Philosophy* (Chicago: University of Chicago Press, 1998), p. 150.

or any other religion are widely ignored. The only official attempt to construct a secular substitute was vitiated by the inability of the moral philosopher on the relevant government committee to recognize the fundamental difference between justice without prefix or suffix and the "social" justice of John Rawls's *Theory of Justice.*

I must sometime send you a copy of the final chapter of my latest and presumably last book, in which I offer a syllabus and a program for moral education in secular schools.[17] This is relevant and important for both the United States and the United Kingdom—to the United States because the Supreme Court has utterly misinterpreted the clause in the Constitution about not establishing a religion, misunderstanding it as imposing a ban on all official reference to religion. In the United Kingdom, any effective program of moral education has to be secular because unbelief is now very widespread.

HABERMAS: In *God and Philosophy,* and in many other places in our discussions too, it seems that your primary motivation for rejecting theistic arguments used to be the problem of evil. In terms of your new belief in God, how do you now conceptualize God's relationship to the reality of evil in the world?

FLEW: Well, absent revelation, why should we perceive anything as objectively evil? The problem of evil is a problem only for Christians. For Muslims everything which human beings perceive as evil, just as much as everything we perceive as good, has to be obediently accepted as produced by the will of Allah. I suppose that the moment when, as a schoolboy of fifteen years, it first appeared to me that the thesis that the universe was created and is sustained by a being of infinite power and goodness is flatly incompatible with the occurrence of massive undeniable and undenied evils in that universe was the first step toward my future career as a philosopher! It was, of course, very much later that I learned of the philosophical identification of goodness with existence!

HABERMAS: In your view, then, God hasn't done anything about evil.

FLEW: No, not at all, other than producing a lot of it.

HABERMAS: Given your theism, what about mind-body issues?

---

[17]Antony Flew, *Social Life and Moral Judgment* (New Brunswick, N.H.: Transaction, 2003).

FLEW: I think those who want to speak about an afterlife have got to meet the difficulty of formulating a concept of an incorporeal person. Here I have again to refer back to my year as a graduate student supervised by Gilbert Ryle, in the year in which he published *The Concept of Mind*.

At that time there was considerable comment, usually hostile, in the serious British press on what was called "Oxford Linguistic Philosophy." The objection was usually that this involved a trivialization of a very profound and important discipline.

I was by this moved to give a talk to the Philosophy Postgraduates Club under the title "Matter Which Matters." In it I argued that, so far from ignoring what Immanuel Kant described as the three great problems of philosophers—God, freedom and immortality—the linguistic approach promised substantial progress toward their solution.

I myself always intended to make contributions in all those three areas. Indeed my first philosophical publication was relevant to the third.[18] Indeed it was not very long after I got my first job as a professional philosopher that I confessed to Ryle that if ever I was asked to deliver the Gifford Lectures I would give them under the title "The Logic of Mortality."[19] They were an extensive argument to the conclusion that it is simply impossible to create a concept of an incorporeal spirit.

HABERMAS: Is such a concept necessarily required for the notion of an afterlife?

FLEW: Dr. Johnson's dictionary defines death as the soul leaving the body. If the soul is to be, as Dr. Johnson and almost if perhaps not quite everyone else in his day believed it to be, something which can sensibly be said to leave its present residence and to take up or be forced to take up residence elsewhere, then a soul must be, in the philosophical sense, a substance rather than merely a characteristic of something else.

My Gifford Lectures were published after Richard Swinburne published his, on *The Evolution of the Soul*.[20] So when mine were reprinted under the title *Merely Mortal? Can You Survive Your Own Death?*[21] I

---

[18]Antony Flew, "Selves," *Mind* (1949): 355–58.
[19]Antony Flew, *The Logic of Mortality* (Oxford: Blackwell, 1987).
[20]Richard Swinburne, *The Evolution of the Soul* (Oxford: Clarendon, 1986).
[21]Antony Flew, *Merely Mortal? Can You Survive Your Own Death?* (Amherst, N.Y.: Prometheus, 2000).

might have been expected to respond to any criticisms which Swinburne had made of my earlier publications in the same area. But the embarrassing truth is that he had taken no notice of any previous relevant writings either by me or by anyone published since World War II. There would not have been much point in searching for books or articles before that date, since Swinburne and I had been the only Gifford lecturers to treat the question of a future life for the sixty years past. Even more remarkably, Swinburne in his Gifford Lectures ignored Bishop Butler's decisive observation: "Memory may reveal but cannot constitute personal identity."[22]

HABERMAS: On several occasions, you and I have dialogued regarding the subject of near-death experiences, especially the specific sort where people have reported verifiable data from a distance away from themselves. Sometimes these reports even occur during the absence of heartbeat or brain waves.[23] After our second dialogue you wrote me a letter and said that "I find the materials about near death experiences so challenging. . . . this evidence equally certainly weakens if it does not completely refute my argument against doctrines of a future life."[24] In light of these evidential near-death cases, what do you think about the possibility of an afterlife—especially given your theism?

FLEW: An incorporeal being may be hypothesized, and hypothesized to possess a memory. But before we could rely on its memory even of its own experiences, we should need to be able to provide an account of how this hypothesized incorporeal being could be identified in the first place and then—after what lawyers call an affluxion of time—reidentified even by himself or herself as one and the same individual spiritual being. Until we have evidence that we have been and presumably—as Dr. Johnson and so many lesser men have believed—are to be identified with such incorporeal spirits, I do not see why near-death experiences should be taken as evidence for the conclusion that human beings will enjoy a future life—or more likely if either of the two great revealed religions is true—suffer eternal torment.

---

[22]Joseph Butler, *Butler's Works,* ed. W. E. Gladstone (Oxford: Clarendon, 1896), 1:387.

[23]For many cases see Gary R. Habermas and J. P. Moreland, *Beyond Death: Exploring the Evidence for Immortality* (Wheaton, Ill.: Crossway, 1998; Eugene, Ore.: Wipf & Stock, 2003), chaps. 7–9.

[24]Letter from Antony Flew, September 6, 2000.

HABERMAS: I agree that near-death experiences do not evidence the doctrines of either heaven or hell. But do you think these evidential cases increase the possibility of some sort of an afterlife—again, given your theism?

FLEW: I still hope and believe there's no possibility of an afterlife.

HABERMAS: Even though you hope there's no afterlife, what do you think of the evidence that there might be such, as perhaps indicated by these evidential near-death cases? And even if there is no clear notion of what sort of body might be implied here, do you find this evidence helpful in any way? In other words, apart from the form in which a potential afterlife might take, do you still find these to be evidence for something?

FLEW: It's puzzling to offer an interpretation of these experiences. But I presume it has got to be taken as extrasensory perceiving by the flesh-and-blood person who is the subject of the experiences in question. What it cannot be is the hypothesized incorporeal spirit which you would wish to identify with the person who nearly died but actually did not. For this concept of an incorporeal spirit cannot properly be assumed to have been given sense until and unless some means has been provided for identifying such spirits in the first place and reidentifying them as one and the same individual incorporeal spirits after the affluxion of time. Until and unless this has been done we have always to remember Bishop Butler's objection: "Memory may reveal but cannot constitute personal identity."

Perhaps I should here point out that, long before I took my first university course in philosophy, I was much interested in what in the United Kingdom, where it began, is still called psychical research, although the term *parapsychology* is now used almost everywhere else. Perhaps I ought here to confess that my first book was brashly entitled *A New Approach to Psychical Research*,[25] and my interest in this subject continued for many years thereafter.

HABERMAS: Actually you have also written to me that these near-death experiences "certainly constitute impressive evidence for the possibility of the occurrence of human consciousness independent of any

---

[25]Antony Flew, *A New Approach to Psychical Research* (London: C. A. Watts, 1953).

occurrences in the human brain."[26]

FLEW: When I came to consider what seemed to me the most impressive of these near-death cases, I asked myself what is the traditional first question to ask about "psychic" phenomena. It is, "When, where and by whom were the phenomena first reported?" Some people seem to confuse near-death experiences with after-death experiences. Where any such near-death experiences become relevant to the question of a future life is when, and only when, they appear to show "the occurrence of human consciousness independent of any occurrences in the human brain."

HABERMAS: Elsewhere, you again very kindly noted my influence on your thinking here, regarding these data being decent evidence for human consciousness independent of "electrical activity in the brain."[27] If some near-death experiences are evidenced, independently confirmed experiences during a near-death state, even in persons whose heart or brain may not be functioning, isn't that quite impressive evidence? Are near-death experiences, then, the best evidence for an afterlife?

FLEW: Oh, yes, certainly. They are basically the only evidence.

HABERMAS: What critical evaluation would you make of the three major monotheisms? Are there any particular philosophical strengths or weaknesses in Christianity, Judaism or Islam?

FLEW: If all I knew or believed about God was what I might have learned from Aristotle, then I should have assumed that everything in the universe, including human conduct, was exactly as God wanted it to be. And this is indeed the case, in so far as both Christianity and Islam are predestinarian, a fundamental teaching of both religious systems. What was true of Christianity in the Middle Ages is certainly no longer equally true after the Reformation. But Islam has neither suffered nor enjoyed either a Reformation or an Enlightenment. In the *Summa Theologiae* we may read:

[26]Letter from Antony Flew, September 6, 2000.
[27]Flew, "God and the Big Bang," p. 2. Habermas's influence on Flew's statement here is noted in Flew's letter of November 9, 2000.

As men are ordained to eternal life throughout the providence of God, it likewise is part of that providence to permit some to fall away from that end; this is called reprobation. . . . Reprobation implies not only fore-knowledge but also is something more.[28]

What and how much that something more is the *Summa contra gentiles* makes clear:

Just as God not only gave being to things when they first began, but is also—as the conserving cause of being—the cause of their being as long as they last. . . . Every operation, therefore, of anything is traced back to Him as its cause.[29]

The Angelic Doctor, however, is always the devotedly complacent apparatchik. He sees no problem about the justice of either the inflicting of infinite and everlasting penalties for finite and temporal offenses, or of their affliction upon creatures for offenses which their Creator makes them freely choose to commit. Thus, the Angelic Doctor assures us:

In order that the happiness of the saints may be more delightful to them and that they may render more copious thanks to God . . . they are allowed to see perfectly the sufferings of the damned. . . . Divine justice and their own deliverance will be the direct cause of the joy of the blessed, while the pains of the damned will cause it indirectly. . . . [T]he blessed in glory will have no pity for the damned.[30]

The statements of predestinarianism in the Qur'an are much more aggressive and unequivocal than even the strongest in the Bible. Compare the following from the Qur'an with that from Romans 9.

As for the unbelievers, alike it is to them
Whether thou hast warned them or hast not warned them
They do not believe.[31]

God has set a seal on their hearts and on the hearing
And on the eyes is a covering
And there awaits them a mighty chastisement.[32]

In the United Kingdom the doctrine of hell has for the last century or

---

[28]Thomas Aquinas *Summa Theologiae* I.q.23.a.3.
[29]Thomas Aquinas *Summa contra gentiles*. 3.67.
[30]Thomas Aquinas *Summa Theologiae* III.supp.94.a.1–3.
[31]Qur'an 2, trans. Arthur J. Arberry (Oxford: Oxford University Press, 1998).
[32]Qur'an 5.

more been progressively deemphasized, until in 1995 it was explicitly and categorically abandoned by the Church of England. It would appear that the Roman Catholic Church has not abandoned either the doctrine of hell nor predestination.

Thomas Hobbes spent a very large part of the forty years between the first publication of the King James Bible and the first publication of his own *Leviathan* engaged in biblical criticism, one very relevant finding of which I now quote:

> And it is said besides in many places [that the wicked] shall go into everlasting fire; and that the worm of conscience never dieth; and all this is comprehended in the word everlasting death, which is ordinarily interpreted everlasting life in torments. And yet I can find nowhere that any man shall live in torments everlastingly. Also, it seemeth hard to say that God who is the father of mercies; that doth in heaven and earth all that he will, that hath the hearts of all men in his disposing; that worketh in men both to do, and to will; and without whose free gift a man hath neither inclination to good, nor repentance of evil, should punish men's transgressions without any end of time, and with all the extremity of torture, that men can imagine and more.[33]

As for Islam, it is, I think, best described in a Marxian way as the uniting and justifying ideology of Arab imperialism. Between the New Testament and the Qur'an there is (as it is customary to say when making such comparisons) no comparison. Whereas markets can be found for books on reading the Bible as literature, to read the Qur'an is a penance rather than a pleasure. There is no order or development in its subject matter. All the chapters (the suras) are arranged in order of their length, with the longest at the beginning. However, since the Qur'an consists in a collection of bits and pieces of putative revelation delivered to the prophet Mohammad by the Archangel Gabriel in classical Arab on many separate but unknown occasions, it is difficult to suggest any superior principle of organization.

One point about the editing of the Qur'an is rarely made, although it would appear to be of very substantial theological significance. For every sura is prefaced by the words "In the Name of God, the Merciful, the Compassionate." Yet there are references to hell on at least 255 of the

---

[33]Thomas Hobbes, *Leviathan,* ed. J. C. A. Gaskin (Oxford: Oxford University Press, 1998), p. 416.

669 pages of Arberry's rendering of the Qur'an[34] and quite often pages
have two such references.

Whereas St. Paul, who was the chief contributor to the New Testament, knew all the three relevant languages and obviously possessed a
first-class philosophical mind, the Prophet, though gifted in the arts of
persuasion and clearly a considerable military leader, was both doubtfully literate and certainly ill-informed about the contents of the Old
Testament and about several matters of which God, if not even the least
informed of the Prophet's contemporaries, must have been cognizant.

This raises the possibility of what my philosophical contemporaries
in the heyday of Gilbert Ryle would have described as a knock-down
falsification of Islam: something which is most certainly not possible in
the case of Christianity. If I do eventually produce such a paper it will
obviously have to be published anonymously.

HABERMAS: What do you think about the Bible?

FLEW: The Bible is a work which someone who had not the slightest
concern about the question of the truth or falsity of the Christian religion could read as people read the novels of the best novelists. It is an
eminently readable book.

HABERMAS: You and I have had three dialogues on the resurrection of
Jesus. Are you any closer to thinking that the resurrection could have
been a historical fact?

FLEW: No, I don't think so. The evidence for the resurrection is better
than for claimed miracles in any other religion. It's outstandingly different
in quality and quantity, I think, from the evidence offered for the occurrence of most other supposedly miraculous events. But you must remember that I approached it after considerable reading of reports of psychical
research and its criticisms. This showed me how quickly evidence of remarkable and supposedly miraculous events can be discredited.

What the psychical researcher looks for is evidence from witnesses, of
the supposedly paranormal events, recorded as soon as possible after
their occurrence. What we do not have is evidence from anyone who
was in Jerusalem at the time, who witnessed one of the allegedly miracu-

---

[34]This is the version of the Qur'an as "interpreted" by Arthur Arberry, in the Oxford University Press edition.

lous events, and recorded his or her testimony immediately after the occurrence of that allegedly miraculous event. In the 1950s and 1960s I heard several suggestions from hard-bitten young Australian and American philosophers of conceivable miracles the actual occurrence of which, it was contended, no one could have overlooked or denied. Why, they asked, if God wanted to be recognized and worshipped, did God not produce a miracle of this unignorable and undeniable kind?

HABERMAS: So you think that, for a miracle, the evidence for Jesus' resurrection is better than other miracle claims?

FLEW: Oh yes, I think so. It's much better, for example, than that for most if not all of the, so to speak, run-of-the-mill Roman Catholic miracles. On this see, for instance, D. J. West.[35]

HABERMAS: You have made numerous comments over the years that Christians are justified in their beliefs such as Jesus' resurrection or other major tenets of their faith. In our last two dialogues I think you even remarked that for someone who is already a Christian there are many good reasons to believe Jesus' resurrection. Would you comment on that?

FLEW: Yes, certainly. This is an important matter about rationality which I have fairly recently come to appreciate. What it is rational for any individual to believe about some matter which is fresh to that individual's consideration depends on what he or she rationally believed before they were confronted with this fresh situation. For suppose they rationally believed in the existence of a God of any revelation; then it would be entirely reasonable for them to see the fine-tuning argument as providing substantial confirmation of their belief in the existence of that God.

HABERMAS: You've told me that you have a very high regard for John and Charles Wesley and their traditions. What accounts for your appreciation?

FLEW: The greatest thing is their tremendous achievement of creating the Methodist movement mainly among the working class. Methodism made it impossible to build a really substantial Communist Party in Brit-

---

[35]D. J. West, *Eleven Lourdes Miracles* (London: George Duckworth, 1957).

ain and provided the country with a generous supply of men and women of sterling moral character from mainly working class families. Its decline is a substantial part of the explosions both of unwanted motherhood and of crime in recent decades. There is also the tremendous determination shown by John Wesley in spending year after year riding for miles every day, preaching more than seven sermons a week and so on. I have only recently been told of John Wesley's great controversy against predestination and in favor of the Arminian alternative. Certainly John Wesley was one of my country's many great sons and daughters. One at least of the others was raised in a Methodist home with a father who was a local preacher.

HABERMAS: Don't you attribute some of your appreciations for the Wesleys to your father's ministry? Haven't you said that your father was the first non-Anglican to get a doctorate in theology from Oxford University?

FLEW: Yes to both questions. Of course it was because my family's background was that of Methodism. Yes, my father was also president of the Methodist Conference for the usual single-year term, and he was the Methodist representative of one or two other organizations. He was also concerned for the World Council of Churches. Had my father lived to be active into the early 1970s, he would have wanted at least to consider the question of whether the Methodist Church ought not to withdraw from the World Council of Churches. That had by that time apparently been captured by agents of the USSR.[36]

HABERMAS: What do you think that Bertrand Russell, J. L. Mackie and A. J. Ayer would have thought about these theistic developments, had they still been alive today?

FLEW: I think Russell certainly would have had to notice these things. I'm sure Mackie would have been interested too. I never knew Ayer very well, beyond meeting him once or twice.

HABERMAS: Do you think any of them would have been impressed in the direction of theism? I'm thinking here, for instance, about Russell's

---

[36]Bernard Smith, *The Fraudulent Gospel: Politics and the World Council of Churches* (London: Foreign Affairs, 1977).

famous comments that God hasn't produced sufficient evidence of his existence.[37]

FLEW: Consistent with Russell's comments that you mention, Russell would have regarded these developments as evidence. I think we can be sure that Russell would have been impressed too, precisely because of his comments to which you refer. This would have produced an interesting second dialogue between him and that distinguished Catholic philosopher Frederick Copleston.

HABERMAS: In recent years you've been called the world's most influential philosophical atheist. Do you think Russell, Mackie or Ayer would have been bothered or even angered by your conversion to theism? Or do you think that they would have at least understood your reasons for changing your mind?

FLEW: I'm not sure how much any of them knew about Aristotle. But I am almost certain that they never had in mind the idea of a God who was not the God of any revealed religion. But we can be sure that they would have examined these new scientific arguments.

HABERMAS: C. S. Lewis explained in his autobiography that he moved first from atheism to theism and only later from theism to Christianity. Given your great respect for Christianity, do you think that there is any chance that you might in the end move from theism to Christianity?

FLEW: I think it's very unlikely, due to the problem of evil. But, if it did happen, I think it would be in some eccentric fit and doubtfully orthodox form: regular religious practice perhaps but without belief. If I wanted any sort of future life, I should become a Jehovah's Witness. But some things I am completely confident about. I would never regard Islam with anything but horror and fear because it is fundamentally committed to conquering the world for Islam. It was because the whole of Palestine was part of the Land of Islam that Muslim Arab armies moved in to try to destroy Israel at birth, and why the struggle for the return of the still surviving refugees and their numerous descendents continues to this day.

---

[37]See, for example, Bertrand Russell, *Bertrand Russell Speaks His Mind,* ed. Woodrow Wyatt (New York: Bard Books, 1960), pp. 19-20.

HABERMAS: I ask this last question with a smile, Tony. But just think what would happen if one day you were pleasantly disposed toward Christianity and all of a sudden the resurrection of Jesus looked pretty good to you?

FLEW: Well, one thing I'll say in this comparison is that, for goodness sake, Jesus is an enormously attractive charismatic figure, which the Prophet of Islam most emphatically is not.[38]

---

[38]Permission was granted by the editor of *Philosophia Christi* to reprint this interview between Gary Habermas and Antony Flew from the Winter 2004 issue. More about the interview can be found at <www.epsociety.org>. The complete story of Antony Flew's movement from atheism to theism is told in his book *There Is a God* (San Francisco: HarperOne, 2007), winner of the 2008 *Christianity Today* Book of the Year award for apologetics.

Appendix

The Dawkins Confusion: Naturalism "Ad Absurdum"
A Review of Richard Dawkins's The God Delusion

ALVIN PLANTINGA

Richard Dawkins is not pleased with God:

> The God of the Old Testament is arguably the most unpleasant character in all of fiction: jealous and proud of it; a petty, unjust unforgiving control-freak; a vindictive, bloodthirsty ethnic cleanser; a misogynistic, homophobic, racist, infanticidal, genocidal, filicidal, pestilential, megalomaniacal. . . .

No need to finish the quotation; you get the idea. Dawkins seems to have chosen God as his sworn enemy. (Let's hope for Dawkins's sake God doesn't return the compliment.)

The God Delusion is an extended diatribe against religion in general and belief in God in particular; Dawkins and Daniel Dennett (whose recent *Breaking the Spell* is his contribution to this genre) are the touchdown twins of current academic atheism.[39] Dawkins has written his book, he says, partly to encourage timorous atheists to come out of the closet. He and Dennett both appear to think it requires considerable courage to attack religion these days; says Dennett, "I risk a fist to the

---

[39]A third book along these lines, *The End of Faith*, has recently been written by Sam Harris, and more recently still a sequel, *Letter to a Christian Nation*, so perhaps we should speak of the touchdown triplets—or, given that Harris is very much the junior partner in this enterprise (he's a grad student) maybe the "Three Bears of Atheism"?

face or worse. Yet I persist." Apparently atheism has its own heroes of the faith—at any rate its own self-styled heroes. Here it's not easy to take them seriously; religion-bashing in the current Western academy is about as dangerous as endorsing the party's candidate at a Republican rally.

Dawkins is perhaps the world's most popular science writer; he is also an extremely *gifted* science writer. (For example, his account of bats and their ways in his earlier book *The Blind Watchmaker* is a brilliant and fascinating tour de force.) *The God Delusion*, however, contains little science; it is mainly philosophy and theology (perhaps "atheology" would be a better term) and evolutionary psychology, along with a substantial dash of social commentary decrying religion and its allegedly baneful effects. As the above quotation suggests, one shouldn't look to this book for evenhanded and thoughtful commentary. In fact the proportion of insult, ridicule, mockery, spleen and vitriol is astounding. (Could it be that his mother, while carrying him, was frightened by an Anglican clergyman on the rampage?) If Dawkins ever gets tired of his day job, a promising future awaits him as a writer of political attack ads.

Now despite the fact that this book is mainly philosophy, Dawkins is not a philosopher; he's a biologist. Even taking this into account, however, much of the philosophy he purveys is at best jejune. You might say that some of his forays into philosophy are at best sophomoric, but that would be unfair to sophomores; the fact is (grade inflation aside), many of his arguments would receive a failing grade in a sophomore philosophy class. This, combined with the arrogant, smarter-than-thou tone of the book, can be annoying. I shall put irritation aside, however, and do my best to take Dawkins's main argument seriously.

Chapter three, "Why There Almost Certainly Is No God," is the heart of the book. Why does Dawkins think there almost certainly isn't any such person as God? It's because, he says, the existence of God is monumentally improbable. How improbable? The astronomer Fred Hoyle famously claimed that the probability of life arising on earth (by purely natural means, without special divine aid) is less than the probability that a flightworthy Boeing 747 should be assembled by a hurricane roaring through a junkyard. Dawkins appears to think the probability of the existence of God is in that same neighborhood—so small as to be negligible for all practical (and most impractical) purposes. Why does he think so?

Here Dawkins doesn't appeal to the usual antitheistic arguments—the argument from evil, for example, or the claim that it's impossible that there be a being with the attributes believers ascribe to God.[40] So why does he think theism is enormously improbable? The answer: if there were such a person as God, he would have to be enormously complex, and the more complex something is, the less probable it is: "However statistically improbable the entity you seek to explain by invoking a designer, the designer himself has got to be at least as improbable. God is the Ultimate Boeing 747." The basic idea is that anything that knows and can do what God knows and can do would have to be incredibly complex. In particular, anything that can create or design something must be at least as complex as the thing it can design or create. Putting it another way, Dawkins says a designer must contain at least as much information as what it creates or designs, and information is inversely related to probability. Therefore, he thinks, God would have to be monumentally complex, hence astronomically improbable; thus it is almost certain that God does not exist.

But why does Dawkins think God is complex? And why does he think that the more complex something is, the less probable it is? Before looking more closely into his reasoning, I'd like to digress for a moment; this claim of improbability can help us understand something otherwise very perplexing about Dawkins's argument in his earlier and influential book *The Blind Watchmaker*. There he argues that the scientific theory of evolution shows that our world has not been designed—by God or anyone else. This thought is trumpeted by the subtitle of the book: *Why the Evidence of Evolution Reveals a Universe Without Design*.

How so? Suppose the evidence of evolution suggests that all living creatures have evolved from some elementary form of life: how does that show that the universe is without design? Well, if the universe has not been designed, then the process of evolution is unguided, unorchestrated by any intelligent being; it is, as Dawkins suggests, blind. So his claim is that the evidence of evolution reveals that evolution is unplanned, unguided, unorchestrated by any intelligent being.

---

[40]Dawkins does bring up (p. 54), apparently approvingly, the argument that God can't be both omniscient and omnipotent: if he is omniscient, then he can't change his mind, in which case there is something he can't do, so that he isn't omnipotent.

But how could the evidence of evolution reveal a thing like that? After all, couldn't it be that God has directed and overseen the process of evolution? What makes Dawkins think evolution is unguided? What he does in *The Blind Watchmaker*, fundamentally, is three things. First, he recounts in vivid and arresting detail some of the fascinating anatomical details of certain living creatures and their incredibly complex and ingenious ways of making a living; this is the sort of thing Dawkins does best. Second, he tries to refute arguments for the conclusion that blind, unguided evolution could not have produced certain of these wonders of the living world—the mammalian eye, for example, or the wing. Third, he makes suggestions as to how these and other organic systems could have developed by unguided evolution.

Suppose he's successful with these three things: how would that show that the universe is without design? How does the main argument go from there? His detailed arguments are all for the conclusion that it is biologically possible that these various organs and systems should have come to be by unguided Darwinian mechanisms (and some of what he says here is of considerable interest). What is truly remarkable, however, is the form of what seems to be the main argument. The premise he argues for is something like this:

(1) We know of no irrefutable objections to its being biologically possible
    that all of life has come to be by way of unguided Darwinian processes.

Dawkins supports that premise by trying to refute objections to its being biologically possible that life has come to be that way. His conclusion, however, is

(2) All of life has come to be by way of unguided Darwinian processes.

It's worth meditating, if only for a moment, on the striking distance, here, between premise and conclusion. The premise tells us, substantially, that there are no irrefutable objections to its being possible that unguided evolution has produced all of the wonders of the living world; the conclusion is that it is true that unguided evolution has indeed produced all of those wonders. The argument form seems to be something like

(1) We know of no irrefutable objections to its being possible that p.
(2) Therefore p is true.

Philosophers sometimes propound invalid arguments (I've propounded a few myself); few of those arguments display the truly colossal distance between premise and conclusion sported by this one. I come into the departmental office and announce to the chairman that the dean has just authorized a $50,000 raise for me; naturally he wants to know why I think so. I tell him that we know of no irrefutable objections to its being possible that the dean has done that. My guess is he'd gently suggest that it is high time for me to retire.

Here is where that alleged massive improbability of theism is relevant. If theism is false, then (apart from certain weird suggestions we can safely ignore) evolution is unguided. But it is extremely likely, Dawkins thinks, that theism is false. Hence it is extremely likely that evolution is unguided—in which case to establish it as true, he seems to think, all that is needed is to refute those claims that it is impossible. So perhaps we can think about his *Blind Watchmaker* argument as follows: he is really employing as an additional if unexpressed premise his idea that the existence of God is enormously unlikely. If so, then the argument doesn't seem quite so magnificently invalid. (It is still invalid, however, even if not quite so magnificently—you can't establish something as a fact by showing that objections to its possibility fail, and adding that it is very probable.)

Now suppose we return to Dawkins's argument for the claim that theism is monumentally improbable. As you recall, the reason Dawkins gives is that God would have to be enormously complex, and hence enormously improbable ("God, or any intelligent, decision-making calculating agent, is complex, which is another way of saying improbable"). What can be said for this argument?

Not much. First, is God complex? According to much classical theology (Thomas Aquinas, for example) God is simple, and simple in a very strong sense, so that in him there is no distinction of thing and property, actuality and potentiality, essence and existence, and the like. Some of the discussions of divine simplicity get pretty complicated, not to say arcane.[41] (It isn't only Catholic theology that declares God simple; according to the Belgic Confession, a splendid expression of Reformed Christianity, God is "a single and simple spiritual being.") So first, ac-

---

[41]See my *Does God Have a Nature?* Aquinas Lecture 44 (Marquette: Marquette University Press, 1980).

cording to classical theology, God is simple, not complex.[42]

More remarkable, perhaps, is that according to Dawkins's own definition of complexity, God is not complex. According to his definition (set out in *The Blind Watchmaker*), something is complex if it has parts that are "arranged in a way that is unlikely to have arisen by chance alone." But of course God is a spirit, not a material object at all, and hence has no parts.[43] A fortiori (as philosophers like to say) God doesn't have parts arranged in ways unlikely to have arisen by chance. Therefore, given the definition of complexity Dawkins himself proposes, God is not complex.

So first, it is far from obvious that God is complex. But second, suppose we concede, at least for purposes of argument, that God *is* complex. Perhaps we think the more a being knows, the more complex it is; God, being omniscient, would then be highly complex. Perhaps so; still, why does Dawkins think it follows that God would be improbable? Given *materialism* and the idea that the ultimate objects in our universe are the elementary particles of physics, perhaps a being that knew a great deal would be improbable—how could those particles get arranged in such a way as to constitute a being with all that knowledge? Of course we aren't *given* materialism. Dawkins is arguing that theism is improbable; it would be dialectically deficient *in excelsis* to argue this by appealing to materialism as a premise. *Of course* it is unlikely that there is such a person as God if materialism is true; in fact materialism logically entails that there is no such person as God; but it would be obviously question-begging to argue that theism is improbable because materialism is true.

So why think God must be improbable? According to classical theism, God is a necessary being; it is not so much as possible that there should be no such person as God; he exists in all possible worlds. But if God is a necessary being, if he exists in all possible worlds, then the probability that he exists, of course, is 1, and the probability that he

---

[42]The distinguished Oxford philosopher (Dawkins calls him a theologian) Richard Swinburne has proposed some sophisticated arguments for the claim that God is simple. Dawkins mentions Swinburne's argument but doesn't deign to come to grips with it; instead he resorts to ridicule (pp. 110-11).

[43]What about the Trinity? Just how we are to think of the Trinity is of course not wholly clear; it is clear, however, that it is false that in addition to each of the three persons of the Trinity, there is also another being of which each of those persons is a part.

does not exist is 0. Far from its being improbable that he exists, his existence is maximally probable. So if Dawkins proposes that God's existence is improbable, he owes us an argument for the conclusion that there is no necessary being with the attributes of God—an argument that doesn't just start from the premise that materialism is true. Neither he nor anyone else has provided even a decent argument along these lines; Dawkins doesn't even seem to be aware that he *needs* an argument of that sort.

A second example of Dawkinsian-style argument. Recently a number of thinkers have proposed a new version of the argument from design, the so-called fine-tuning argument. Starting in the late 1960s and early 1970s, astrophysicists and others noted that several of the basic physical constants must fall within very narrow limits if there is to be the development of intelligent life—at any rate in a way anything like the way in which we think it actually happened. For example, if the force of gravity were even slightly stronger, all stars would be blue giants; if even slightly weaker, all would be red dwarfs; in neither case could life have developed. The same goes for the weak and strong nuclear forces; if either had been even slightly different, life—at any rate life of the sort we have—could probably not have developed. Equally interesting in this connection is the so-called flatness problem: the existence of life also seems to depend very delicately upon the rate at which the universe is expanding. Thus Stephen Hawking:

> Reduction of the rate of expansion by one part in 1012 at the time when the temperature of the Universe was 1010 K would have resulted in the Universe's starting to recollapse when its radius was only 1/3000 of the present value and the temperature was still 10,000 K.[44]

That would be much too warm for comfort. Hawking concludes that life is possible only because the universe is expanding at just the rate required to avoid recollapse. At an earlier time, he observes, the fine-tuning had to be even more remarkable:

> We know that there has to have been a very close balance between the competing effect of explosive expansion and gravitational contraction

---

[44]Stephen Hawking, "The Anisotropy of the Universe at Large Times," in *Confrontation of Cosmological Theories with Observational Data*, ed. M. S. Longair (New York: Springer, 2002), p. 285.

which, at the very earliest epoch about which we can even pretend to speak (called the Planck time, 10-43 sec. after the big bang), would have corresponded to the incredible degree of accuracy represented by a deviation in their ratio from unity by only one part in 10 to the sixtieth.[45]

One reaction to these apparent enormous coincidences is to see them as substantiating the theistic claim that the universe has been created by a personal God, and as offering the material for a properly restrained theistic argument—hence the fine-tuning argument.[46] It's as if there is a large number of dials that have to be tuned to within extremely narrow limits for life to be possible in our universe. It is extremely unlikely that this should happen by chance but much more likely that this should happen if there is such a person as God.

Now in response to this kind of theistic argument, Dawkins, along with others, proposes that possibly there are very many (perhaps even infinitely many) universes, with very many different distributions of values over the physical constants. Given that there are so many, it is likely that *some* of them would display values that are life-friendly. So if there are an enormous number of universes displaying different sets of values of the fundamental constants, it's not at all improbable that some of them should be "fine-tuned." We might wonder how likely it is that there *are* all these other universes and whether there is any real reason (apart from wanting to blunt the fine-tuning arguments) for supposing there are any such things.[47] But concede for the moment that indeed there are many universes and that it is likely that some are fine-tuned and life-friendly. That still leaves Dawkins with the following problem: even if it's likely that *some* universes should be fine-tuned, it is still improbable that *this* universe should be fine-tuned. Name our universe *alpha*: the odds that *alpha* should be fine-tuned are exceedingly, astronomically low, even if it's likely that some universe or other is fine-tuned.

What is Dawkins's reply? He appeals to "the anthropic principle," the

---

[45]John Polkinghorne, *Science and Creation: The Search for Understanding* (New York: Random House, 1989), p. 22.

[46]One of the best versions of the fine-tuning argument is proposed by Robin Collins in "A Scientific Argument for the Existence of God: The Fine-Tuning Design Argument," in *Reason for the Hope Within*, ed. Michael J. Murray (Grand Rapids: Eerdmans, 1999), pp. 47-75.

[47]See my review of Daniel Dennett's *Darwin's Dangerous Idea* in *Books & Culture*, May/June 1996.

thought that the only sort of universe in which we could be discussing this question is one which is fine-tuned for life:

> The anthropic answer, in its most general form, is that we could only be discussing the question in the kind of universe that was capable of producing us. Our existence therefore determines that the fundamental constants of physics had to be in their respective Goldilocks [life-friendly] zones.

Well, of *course* our universe would have to be fine-tuned, given that we live in it. But how does that so much as begin to explain why it is that *alpha* is fine-tuned? One can't explain this by pointing out that we are indeed here—anymore than I can "explain" the fact that God decided to create me (instead of passing me over in favor of someone else) by pointing out that if God had not thus decided, I wouldn't be here to raise that question. It still seems striking that these constants should have just the values they do have; it is still monumentally improbable, given chance, that they should have just those values; and it is still much less improbable that they should have those values if there is a God who wanted a life-friendly universe.

One more example of Dawkinsian thought. In *The Blind Watchmaker* he considers the claim that since the self-replicating machinery of life is required for natural selection to work, God must have jump-started the whole evolutionary process by specially creating life in the first place—by specially creating the original replicating machinery of DNA and protein that makes natural selection possible. Dawkins retorts as follows:

> This is a transparently feeble argument, indeed it is obviously self-defeating. Organized complexity is the thing that we are having difficulty in explaining. Once we are allowed simply to *postulate* organized complexity, if only the organized complexity of the DNA/protein replicating machine, it is relatively easy to invoke it as a generator of yet more organized complexity. . . . But of course any God capable of intelligently designing something as complex as the DNA/protein machine must have been at least as complex and organized as that machine itself. . . . To explain the origin of the DNA/protein machine by invoking a supernatural Designer is to explain precisely nothing, for it leaves unexplained the origin of the Designer.

In *Darwin's Dangerous Idea*, Daniel Dennett approvingly quotes this passage from Dawkins and declares it an "unrebuttable refutation, as devastating today as when Philo used it to trounce Cleanthes in Hume's

Dialogues two centuries earlier." Now here in *The God Delusion* Dawkins approvingly quotes Dennett approvingly quoting Dawkins, and adds that Dennett (i.e., Dawkins) is entirely correct.

Here there is much to say, but I'll say only a bit of it. First, suppose we land on an alien planet orbiting a distant star and discover machinelike objects that look and work just like tractors; our leader says, "There must be intelligent beings on this planet who built those tractors." A first-year philosophy student on our expedition objects: "Hey, hold on a minute! You have explained nothing at all! Any intelligent life that designed those tractors would have to be at least as complex as they are." No doubt we'd tell him that a little learning is a dangerous thing and advise him to take the next rocket ship home and enroll in another philosophy course or two. For of course it is perfectly sensible, in that context, to explain the existence of those tractors in terms of intelligent life, even though (as we can concede for the moment) that intelligent life would have to be at least as complex as the tractors. The point is we aren't trying to give an *ultimate* explanation of organized complexity, and we aren't trying to explain organized complexity *in general;* we are only trying to explain one particular manifestation of it (those tractors). And unless you are trying to give an ultimate explanation of organized complexity, it is perfectly proper to explain one manifestation of organized complexity in terms of another. Similarly, in invoking God as the original creator of life, we aren't trying to explain organized complexity *in general* but only a particular kind of it, that is, terrestrial life. So even if (contrary to fact, as I see it) God himself displays organized complexity, we would be perfectly sensible in explaining the existence of terrestrial life in terms of divine activity.

A second point: Dawkins (and again Dennett echoes him) argues that "the main thing we want to explain" is "organized complexity." He goes on to say that "the one thing that makes evolution such a neat theory is that it explains how organized complexity can arise out of primeval simplicity," and he faults theism for being unable to explain organized complexity. Now *mind* would be an outstanding example of organized complexity, according to Dawkins, and of course (unlike with organized complexity) it is uncontroversial that God is a being who thinks and knows; so suppose we take Dawkins to be complaining that theism doesn't offer an explanation of mind. It is obvious that theists won't be able to give an ultimate explanation of mind, because, naturally enough, there isn't any explanation of the existence of God. Still, how is that a point against theism?

Explanations come to an end; for theism they come to an end in God. Of course the same goes for any other view; on *any* view explanations come to an end. The materialist or physicalist, for example, doesn't have an explanation for the existence of elementary particles: they just are. So to claim that what we want or what we need is an ultimate explanation of mind is, once more, just to beg the question against theism; the theist neither wants nor needs an ultimate explanation of personhood, or thinking, or mind.

Toward the end of the book, Dawkins endorses a certain limited skepticism. Since we have been cobbled together by (unguided) evolution, it is unlikely, he thinks, that our view of the world is overall accurate; natural selection is interested in adaptive behavior, not in true belief. But Dawkins fails to plumb the real depths of the skeptical implications of the view that we have come to be by way of unguided evolution. We can see this as follows. Like most naturalists, Dawkins is a materialist about human beings: human persons are material objects; they are not immaterial selves or souls or substances joined to a body, and they don't contain any immaterial substance as a part. From this point of view, our beliefs would be dependent on neurophysiology, and (no doubt) a belief would just be a neurological structure of some complex kind. Now the neurophysiology on which our beliefs depend will doubtless be adaptive; but why think for a moment that the beliefs dependent on or caused by that neurophysiology will be mostly true? Why think our cognitive faculties are reliable?

From a theistic point of view, we'd expect that our cognitive faculties would be (for the most part, and given certain qualifications and caveats) reliable. God has created us in his image, and an important part of our image bearing is our resembling him in being able to form true beliefs and achieve knowledge. But from a naturalist point of view the thought that our cognitive faculties are reliable (produce a preponderance of true beliefs) would be at best a naive hope. The naturalist can be reasonably sure that the neurophysiology underlying belief formation is adaptive, but nothing follows about the truth of the beliefs depending on that neurophysiology. In fact he'd have to hold that it is unlikely, given unguided evolution, that our cognitive faculties are reliable. It's as likely, given unguided evolution, that we live in a sort of dream world as that we actually know something about ourselves and our world.

If this is so, the naturalist has a defeater for the natural assumption that his cognitive faculties are reliable—a reason for rejecting that belief, for no longer holding it. (Example of a defeater: suppose someone once told me that you were born in Michigan and I believed her; but now I ask you, and you tell me you were born in Brazil. That gives me a defeater for my belief that you were born in Michigan.) And if he has a defeater for that belief, he also has a defeater for any belief that is a product of his cognitive faculties. But of course that would be all of his beliefs—including naturalism itself. So the naturalist has a defeater for naturalism; naturalism, therefore, is self-defeating and cannot be rationally believed.

The real problem here, obviously, is Dawkins's naturalism, his belief that there is no such person as God or anyone like God. That is because naturalism implies that evolution is unguided. So a broader conclusion is that one can't rationally accept both naturalism and evolution; naturalism, therefore, is in conflict with a premier doctrine of contemporary science. People like Dawkins hold that there is a conflict between science and religion because they think there is a conflict between evolution and theism; the truth of the matter, however, is that the conflict is between science and naturalism, not between science and belief in God.

The God Delusion is full of bluster and bombast, but it really doesn't give even the slightest reason for thinking belief in God is mistaken, let alone a "delusion." The naturalism that Dawkins embraces, furthermore, in addition to its intrinsic unloveliness and its dispiriting conclusions about human beings and their place in the universe, is in deep self-referential trouble. There is no reason to believe it; and there is excellent reason to reject it.

Contributors

Michael J. Behe is professor of biochemistry at Lehigh University and a senior fellow of the Discovery Institute's Center for Science and Culture. He is one of the leaders in the intelligent design movement. His works include *Darwin's Black Box: The Biochemical Challenge to Evolution* and *The Edge of Evolution: The Search for the Limits of Darwinism*.

Paul Copan is Pledger Family Chair of Philosophy and Ethics at Palm Beach Atlantic University. He has edited, with Paul K. Moser, *The Rationality of Theism* and, with Chad Meister, *Philosophy of Religion: Classic and Contemporary Issues*. He has coauthored with William Lane Craig *Creation Out of Nothing: A Biblical, Philosophical, and Scientific Exploration*, and has written works related to the philosophy of religion including *True for You, But Not for Me* and *That's Just Your Interpretation*.

William Lane Craig is Research Professor of Philosophy at the Talbot School of Theology. One of the most widely published philosophers of religion of our day, he is the author of *The Kalam Cosmological Argument*, *Theism, Atheism, and Big Bang Cosmology*, and *God, Time, and Eternity*, as well as over a hundred articles in professional journals of philosophy and theology, including *The Journal of Philosophy, American Philosophical Quarterly, Philosophical Studies, Philosophy* and the *British Journal for Philosophy of Science*.

Antony Flew is former professor of philosophy at the University of Oxford and the University of Reading. He was one of the most renowned atheists of the twentieth century, although he has since rejected atheism and now believes in some kind a grand designer of the universe. His many books include *There Is a God: How the World's Most Notorious Atheist Changed His Mind*, *God and Philosophy*, and (coauthored with William Lane Craig) *Does God Exist? The Craig-Flew Debate*.

Gary R. Habermas is Distinguished Research Professor and chair of the department of philosophy and theology at Liberty University. He has written over one hundred articles and reviews, and dozens of books, including *The Historical Jesus: Ancient Evidence for the Life of Christ*, *The Risen Jesus and Future Hope*, and (with Antony Flew) *Resurrected? An Atheist & Theist Dialogue*.

Alister McGrath is professor of theology, ministry and education, and head of the Center for Theology, Religion and Culture at King's College London, and president of the Oxford Center for Christian Apologetics. He has published many books and articles on theology and science and specifically on topics related to the New Atheism, including *The Dawkins Delusion*, *Dawkins's God: Genes, Memes, and the Meaning of Life*, and *The Twilight of Atheism: The Rise and Fall of Disbelief in the Modern World*.

Scot McKnight is Karl A. Olsson Professor in Religious Studies at North Park University. He has written or edited more than twenty books, including *Interpreting the Synoptic Gospels*, *The Jesus Creed, Jesus and His Death*, and (with James Dunn) *The Historical Jesus in Current Study*. He has also published widely in scholarly journals, and is regularly interviewed on national radio and television.

Chad Meister is director of philosophy at Bethel College and vice president of the Evangelical Philosophical Society. His publications include *Building Belief: Constructing Faith from the Ground Up*, *The Oxford Handbook of Religious Diversity*, *The Cambridge Companion to Christian Philosophical Theology* (coedited with Charles Taliaferro) and *Evil: A Guide for the Perplexed* (forthcoming).

Mark Mittelberg is a bestselling author, international speaker, and leading strategist and consultant in evangelism and apologetics. He is the author of *Choosing Your Faith* and *Becoming a Contagious Church*, the primary author of the recently updated *Becoming a Contagious Christian* training course, and contributing editor of *The Journey: A Bible for the Spiritually Curious*.

J. P. Moreland is Distinguished Professor of Philosophy at Biola University. He has authored, edited or contributed to thirty books, including *Kingdom Triangle*, *Naturalism: A Critical Analysis*, *Universals*, and *Philosophy of Religion: A Reader and Guide*. He has also published over sixty articles in professional journals, including the *American Philosophical Quarterly*, *Australasian Journal of Philosophy*, *Religious Studies*, and *Faith and Philosophy*.

Paul K. Moser is professor and chair of philosophy at Loyola University of Chicago. He is the author of *Philosophy After Objectivity*, *Knowledge and Evidence*, and *Empirical Justification*. He is the editor of *The Oxford Handbook of Epistemology*, *A Priori Knowledge*, *Rationality in Action*, *Jesus and Philosophy* (Cambridge series), and *The Elusive God*, among other works. His articles have appeared in the *American Philosophical Quarterly*, *Synthese*, *Erkenntnis*, *Analysis* and *Noûs*, among other journals.

Michael J. Murray is the Arthur and Katherine Shadek Professor of Humanities and Philosophy, and chair of the philosophy department at Franklin and Marshall College. His books include *Philosophy of Religion* (with Michael Rea), and two edited volumes: *Philosophy of Religion: The Big Questions* (with Eleonore Stump) and *Reason for the Hope Within*. He has also published in numerous journals including *Philosophy and Phenomenological Research* and the *American Philosophical Quarterly*.

Alvin Plantinga is John A. O'Brien Professor of Philosophy at the University of Notre Dame. He has been called "the most important philosopher of religion now writing." His many publications include *God, Freedom and Evil*, *God and Other Minds*, and *Warranted Christian Belief*.

John Polkinghorne is emeritus president of Queen's College, Cambridge, a fellow of the Royal Society and an Anglican priest. He has written numerous articles and authored/edited many books exploring the relationship between science and religion, including *The Faith of a Physicist*, *Belief in God in an Age of Science*, *Science and the Trinity*, and *Exploring Reality*.

Charles Taliaferro is professor of philosophy at St. Olaf College. His books include *Evidence and Faith: Philosophy and Religion Since the Seventeenth Century*, *Contemporary Philosophy of Religion*, and *Consciousness and the Mind of God*. He has published papers in *Religious Studies*, *Faith and Philosophy*, the *International Journal for Philosophy of Religion*, *Sophia*, and elsewhere.

Jerry L. Walls is professor of philosophy of religion at Asbury Seminary. Among his books are *Hell: The Logic of Damnation*, *Heaven: The Logic of Eternal Joy*, and *C. S. Lewis and Francis Schaeffer: Lessons for a New Century from the Most Influential Apologists of Our Time*. He is also editor of *The Oxford Handbook of Eschatology*.

Index